THE TENNYSONS

THE TENNYSONS

BACKGROUND TO GENIUS

CHARLES TENNYSON

AND

HOPE DYSON

MACMILLAN

SBN 333 17702 9

First published 1974 *by*
MACMILLAN LONDON LTD
London and Basingstoke
Associated companies in New York
Dublin Melbourne Johannesburg and Madras

Printed in Great Britain by
JOHN SHERRATT AND SON LTD
St Ann's Press, Park Road, Altrincham
Cheshire WA14 5QQ

THIS BOOK IS DEDICATED TO

CAPTAIN F. B. ff. SHEPPARD O.B.E., D.L.

Chairman of the Tennyson Society from its foundation until his death in 1972, with affection and gratitude.

CONTENTS

	The Somersby Tennysons	8
	Preface	9
1	Beginnings at Holderness and Grimsby	11
2	George Tennyson: a Lincolnshire gentleman	20
3	George Tennyson and His Children	32
4	Young George	39
5	The Unhappy Doctor	55
6	The 'Man of Sorrow'	70
7	Bayons and Arthur Hallam	79
8	Bayons Manor and High Beech	87
9	'This Extraordinary Brood'	100
	(i) Frederick, Charles and Alfred	100
	(ii) Edward, Septimus, Arthur and Horatio	118
	(iii) The Somersby Sisters and Matthew Allen	143
10	Mary and Emily	160
11	Matilda and Cecilia	168
12	Uncle and Aunts	177
	Epilogue	195
	Appendix Tennyson's Conversation	197
	Select Bibliography	209
	Index	215

THE SOMERSBY TENNYSONS

Children of George Clayton Tennyson (1778–1831) and Elizabeth Fytche (1781–1865), who were married 6th August 1805.

Name	Birth	Marriage	Death
Frederick	5th June 1807	1839 Maria Giuliotti	26th February 1898 (d. 22nd January 1884
Charles	4th July 1808	24th May 1836 Louisa Sellwood	25th April 1879 (d. 20th May 1879)
Alfred	6th August 1809	13th June 1850 Emily Sellwood	6th October 1892 (d. 10th August 1896)
Mary	11th September 1810	7th July 1851 Alan Ker	4th April 1884 (d. 20th March 1885)
Emilia	25th October 1811	24th January 1842 Captain Richard Jesse, R.N.	24th January 1887
Edward	January 1813		1890
Arthur	12th May 1814	22nd May 1860 Harriet West 7th December 1882 Emma Louisa Maynard	27th June 1899 (d. 17th June 1881) (d. 31st August 1919)
Septimus	10th September 1815		8th September 1866
Matilda	13th September 1816		1913
Cecilia	10th October 1817	14th October 1842 Edmund Law Lushington, D.C.L.	18th March 1909 (d. 13th July 1893)
Horatio	25th September 1819	16th April 1857 Charlotte Maria Elwes 8th December 1870 Catherine West	2nd October 1899 (d. 31st October 1868)

PREFACE

THIS book is not a biography of one person or of a number of persons. It is the history of a family, including both the not uncommon story of a gradual climb up the social ladder, and the very uncommon story of sudden explosion of genius.

Parts of the book are founded on articles by one of the authors, viz. 'Alfred's Father' *Cornhill Magazine*, CLIII April 1936, 426–49 and 'The Somersby Tennysons' *Victorian Studies* Christmas Supplement 1963, Indiana University, Bloomington, Indiana, U.S.A. We are grateful to both *The Twentieth Century* and to *Victorian Studies* for permission to make use of these essays and to *The Twentieth Century* for permission to include the appendix 'Tennyson's Conversation' which first appeared in the issue of January 1959.

We have made considerable use of two recently published books – *A History of Grimsby* by Edward Gillett (Oxford University Press, 1970) and *Grimsby and the Haven Company* by Gordon Jackson (Grimsby Public Libraries, 1971). We are grateful to the authors of both for much help most generously afforded. We have also drawn much material from Dr John Parkinson's Diary. The author of this, who compiled his diary between the years 1790–1830, knew many of the people referred to in this book. The Diary is at the moment being studied by scholars through whose kindness we have been enabled to extract a considerable amount of very relevant information from its pages. For this we desire to tender grateful thanks to Mr William Collier who has already edited a section of the diary under the title *A Tour in Russia, Siberia and the Crimea 1792–1794* (Frank Cass & Co, 1971), to Mr Alan Dowling of the Public Library, Scunthorpe, to Mr E. H. Trevitt of the Public Library, Grimsby and to Mr Michael Kirkby now Curator of the Bowes Museum at Barnard Castle, formerly head of the Museum at Scunthorpe.

We also wish to express our gratitude to the staff of The Tennyson Research Centre at the Central Library, Lincoln, and to the Lincolnshire Archives Office for the very great help which they have ungrudgingly given us. We are also most grateful to Sir Francis Hill, historian of Lincoln, for valuable advice and assistance and to Major A. Tennyson D'Eyncourt and Captain Walter Tennyson D'Eyncourt for much helpful co-operation.

CHAPTER ONE

BEGINNINGS AT HOLDERNESS AND GRIMSBY

THE Tennyson family and name seem to have sprung from South Holderness in Yorkshire, on the north bank of the Humber between Hull and the sea. The origin of the name Holderness is thought to be 'the Headland of the Hold', the Hold having been an important administrative officer in the Daneland. The name Tennyson is also probably Danish. The Tennyson Research Centre at Lincoln owns a letter from the great historian F. W. Maitland suggesting that the name might be traced back to Ithuneson, meaning the son of Idonea, a matronymic which he had discovered in an early Holderness document. A simpler derivation was suggested a few years ago by a young man in North Carolina called John Tennyson, who said that his father, a Danish immigrant called Thoenissen, had got so tired of trying to explain to Americans how to spell his name that he changed it to one better known.

Holderness is generally defined as covering south-east Yorkshire between the Wolds and the Humber. Of this area the Tennyson country occupies only a narrow strip along the left bank of the river between Hull and Spurn Head. It is not perhaps very exciting country, being flat and treeless and bitterly exposed to the mists and gales of the North Sea, but it has a long and varied history, and, at Hedon and Patrington, two of the finest mediaeval parish churches in a country whose parish churches are amongst the wonders of the world. This twenty-mile strip must in mediaeval times have been both populous and active, the people toiling hard both by land and sea to make a living. Signs of this dual activity are still evident, oars, boats and nets being no less familiar tools than ploughs and harrows. Indeed it is even said that there are many gate posts of whale-bone to remind one of Hull's

once important whaling industry, and the water has played strange
tricks with the land; witness the great shingle ridge which it has built
up between Paul and Patrington, and the 'sunk island', which seems
to have appeared first as a low mud bank in the river in the reign of
Charles II but now contains 6,000 acres of good mainland with a church
and a village built on it. There are many villages, hamlets and small
towns in this long-settled mainland area – Preston and Hedon (almost
continuous) three or four miles from Hull on the west; Paul, Thorgumbold and Boarhousehill between Hedon and the river; Ryhill, Keyingham, Ottringham, Burstwick, Halsham, Winestead (where
Andrew Marvell was born at the Rectory in 1621), Patrington, where
the church is dedicated to Saint Patrick and there are traditions of
connexion with the Saint, Welwick, Skeffling, Easington, Kilnsea (just
short of Spurn Head), and, northwards up the coast beyond Hollyon
and Holmpton, Withernsea, now a pleasant seaside resort. In all these
towns, villages and hamlets (particularly those in the western half of
the district) the archives of the sixteenth, seventeenth and eighteenth
centuries record marriages and baptisms of Tennysons, Tenisons,
Tenysons or Tennisons, and probates of their wills, the latter presumably indicating a certain level of middle-class prosperity. In and
around Preston, Hedon, Paul, Ryhill, Thorgumbold, Boarhousehill
and Keyingham the concentration appears to be thickest and there is a
record of a John Tenison of Paul-flete bringing an action for the
recovery of goods in 1343.

There are still Tennysons living in the district, some spelling the
name with an 'i', some with a 'y', some with one 'n', some with two.
Most of the men seem to be labourers or craftsmen emerging or not
long emerged from illiteracy, though there are some nineteenth-
century tombs in the church yard at Ottringham and in Easington
Church which suggest a greater affluence, and there was until recently
one William who had made money in and after the First World War
and bought land at Welwick and Kilnsea and whose name was in the
telephone book. None of the Tennyson families at present residing in
the district appears to claim any connexion with the poet, though in
moments of exuberance claims of descent from him may have been
made in public bars or cottage kitchens. The spelling of the name

appears to have no significance, the spelling of both personal and place
names in the district being remarkably erratic. In the Hull telephone
book there are several 'Tennisons' and one 'Tennyson', and a few
years ago a cousin of the male author of this book, another Charles,
was told by the barmaid of a Hull pub with whom he was chatting
that he had the same name as her boy friend.

The most interesting fact about the Tennysons of Holderness –
however spelt – is their almost complete lack of distinction during the
centuries preceding the eighteenth. The only names of distinction
amongst them that can be found are those of the three episcopal
cousins – Richard Tenison, Bishop of Meath (1640–1705); Edward
Tenison, Bishop of Ossory (1673–1735) and Thomas Tenison, Archbishop of Canterbury (1636–1715), who founded a well-known London
grammar school, endowed the first public library in England and
preached Nell Gwyn's funeral sermon. Their ancestors are known to
have left Holderness for Cambridgeshire towards the end of the
sixteenth century, but although it is said that the poet's grandfather
claimed descent from the Archbishop, and his son, the poet's father,
owned quite a good contemporary portrait of him, now in the Usher
Art Gallery, Lincoln, there appears to be no direct evidence for the
claim.

The first ancestor of the poet who can be traced is Ralph Tennyson
who died in 1735. Hallam, Lord Tennyson, in his memoir of his father
speaks of a Lancelot Tennyson of Preston and credits a Ralph with
having raised a troop of horse to support William III – on what
evidence is not known. Boyle in his history of Hedon says there had
been a 'Tennyson Close' there in 1643, which suggests that the family
may have had some local importance in the early seventeenth century,
but no further record of this remains. For our present purpose the first
Tennyson to whom we need devote any attention is Ralph, who
crossed the river in about 1715 to settle at Barton-on-Humber in
Lincolnshire. He was a solicitor, who must have prospered profession-
ally, for the house in which he lived at Barton is still known as Tennyson House. Incidentally this Ralph cannot have raised the troop of
horse mentioned by Hallam, Lord Tennyson, for he was still alive in
1767, 79 years after William III landed at Torbay. Ralph, who may be

regarded as the first Tennyson to settle in Lincolnshire, died at Brigg
and was then described as of Barton, Wrawby and Brigg. It therefore
seems probable that he owned property in all three Lincolnshire
towns. He had three sons: Ralph, Michael and William. Ralph, the
second, who also became a solicitor, settled in Grimsby, fifteen miles
from Barton, where he apparently prospered for he became alderman,
was elected mayor in 1747 and continued active in municipal affairs
until his death twenty years later.

What was more important for the history of the Tennyson family,
he formed a close alliance with the Claytons, who had for a hundred
years or more been the most important family in Grimsby. This is not
saying much, for Grimsby, which in mediaeval times had been a considerable port, was in the 1740s, according to John Wesley who visited
it several times, 'no bigger than a middling village, containing a small
number of half-starved inhabitants'. Indeed the population, now about
100,000, was right up to the mid-eighteenth century probably less
than a thousand. The town had in fact suffered in its most severe form
the misfortune which had impoverished so many of the east coast wool
ports after the discovery of America had turned the direction of our
trade from east to west. In the eighteenth century nothing remained of
Grimsby's once-important trade in wool, wine and fish, and 'the
haven', a mile-long narrow creek connecting the town with the River
Humber, had become so silted up with sludge from the river that it
was of very little use. In consequence most of the available trade went
through the port of Hull ten miles up the river to the north. But the
borough still enjoyed one relic of its former importance. Under a
charter of King John it was entitled to send two members to Parliament,
and during the highly political eighteenth century the manipulation of
parliamentary elections became the most important common concern
of Grimsby's inhabitants. The right to vote was confined to freemen
of the borough and by this time could only be secured by being the son
or apprentice of a freeman or marrying a freeman's widow or daughter.
Freemen sold their votes without shame or concealment, and as the
mayor and aldermen had much power both in relation to parliamentary
elections and commercial and administrative affairs municipal elections
also became of great importance.

The Claytons, besides being the most important family in Grimsby, had considerable interests in London and the Far East and connexions with the Continent and were ambitious, far-seeing and unscrupulous. From the end of the seventeenth century onwards they bought up lands in and around the little old town, which still lay isolated in the surrounding marsh, and, politically, grew to be 'predominant by sheer ruthlessness, thus ensuring that they would become the channel through which funds dispensed by Parliamentary candidates would have to flow.'*

From the beginning of the eighteenth century one at least of the two Members of Parliament representing the Borough had generally been a Clayton nominee; the first Clayton mayor had been elected in 1667, after which date there was always at least one alderman from the family, and Claytons filled the mayor's seat eighteen times between 1700 and 1769.

The leaders of the Clayton family at the time when Ralph Tennyson II came to Grimsby were two brothers, Christopher and George, descendants of another Christopher who, starting as a yeoman farmer with interests in trade and shipping, had become the only merchant in the little town. George had in 1719 made a marriage (destined to have a remarkable influence on the outlook and ambitions of the Tennyson family) with Dorothy, daughter of Christopher Hildyard of Kelstern near Louth, 15 or 16 miles to the south. The Hildyards were a family of landed proprietors who also owned property in Holderness and claimed descent from both Edward I and Edward III and from Barons d'Eyncourt of two separate creations. George and Dorothy Clayton's daughter Elizabeth married in 1745 Michael Tennyson (younger brother of Ralph, the Mayor), an 'apothecary' who had gone back to Hedon in Holderness to practise. The word 'apothecary' originally meant 'shopkeeper' or 'warehouseman' and was gradually restricted to sellers of drugs. After securing protection by statute in 1543, they gradually strengthened their position and rights to practise medicine. In his will Michael Tennyson described himself as surgeon. He was apparently a man of substance, owning property at Hundleby and Stainton in Lincolnshire and at Preston in Holderness, besides one of

* See *A History of Grimsby* by Edward Gillett, London, Oxford University Press, 1970, p. 151.

the staithes in the High Street at Hull which were in general owned only by the richer Hull merchants. When he died he left his son George £700 a year, besides providing for his only other child, a daughter, Anne Raines.

Michael Tennyson had no doubt been introduced to the Claytons by Ralph, who in 1741 had, after the death of Elizabeth's father, George Clayton, married Dorothy Hildyard as her second husband and no doubt owed his election as alderman and mayor to this marriage. The closeness of the relations between the Tennysons and the Claytons is emphasised by the fact that William, the youngest of the three Tennyson brothers, also married a Clayton relict – Susan, widow of Christopher, who had died in 1731.

The only letter of Elizabeth, Michael's wife, which survives suggests that, however aristocratic her ancestry, she was not a lady of much education.

My dear,

I am very sorry that you should make your Self so uneasy as I thank God that I am mutch better than I was when I left Headon and I am in great hopes it will continue so that I shall be able to retorn in a very little time it gives me great pleasure to here that you and my Dear Babys is well which pray God continue and when I have the pleasure to retorn I shall think myself happy I am just a going out with Mrs Clambers so I have not time to write any more but believe me to be youre affectionate wife till death

ELIZ TENNYSON

Beverley July 16, 1754
pray make my compliments to all Friends

Poor Elizabeth, she died within six months, on 6th January 1755, and her husband, who lived till 6th October 1769, never married again. Her 'Dear Babys' were two, George and Anne, George being the first Tennyson ancestor of whom we have any detailed knowledge. On him, owing to a general failure of Clayton issue, there was to devolve before the end of the century most of the Clayton property and power.

The failure of issue in so strong and rugged a stock is remarkable, but there are signs in the few records which have come down to us of a mental abnormality amongst the male members of the family which may have masked a constitutional weakness. We first hear of the family in connexion with the South Sea Bubble disaster, in which at least one of them was involved. This was Christopher (1687–1737) already mentioned as a leader of the family at the time of Ralph Tennyson II's move to Grimsby. He had been appointed confidential clerk to the very astute and plausible cashier of the Company, Robert Knight, and was probably involved in many of Knight's malpractices. After the Parliamentary Committee's activities had caused his chief to fly the country, Christopher Clayton got into serious trouble for forcibly interfering with one of the inquiry's witnesses, laying violent hands on his face, squeezing his jaws very hard and threatening to be the death of him 'if he discovered anything'. For this Christopher Clayton was imprisoned by order of the Committee. Violence to one who was in effect a witness for the prosecution was not a very safe or sensible proceeding.

Another Christopher, nephew of this Christopher (son of his brother George (1694–1741?) above-mentioned) was early involved in family litigation, being in 1762 defendant in a suit bronght in the Court of Chancery by his brother-in-law Michael Tennyson, probably in connexion with Christopher's administration as executor of his synonymous uncle's estate. We know nothing of this litigation but the evidence taken on commission in the course of another chancery suit involving the Tennyson and Clayton families has come down to us.

This was a suit brought by the younger Christopher, who had been defendant in Michael Tennyson's suit, against Joseph Foster, a clergy-man, and his wife Susannah, asking that the will of the late David Clayton (uncle of the plaintiff Christopher) might be declared null and void, as having been obtained by undue influence on the part of Susannah Foster in whose favour it was made. It seems that David Clayton, who had been for many years a salesman in Smithfield and in very poor circumstances, had inherited considerable property from the elder Christopher, and had returned to Grimsby in about 1760 suffering from some paralytic complaint, to live with and be looked after by Susannah (then Susannah Wright) who had been his housekeeper for several years. David, who had died in 1765, had made a will in 1763 and cancelled this in 1764 by one leaving everything he possessed to Susannah. Later in the year he became apprehensive about the validity of the devise in his will of some of his real estate and insisted on his title being strengthened by carrying out a now long extinct procedure known as a 'Recovery'. Most of the evidence recorded before the Commission related to this procedure. It seems that it took place very late at night on 19th November 1764, when David Clayton was carried from the house, where Susannah looked after him, to an inn nearby, which belonged to David and was kept by John Bowes as his tenant. Ralph Tennyson, Michael's elder brother, who had once been Mayor of Grimsby, was living at the inn. He had long been suffering from 'a despondency' and had not left his bed for two years. As a solicitor Ralph Tennyson was no doubt qualified to conduct the proceedings; another present was William Hildyard, also an attorney and therefore similarly qualified. John Bowes was uneasy, feeling that he had been chosen to witness the proceedings because he was a tenant of David Clayton and therefore subject to his control. When all had signed the documents he said to Foster, the parson, that he didn't know what he had signed. 'Hah, Hah!' replied the parson. 'Nor I neither.'

The circumstances attending the making of the will and the carrying out of the 'Recovery' were certainly suspicious, and the part played in it by the Tennyson family is strange. We have noted the aged and despondent Ralph's part. He was not called as a witness – perhaps he had died before the date of the Commission – but Michael and William, his brothers, both gave evidence, the first for the complainant, the second for the defendants. Michael may be thought to have been prejudiced against David Clayton, because his son George had been given a legacy under David's will of 1763, but on the testator's very definite instructions this had been cancelled in the will of 1764. Michael Tennyson, the apothecary, stated that he considered David to have been insane during the last years of his life. Other witnesses felt that, while very infirm in body and easily moved to tears, his mind was perfectly clear. Almost all however agreed that he was liable to violent outbursts of passion ('frequently and uncommonly addicted' said one witness

giving evidence on his behalf) during which he would curse and swear
– calling even Susannah 'a damned bitch' – and certainly could not then
be thought capable of reasonable decisions.

Was this tendency a result of David Clayton's paralytic illness, or
was it a Clayton characteristic? We have no conclusive evidence, but
the elder Christopher's behaviour in the South Sea Bubble inquiry
makes one inclined to think the latter, and the following entry in a
notebook of the younger Christopher, made in a diary which he kept,
under the date 24th July 1764, makes one feel that young Christopher
had little more self control than old Christopher or David:

As to the sanctity of an Oath infamous W. gave no Notion of it – All
their concern in giving evidence is not how to prove but how to
express what they say; they never appear in a cause but with the
resolution to hurt nor ever consider what words are proper for any
oath, but what are proper to do mischief taking it for the last disgrace
to be baffled confuted outdone in swearing, in short those sort of
people look on an oath as a mere jest, place all their credit livelihood,
praise on the success of an impudent Lye – one of the most memorable
flagrant perjuries which his crimes forged, dangers prepared – Kingdom
has ever known that my mother/father [sic] dyed in Bedlam and that
I was almost as mad as he – that we [meaning S.W.] had got him fast,
that a little swearing would do for him and Co.

Parson Foster offers to lay £5 Mr Clayton durst not carry on a suit
against Sus. Wright.

The entry is written in a very uncontrolled and illegible hand and it is
hard to be sure of the text. It certainly suggests a mind on the verge of
insanity and makes one wonder what effect the Clayton inheritance
might have had on Michael Tennyson's descendants.

CHAPTER TWO

GEORGE TENNYSON: A LINCOLNSHIRE GENTLEMAN

GEORGE Tennyson, only son of Michael and Elizabeth, was born at Hedon on 7th February 1750. It seems that Michael had already begun to acquire an aura of gentility from his marriage to the Clayton heiress, for William Gray, afterwards a well-known solicitor at York where he lived in what is still known as Gray's Court next to the Treasurer's House, recalled that at the Dame's School, to which they were both sent, young George was never beaten by the Dame, Betsy Dales, because he was 'a gentleman's son'. Whenever he had to be punished – and he was of a rebellious disposition – punishment was administered by tying him to the Dame's bed-post. At school at Beverley where he was sent after Betsy Dales', he was reckoned inordinately proud and nick-named 'Dindon' the Turkey Cock. Both he and William Gray were in due course apprenticed to a Hedon solicitor, called Iveson, whom George left in 1773, almost immediately setting up in practice at Market Rasen, a strategically placed town about half-way between Lincoln and Grimsby and within easy reach of Barton, Gainsborough, Caistor and Louth. Immediately after settling at Rasen George married Mary Turner, daughter of a quite important landed family at Caistor. In 1779 his Uncle William joined him as partner. His connexion with the Hildyards no doubt helped him to build up a good practice with the local landowners and he soon added banking to his activities, there being no bank at Rasen at the time. The partnership with William also helped him to establish close links with Grimsby, though the Clayton influence there was giving way to that of the Pelhams of Brocklesby, who were to be elevated to the peerage as Barons Yarborough towards the end of the century.

In fact the year 1774 during which George Tennyson settled at Market Rasen had been the first year to mark Brocklesby's challenge to the Claytons, for it saw the election to Parliament as one of the members for Grimsby of Evelyn Anderson, the younger brother of Anderson-Pelham who had succeeded in 1763, the year in which he went to Eton, to the family estate at Brocklesby about ten miles away. Anderson-Pelham was not only one of the richest commoners in England; he was astute, restless and ambitious, and the Claytons stood in his way. In 1780, and again in 1784, he won both the Grimsby seats; but the Clayton power was not yet broken. During the remaining years of the century, owing to general failure of issue, it gradually passed, with the Clayton property, more and more into the hands of George Tennyson, who became not only a man of considerable wealth (his uncle Christopher Clayton, who died in 1794, leaving him property worth not less than two thousand a year) but also the protagonist of the 'Red' (Tory) party in Grimsby against the Whig 'Blue' of the Pelhams. The main field of battle was the parliamentary one and here the two opponents were well matched – Pelham the great aristocrat and landowner with 55,000 acres at his back, George Tennyson, the astute lawyer, with the Clayton influence behind him and a highly confidential relationship to half the landowners in the county. Some disliked him and suspected him as *nouveau riche*, and as a man who might be assumed always to have an ulterior motive. His enemies would tell of having seen him sweeping out his Uncle William's office at Barton-on-Humber and would laugh at his alleged social inadequacies. But he was an exceedingly astute lawyer who won both the confidence and friendship of his clients and steadily strengthened his position, both personal and political, in Grimsby and the northern part of the county during the last twenty years of the century.

Eighteenth-century Grimsby was famous for the bitterness of its electoral contests and the number of election petitions which these produced. To a freeman a parliamentary election 'was his life and existence'. Votes were freely sold to the candidates and not always cast for the candidate who had paid for them and whose colours the voter was wearing. Members of the candidate's election committee were given lists (called 'billets') of voters who had promised support and those named on them 'lived like fighting cocks' during the period of the canvass. Sometimes doubtful voters were isolated in places where they could be safely looked after. As the date of an election drew near marriages between freemen's daughters and potential voters were arranged – often without consulting the bride, who was taken to the church in charge of two political bravos, while two others looked after the bridegroom, ingenious devices sometimes being adopted to conceal from him the lady's physical imperfections, so that a man might be surprised, after the election was over, to find that his wife had a wooden leg.

Amongst the most notorious of all Grimsby elections was that which took place in 1790. This was said to have cost the candidates not less than £80,000 and to have killed off a quarter of the electors. It led to an election petition which was heard by a committee of the House of Commons from 8th March to 10th April 1793, fifty-three witnesses giving evidence enough to fill 259 folio pages.

George Tennyson and his Uncle Christopher Clayton were the leaders of the 'Reds' in the contest, their candidates being the Hon. John Wellesley-Pole, the Duke of Wellington's elder brother, and Robert Wood, who owned the house in Putney where Edward Gibbon was born. The report of the evidence shews that George Tennyson took a very active part in the election. A very characteristic episode relates to one William Rodenhurst, then living at Greenwich, who had been a servant of Christopher Clayton in Grimsby and had then courted Ann Cook, daughter of a freeman. Christopher Clayton had done his best to encourage the marriage and promised Rodenhurst twenty pounds at every election if he could secure the Freedom. However the Cook family did not favour Rodenhurst, who fell ill, losing the use of his limbs (according to his own account), and left Grimsby in disgust, apparently considering himself ill-used by Christopher Clayton. In 1790 the Pelham party got hold of him and brought him back to Grimsby promising him good money for his vote if he could marry Ann and secure the Freedom. Ann, whom he had left pregnant, was willing to accept him, though her brothers threatened to kill him if he persisted in his suit. George Tennyson and his uncle Christopher now stepped in offering Rodenhurst fifty pounds to postpone the wedding until after the election. This he refused and set off for Brigg to procure a special licence, whereupon George, with the consent of the bride's family, carried her off and locked her up until the crisis was over. There is little trace of humour in George Tennyson's surviving correspondence, but one can imagine him chuckling grimly at the success of his man œuvre.

The report of the inquiry fully confirms the almost insane violence of the Clayton character. The unfortunate William Rodenhurst thus describes an interview with Christopher, after his return to Grimsby before the election:

He damned my blood and said I was come to be an enemy against him – I said I had no right to be in his party at all, for he used me very ill, when I lived with him – He turned me out when I had the use of my limbs taken off me and if I had not had a little money I should have laid in the street. . . . when I was taken ill he took me before the Mayor to take my cloaths off, when I was 200 miles from every parent; but they were my own.

The result of the inquiry was a finding that no one had been elected, the votes cast being exactly equal on both sides.

The next year, 1794, Christopher Clayton died and George Tennyson, released from bondage to the violent and erratic uncle upon whom his fortunes had so critically depended, immediately made an arrangement with Lord Yarborough designed to reduce political competition in the future. To quote his own words, 'While my Uncle Clayton was alive I was obliged in compliance with his wishes to oppose Lord Y but when he died we came to an explanation and I dare [say] we shall never be at variance more.'

However the arrangement only lasted for two elections and in 1802 Dr Parkinson reports George as saying that he did not care a damn for Lord Yarborough and only joined him to get an enclosure at Scartho and the haven at Grimsby and that in his heart he was as much a 'Red' as ever.

The result of the agreement during its short life was a marked improvement in the relations between the Tennysons and Brocklesby. By 1802 George was established as a country gentleman. His behaviour

now became more decorous and he seems for some years to have taken
less interest in party politics. But he maintained his interest in Grimsby.
Indeed the work which occupied him more continuously than any
other during the last years of the century was concerned with the
improvement of Grimsby Haven.

The first proposals for this, in 1787, seem to have been made on his
initiative. Although the overriding aim was to divert traffic from the
long-established port of Hull higher up the Humber, the scheme no
doubt had in part political objectives. Grimsby voters might be
expected to shew gratitude to those whose plans brought them new
prosperity and the docks would provide jobs with which to reward
political supporters. But George had his own economic advantage also
in view. The Claytons had a good deal of property adjacent to the
Haven, which gradually fell into his lap, and he himself rounded off
these properties by new acquisitions. If the Haven could be improved
and deepened and brought nearer to the old town, all these properties
would benefit and he might hope that new housing estates would
grow up on these same properties which would provide tenancies for
'Red' voters. From the beginning the Haven scheme proved of most
interest not to merchants but to the north Lincolnshire landowners,
who were keen to have easier access for timber and other imports
required for their estates. One effect of the campaign was to make
George Tennyson, who as yet owned a mere four or five thousand
acres, many friends among the great landowners. Lord Yarborough,
with his 55,000 acres, could not refuse to back the scheme, and its
development brought him and George Tennyson into social relations
which were quite friendly, though on Lord Yarborough's side probably
rather contemptuous. Aynscough Boucherett of North Willingham
was more genuinely friendly, as was his close friend John Julius
Angerstein, of Stainton le Vale, perhaps the greatest marine insurance
man in history, whose collection of pictures was to form the nucleus of
the National Gallery in London. The Reverend Marmaduke Alington
of Swinhope, Philip Skipworth of Aylesby and the Heneages of
Hainton also became supporters and friends.

This was a time when the beginnings of the Industrial Revolution
were stimulating dock extensions and constructions all round our

shores, both for the importation of materials and the export of industrial products. But technical knowledge and experience were scanty and the pioneers encountered many obstacles. This was certainly so at Grimsby where physical conditions were particularly difficult, and although the first scheme was put forward in 1787 it was not until John Rennie was appointed ten years later (probably on George Tennyson's suggestion) that real progress began to be made. Industrial finance was also in its infancy and many difficulties were experienced, first in securing the necessary acts of parliament and then in raising the capital authorized. The brunt fell upon George Tennyson who had more personal interests at stake than most of his collaborators and found himself, owing to his profession and political involvement, carrying most of the responsibility. It is not surprising that, a year after the Dock had been officially opened in December 1800, he is found confessing to a friend that the Grimsby Dock had been such a plague to him that, with the consent of the other subscribers, he would freely sell it as an assistant dock to Hull.

In fact the Grimsby Haven Company was never successful until the railway came and took it over in the middle 1840s, by which time it had spent the whole of its £68,000 capital and owed £136,000 in addition. The reason for this failure is clear, though the promoters, George Tennyson amongst them, do not seem to have perceived it. There was a great need of docks to carry on the country's rapidly increasing trade and the Grimsby docks constructed by George and his friends were, at the time of their construction, the largest in the country and designed by the country's finest dock engineer. But for commercial purposes Grimsby had no hinterland. It had no connexion with the great manufacturing industries of Yorkshire and Lancashire and there was no local raw material for it to export. It was not until the 1840s, when the Sheffield, Ashton-under-Lyne and Manchester Railway decided to extend to Grimsby, take over the old Haven Company and build a new and much larger port, that Grimsby's difficulties were solved. But by that time George Tennyson had been dead ten years.

Fortunately for him George Tennyson proved much more successful in many of the other activities which he carried on while trying to establish the Grimsby Dock and Haven. His Uncle William died in

1787 leaving him the pleasant white house on the Caistor Road just outside the little town of Market Rasen, in which he had settled. The house still stands and is known as The Grove. George now took a partner and the firm of Tennyson & Main became one of the most successful in north Lincolnshire, taking a foremost part in the enclosure movement which was gathering strength in that part of the country during the last twenty years of the eighteenth century. In this work George's exceptional knowledge of manorial rights and customs was of great value. He soon began to be regarded as a man of unusual learning and this reputation was enhanced when a large hoard of Henry II coins was discovered on one of his farms and he presented an example of each type to the British Museum. He bought land steadily when prices were low during the French and American wars and soon became a formidable figure in county society.

His style of correspondence, even with important clients, was uncompromising – for example: 'Sir, You are a man of leisure and I am not and have no time for peevish and ill-tempered correspondence' and 'I flatter myself it is no part of my character to resist the payment of any money that I may owe or on any account to submit to the payment of money I ought not to pay, therefore when I read your letters I am at a loss to know upon what you presume'. Even to the great Lord Yarborough who was proving somewhat remiss in the payment of an account, in connexion with which George was acting for him, he could write, 'I do not feel myself at ease on this subject and unless money is paid very soon on account, I must advance the interest to the creditors myself and wait the event, for it is painful to me to be suspected for a moment of impropriety in my profession, in my capacity of Justice or in any other respect'.

On 7th September 1798 Dr Parkinson records a conversation between George and Lord Yarborough: *George* 'It would be well, my Lord, if you could be taught to say No and Mr Vyner to say Yes'. *Lord Yarborough* 'God! I shall remember your remark. If I had done so I should have avoided many a scrape'.

In fact his world must have seen him very much as did Sir Thomas Lawrence, who painted his portrait in 1801 – fair, fresh-coloured, handsome, alert, practical and uncompromising – but not a man likely to be the grandfather of poets. Indeed he had no interest whatever in the imaginative side of life and his total indifference to religion distressed his gentle wife and his friend William Gray, a devoted churchman who spent his life in the shadow of York Minster. George's attitude to religion was evidently widely known and commented on, for when Dr Parkinson heard that he had begun reading the Bible he recorded the event in his diary (16th January 1802).

But George Tennyson's apparent hardness and self-control masked a morbid and ungovernable sensibility. This shewed itself partly in an extreme fussiness about his health – perhaps with some reason, for, although according to family tradition he was a staunch teetotaller, he became a martyr to gout at a comparatively early age. He was also easily depressed and liable to moods of indecision and fretfulness, stuttering when embarrassed and easily losing self-control. This tendency perplexed his friends who found it hard to understand why he so often allowed his vanity or vexation or fears of defeat to provoke him to impolitic answers or actions. His daughter-in-law Fanny came nearer to the truth when she wrote many years later, 'It is his nature to be active and when in the course of everyday events things do not go smoothly his mind is perturbed and that morbid sensibility prevails'. In such moods he would explode into violence and sarcasm which were excessively wounding. He himself gave a slightly different explanation: 'you know I am too much alive to fear and a thousand times to one anticipate what never happens'. It was no doubt for this reason that opponents, such as Lord Yarborough, accused him of timidity and indecisiveness, but his success in so many fields suggests that he did not lack courage and decisiveness when it came to the crunch. There was another, more romantic side to this suppressed sensibility. The Hild-yard pedigree and the half hours spent long ago attached to Betsy Dales' bed-post had left their mark and he seems early in life to have conceived the ambition to restore the Tennyson, or Tennyson-Clayton, family to the more exalted social position to which their ancestry, in his opinion, entitled them.

In 1783 when only thirty-three years old he bought from Sir Wharton Amcotts and his wife one half of the Manor of Beacons at Tealby for £1,000. Four years later, in 1787, he bought the other

half from the Rev. Brownlow Potter for £1,100. This purchase was
to have great importance in the family story, for the manor (the name
of which he quickly changed to what was claimed to have been its
ancient and much more romantic name, 'Bayons' – alleged to be a
corruption of Bayeux) had belonged to Francis, Lord Lovel and
d'Eyncourt, an ancestor of Dorothy Hildyard, and on the high ground
above the small seventeenth-century manor house were the foundations
of what had once been the manorial stronghold. George Tennyson
spoke at times of building a new mansion on the site of the old castle,
but in fact he never carried out this idea, nor did he actually move into
the manor house until about 1801. From that time onward Mr Tennyson of Bayons Manor became every year more and more the well-
established country gentleman, less and less the country solicitor, and
he continued adding to his estates in and around Tealby for the next
thirty years.

By the time George Tennyson had established himself at Bayons,
Mary, his wife, had apparently ceased to count for very much in the
family. She seemed his antithesis in every respect, mental as well as
physical. Her portrait by the famous pastellist John Russell (now at
the Usher Art Gallery, Lincoln) shews a tall dark woman with sensitive
aquiline features and a pensive expression. Family tradition credits her
with skill in music and painting and Alfred remembered her reading
'The Prisoner of Chillon' aloud to him 'very tenderly'. She herself
claimed that the poetic talents of her grandchildren derived from her,
though research has so far failed to find any other hint of creative
talent or sensibility in the Turner family. Mary's most remarkable
relative was, apparently, her brother Samuel, a hard-drinking, gam-
bling, pluralist parson, of whom Hallam, Lord Tennyson records in
his *Memoir* of the poet (Vol. I p. 12) that he one day 'smashed the
bottom of his glass of rum and water on the dinner table as he in-
veighed against "this new-fangled Byron." ' Mary had a strong belief
in the supernatural or supersensual and Dr Parkinson records in one
year (1802) no less than eight stories emanating from her and dealing,
for example, with apparitions at the time of death, death warnings,
'disturbed' houses and visionary conversions. Even her materialist
husband seems to have been impressed by some of these.

Until her mother's death Mary wrote to her continually and with passionate affection, as for example in this undated but probably fairly early letter:

When I receive your letters I feel that inward Joy unspeakable which if you was to deny me off [sic] thro' any misfortune or Illness – which God be praised has never yet been the case – I should be lost indeed as I should lose one of the greatest comforts I now enjoy and I hope will still continue to do so.

The correspondence shews her as deeply affectionate and sincerely religious, with a natural gift for self-expression and she is said also to have written verse, none of which is known to survive. Market Rasen, where the first twenty or more years of her married life were spent, she always found dull and unattractive after Caistor where her early life had evidently been exceptionally happy. Her husband, though in general 'very tender and pittysome', seemed to be always away at his office or pursuing his multifarious objectives at Grimsby or elsewhere. 'We are happy at present', she writes to her mother on 2nd June 1777, 'in having nearly every comfort we can wish for which is a great deal for any one to say and nobody can say with truth they are entirely happy'. Evidently the society of Market Rasen offered few compensations. She detested polite conversation and hated 'the very name of dress'. In the spring of 1784 she writes of having an old gown or two made up again in order to get herself 'vamp'd up for the year'.

In the 1790s George took a lease of part of Deloraine Court, a house belonging to the Dean and Chapter just north of Lincoln Cathedral, no doubt hoping to establish closer relations with the social leaders of the county before establishing himself at Bayons. Perhaps he also hoped to make useful contacts in the campaign to raise funds for the Grimsby Haven Scheme. The attempt was not a success, the close society of Lincoln 'above hill' proving very unresponsive and in 1797 George and his family left Lincoln for Grimsby. The move had probably something to do with the property which George had inherited from Christopher Clayton in 1794 and it seems that the family remained at Grimsby until George moved to Bayons in about 1801.

Her position at Bayons Mary Tennyson no doubt found more agreeable and it is certain that she remained a devoted wife until her death in 1825, looking up to her irritable and dominating husband with a youthful affection and admiration which shine delightfully through those of her letters to him which have survived. After forty-five years of married life she would, when he was away from home, send every evening to the Post Office in order to get his letters at the earliest possible moment. 'On great occasions', she explains to him with charming complacency, 'my activity and anxiety equals if not exceeds your own.'

Her husband seems to have returned her affection as far as his harder and more active nature allowed. She was an excellent manager, always careful of his comfort and health – and it was characteristic of the George Tennysons as of their descendants that they were continually ill or thought themselves ill. Even when he was eighty-three years old and had only just given up riding about his extensive estates on horseback George Tennyson's son Charles had to caution his children never to write to their grandfather as though they thought he was well, as that would irritate him past bearing. Very characteristic of the family was a letter which Mary Tennyson wrote to her younger son eight years before her death:

Most feelingly can I aver that the plague of the bowels is a pest – for the perpetual calculation that is requisite to discriminate right from wrong in the operation of medicine through the great intestinal canal is a work of art and experience to keep our unworthy and perishable materials above ground and this I pray you may all do when we are no more.

Perhaps her sense of humour, a sense in which her husband was conspicuously lacking, helped her to put up with his peculiarities and may indeed have given her a mild sense of superiority, without which she might have found her restricted and too dependent life difficult to endure. So these two apparently incompatible beings preserved through fifty years of married life mutual affection and respect, and when death took Mary Tennyson ten years before her husband his letter to their eldest daughter masked with a truly Roman brevity what was perhaps the deepest and most unselfish emotion that he was ever to feel – 'I saw her dying; I saw her dead; I am alive'. Months afterwards, writing to Charles at the end of January 1826, he refers to his beloved Bayons as 'poor dank and melancholy and ever will be while I live at it; being unhappy in myself, I make all around me if not miserable, quiet and grave'.

CHAPTER THREE

GEORGE TENNYSON
AND HIS CHILDREN

EORGE and Mary Tennyson had four children: Elizabeth born in 1776; Mary born in 1777; George born in 1778 and Charles born in 1784. By what must have been rather a singular arrangement in those days, Mary and George were sent away at a very early age – Mary to live with Mrs Turner, her maternal grandmother, at Caistor until early in 1788, and George to Michael Tennyson in Holderness. The only reasons given in their mother's letters are the rather surprising ones that it would 'save her trouble and expense' and that 'if we had 3 at home we could not do without another servant'. Although there is no evidence that the two children were not happy in their exile, or that they suffered from any feeling of rejection by their parents, one cannot help observing that Mary and George were to prove the two difficult members of the family when they grew up. Perhaps they were too happy with their grandparents and felt the wrench when the time came for them to return to their parents. Though there is no evidence of their father's reaction to their return, one cannot ignore his bad relations with both George and Mary in later years.

Young George seems to have been a difficult child from the beginning. On 17th May 1785 when old Michael Tennyson brought him on a visit to Rasen, his mother wrote 'I am thank God well – if I was otherwise I should be almost ready to run away at this time for our house is all noise and distraction since George and his Grandfather came. I think I never saw a child so rude and ungovernable' and a fortnight later, when she herself is going off on a visit, she writes 'I leave George and his Father and grandfather to keep house if they can but agree'. These references suggest that little George had already established a rather dominant position for a seven-year-old. Perhaps his grandfather spoiled him – as grandfathers are apt to do – for in after life he used to recall with pleasure how old Michael would take him into his bed in the early mornings and talk to him about the stars.

Bessie, the eldest child, was undoubtedly the favourite, and indeed she was her mother's constant companion. She was evidently a very nervous child from her earliest years. In an undated letter (probably written about 1780) her mother writes of one or two frightening nights with her:

screaming exactly as if she had seen something super-natural, tho' she was too young to know anything of spirits and hobgoblins. We all thought she had seen something we did not see. God only knows what it was. It has made a strange impression on her. The Boy stood all amazement in his shirt by the side of me.

Again in March 1787 Mary describes terrible nights with Bessie, now eleven years old. The child, she reports, will only eat lemons and oranges. Two years later the whimsicality of her appetite is again noted. Sometimes she would eat a beef steak to her breakfast; at others she sickened at the sight of victuals and her sleep was such as to give her no refreshment. For half an hour she would be full of complaints. The next they would vanish altogether. No doubt the fussiness about health of both her parents was to some extent responsible for these peculiarities. Her grandfather, the apothecary, certainly blamed her father for her precarious state and would warn him 'every dose of physic that child takes is one more nail in her coffin.' However, Elizabeth survived both the devotion of her parents and the distractions of her distracted family. Inheriting many of her mother's delightful qualities, she grew up deeply sensitive and affectionate.

In 1798 she married Matthew Russell, the jovial son of a self-made coal millionaire who had bought Brancepeth Castle in County Durham from the ancient family of the Nevilles, owned two rotten boroughs which he manipulated in the Whig interest and had political connexions in Grimsby and Lincoln. With Matthew, Elizabeth enjoyed twenty-five years of improbably happy married life, then handed over Brancepeth

B

to her daughter who had married Lord Boyne, and died a humorous mystical octogenarian at Cheltenham in the 1860s.

Mary, the second daughter, who seems as a child to have been much beloved by her grandmother Turner, must have undergone a startling change of character after her return to her parents, becoming morose, moody and difficult. Later she developed a peculiarly aggressive brand of Calvinism, married John Bourne of Dalby, a dissenting squire who lived two or three miles from Somersby, and after the burning-down of their home in 1841 and her husband's death spent the remainder of her life wandering about from one health resort to another, quarrelling furiously and dramatically with landladies and companions and attacking her diseases, which, like all Tennysons, she believed to be many and severe, with 'fierce medicines and strict regimen'.

Neither of the sisters was able to exercise a conciliatory influence on the bitter conflict which was to arise from their father's preference of his second over his elder son.

Charles, George's youngest child, came in 1784. Mary Tennyson was much distressed by the unexpected and, one may suspect, unwanted pregnancy. On 19th December 1783 she writes to her mother of her struggles to remain happy and composed.

I called my reason to aid and said to myself, am not I in the situation of thousands in this respect and half of them don't enjoy one tenth part of the comforts of this world as I now do, then I have great reason to be happy. After which I petitioned the Almighty to bestow upon me a composed mind, for at dead of night I would awake frightened and flutter'd for I scarce knew why till a little recollection brought it to my mind. It was uppermost sleeping and waking. I shall put my whole trust and confidence in *that Being* that can extricate me out of all difficulty.

The birth of little Charles was a crucial event in the history of the Tennyson family for, as the boy grew up, his father developed an almost morbid affection for him and a corresponding dislike for his elder brother, which ultimately led to a decision destined to have incalculable effects on the elder son and his descendants.

The correspondence gives no idea how rapidly this position developed. Young George was sent in 1787 to St Peter's Grammar School at York, where he was remembered for the skill of his verse translations from Latin and Greek. In after years he used to lament that he had not been sent to Eton (no doubt he felt that as the eldest son of a landed family he should have been) as he believed that Eton would have given him a greater fluency and polish in versification. From St Peter's he went in 1794 or 1795 for a year to a Mr Hutchinson at Holywell in Huntingdonshire to be prepared for Cambridge. In 1796 he matriculated at St John's College. Charles followed him to St Peter's in due course and went in 1798 to Louth School until he too passed on to St John's College, Cambridge, where he took his degree in 1804.

The fact that his father was in 1790 and 1791 negotiating for livings to be kept warm for a son or son-in-law does not necessarily mean that he had already decided to make Charles successor to his county estates and social position and to force George into the church. But a letter from Mr Orme, headmaster of Louth School, to Charles's father on 15th December 1800, may possibly have some relevance. In this Mr Orme speaks very favourably of young Charles except with regard to his tendency to extravagance. And even of this he speaks reassuringly, reflecting that 'time and the advice of friends seldom fail in contributing to the check if not the cure of most improprieties. I except one which is seldom cured, I mean that of lifting the hand to the head, which when become habitual is the greatest curse that can befall a young man.' One wonders, in the light of what was to happen later, whether he had heard anything unfavourable about Charles's elder brother who was now in his last year at Cambridge.

Young George ultimately took his degree in the spring of 1801. It was only a pass degree, for the reasons given in a delightfully pompous letter which he wrote to his father on 1st March of that year:

You seem inclined that I should take my degree as speedily as I can yet you are very good to leave it to my determination. Now though I think I could take a good degree by waiting till the regular time, and though I have by a habitual study of Mathematics acquired a pleasure in the acquisition of further knowledge in many branches of them, yet were I to aim at the very highest honours it would require such continual application and exertion and a knowledge of such other parts of them which to me are perfectly disinteresting and which I believe are generally acknowledged to be almost useless, as would neither suit my health, time or inclination. The anxiety I should suffer, the deprivation of better knowledge could only be compensated by the hope of an uncertain and at best a transitory honour.

Little is known about young George's Cambridge career. According to family tradition it was not free from trouble. It is said that he once put a pistol-shot through a window of Trinity College Chapel (the next college to St John's) but luckily escaped detection, though a reward was offered for the discovery of the culprit. The very scanty surviving correspondence suggests that his father was uneasy about his extravagance and suspected idleness. His tutor's report (dated 11th July 1799) of success in the college examination was reassuring but not, apparently, convincing: 'With respect to his general conduct, I should have much the same to say as when I last had the pleasure of writing to you. Notwithstanding a good deal of apparent idleness, it is a proof of real industry that he obtained a place in the first class at our late examination.'

A few months later old George even got his son's former coach, Mr Hutchinson of Holywell, to do a little snooping. Here is Mr Hutchinson's report:

> Holywell. Feb. 11th 1800
> Dear Sir,
> I made inquiry and heard nothing blameable in his conduct. I have since called upon him, always found him reading and so lately as this day week he was so deeply engaged to enter the schools for his degree (which I am persuaded will do him honour) that he declined dining from College. . . . Dining in their rooms is expensive and so is the university, like other places, become. I mention this because, as I recollect, your inquiry chiefly turned on that subject. But I am sure his conduct is proper, and his application always pleasing to him, and his morals pure. I rest satisfied with him as a pupil, and doubt not you to be so through life as a son. . . .

George Tennyson's doubts about his elder son's fitness to become leader of the Tennyson family did not affect his determination to send him into the Church, which he seems to have regarded as an institution created solely to provide incomes for the younger sons of the landed gentry. Nor was he affected by his son's unwillingness to undertake a clerical career for which he considered himself very ill-suited. On 11th May 1801 young George was ordained deacon and no more is heard of him until the autumn when there occurred the mysterious episode of his visit to Russia, which Alfred used to tell, no doubt as he had heard it from his father (see Hallam Lord Tennyson's *Memoir* II 147). On 21st September 1801 Alexander, whose predecessor, the Emperor Paul, had been murdered in March, was to be crowned Czar at Moscow, and Lord St Helens, an old St John's man, was to represent England at the ceremony. Young George Tennyson apparently suggested to his father that he should make a trip to Moscow for the event. His father agreed and young George set out, but unfortunately arrived too late for the ceremony. However he found Lord St Helens at St Petersburg and was invited by him to dine. In the course of dinner young Tennyson said to his host, across a Russian who was sitting between them: 'It is perfectly well-known in England who murdered the Emperor Paul – it was Count so-and-so'. A dead silence fell on the company and after dinner Lord St Helens called young George aside and said to him 'Ride for your life; the man across whom you spoke to me was Count so-and-so'. George immediately took horse and rode across Russia to the Crimea, where he fell ill and lay for some time delirious with no other tendance than that of the wild country people who would dance round his bed with magical incantations. Once in every three months an English courier passed through the village blowing a horn. It all depended on George Tennyson's hearing this horn, whether he would be able to escape from Russia, for he had no money. At last the courier came, young Tennyson heard the horn, arranged for the man to take him and after many adventures got home to England more than five months after he had left it.

Can the story be true? Family papers confirm the visit to Russia with a letter of introduction to Lord St Helens, and the long absence without news. All through November and December there are letters to old George from friends: 'Have you heard anything of poor George?' 'We are truly sorry to find you under alarm about George' and so on. Then on 20th December comes a letter from an officer of the ship on

which the young man had sailed, explaining that owing to the unexpected length of the voyage to St Petersburg and the advancement
of the date for the Coronation by a week the party had arrived too
late to attend the ceremony and that young George, after waiting to see
the Emperor who was to come to St Petersburg on 15th October, had
set off with some friends for Moscow, whence he proposed to make
his way home via Hamburg, arriving about the middle of January.
In fact, he got back early in February 1802. On his way home to
Lincolnshire he stopped a few days at Cambridge to visit his brother
and it is some support for his strange story of adventure in Russia that
Charles found him in alarmingly poor health – 'I think', wrote Charles
to his father on 19th February 1802, 'that had he gone on immediately
it would have been little less than suicide'. However, even with this
support for his story, it is difficult to avoid the feeling that he invented
or at least greatly exaggerated it in order to justify his prolonged
absence. Or did he perhaps invent the story later in a pathetic attempt
to create for his children the romance of George Tennyson, to which
unkind fate had denied reality? His account of his adventures in Italy
nearly thirty years later (see p. 76) certainly supports this possibility.

The evidence available permits no solution of the problem and we
know no more of his activities during the year 1802 until 19th December when he was ordained priest. Two days later he was inducted
Rector of Benniworth near Louth. In August 1805 he married Elizabeth
Fytche, daughter of the Vicar of Louth and niece of a Bishop of
Lincoln, and on the last day of 1806 was instituted Rector of Somersby
and Bag Enderby on the Lincolnshire Wolds twelve miles to the south,
though he did not move into the rectory until 1808 owing to alterations
and extensions which had to be made to the house.

It has been suggested that old George Tennyson did not approve of
his elder son's marriage, but there seems to be no reason for such a
view. The Fytches were a well-established Lincolnshire family.
Elizabeth (or Eliza) was very popular in Louth society and a noted
beauty. She was simple, gentle, evangelically pious, and even if, as
seems only too likely, the marriage had only a very brief period of
happiness, the fault can hardly have been on her side.

CHAPTER FOUR

YOUNG GEORGE

A T THIS point we may pause a moment to survey the position and mutual relations of George Tennyson the elder and his family. At about the time that young George took his degree, his father moved into Bayons Manor, and his brother Charles left Louth School and passed on to Cambridge. Elizabeth, the oldest of the family, had been four or five years married to Matthew Russell.

A letter which the elder son wrote to his father on 14th August 1820, when he was forty-two, suggests that he had first become apprehensive about his father's preference for his younger brother some time during his own residence at Cambridge, and one can well believe that it was during this time that George Tennyson, encouraged by Elizabeth's rich marriage, which brought with it valuable political connexions, and by the promising development of his second son, decided to move into Bayons Manor and begin his campaign to make the Tennysons a county family.

Here is the letter:

Aug. 14th 1820

My dear Father,

I find, to my great disquietude, that you have thought proper to attribute to my suggestion or instigation certain expressions which may or may not have been used by Miss Fytche reflecting on your conduct as a parent. I utterly disdain to exculpate myself from this charge. I did intend to have visited Tealby, but an accusation so unjust, so frequently reiterated and so totally unsubstantiated has so far oppressed my spirits and irritated my feelings that it is impossible I should do so with any pleasure. With the sentiments you yet entertain and have entertained for more than 20 years, I cannot wonder you told Mr Bourne you had not a spark of affection for me. The rude and unprecedented manner in which you first address'd me at Hainton, after a long absence on your return from York (I quote your own words *'Now you great awkward booby are you here'*) holding me up to utter derision before Mr Heneage, his sons and Sir Robert Ainslie. Your language and conduct in innumerable other instances, many of which have made a deep impression on my mind sufficiently prove the truth of your own assertion. You have long injured me by your suspicions. I cannot avoid them, for the fault is not mine. God judge between you and me. You make and have always made a false estimate of me in every respect. You look and have always looked on me with a jaundiced eye, and deeply and experimentally feeling this, I am sure that my visiting you would not contribute to your satisfaction and at the same time would materially injure my own health and comfort. Conscious also that I am thrown into a situation unworthy of my abilities and unbecoming either your fortune or my just pretensions, and resisted in my every wish to promote my own interests or that of my family by removing to a more eligible situation, unaccountably kept in the dark with respect to their future prospects, with broken health and spirits, I find myself little disposed to encounter those unprovoked and sarcastic remarks in which you are so apt to indulge yourself at my expense, remarks which though they may be outwardly borne, are inwardly resented, and prey upon the mind – the injustice, the inhumanity and the impropriety of which every one can see but yourself, which in your last visit were levelled against the father of a large family in the very presence of his children and that father between 40 and 50 years of age. I should not have proceeded thus far had you not by your unjust expressions set fire to the mass which was already disposed to ignite. You may forget or pass off as a jest what penetrates and rankles in the heart; you may break what is already bent, but there is a tribunal before which you and I may speedily appear, more speedily perhaps than either of us desire or expect. There it will be seen whether you through life have treated me with the consideration and kindness which a son has a right to expect from a father and whether (as you have been accustomed to represent me to myself and others) I have been deficient in filial affection and obedience. I am my dear Father, your affectionate son,

G. C. TENNYSON

We quote this letter in full because it throws a strong light on both parties to the dispute. It is characteristic of the son in the bitter clarity with which he recalls the offences of his father while entirely ignoring any possible shortcomings of his own, and characteristic of the father in the morbid sensibility and irritability which it suggests. Taking the words 'you great awkward booby' (which one must believe were actually spoken) with what we know of young George from other sources, one gets the rather formidable impression of a tall, swarthy, untidy, awkward boy, with tricks of voice and gesture suggesting a highly nervous temperament, excessive sensibility and marked intolerance of convention and discipline. No doubt the contrast with the able, pliant, conventional, affectionate younger son, who was just then emerging into manhood, made a powerful impression on the ambitious and strong-willed father. It seems therefore highly probable that George Tennyson's decision to give his second son preference crystallized during the elder brother's time at Cambridge. The mysterious Russian adventure is not inconsistent with this. George Tennyson was, like most men who are laboriously engaged in building up a fortune, very close-fisted about money. The Russian trip must have been very expensive, and it may well be that the father agreed to meet the expense as a sop to his conscience, which cannot have been entirely easy about his treatment of his elder son, while the son may have prolonged his trip to five months in a resentful determination to have a really worthwhile last fling before settling down to the humdrum life to which his father was condemning him. The reference in young George's letter to his father's resistance to his removal 'to a more eligible situation' suggests that, when old George secured the living of Grimsby for him in 1815, the son may have wanted to move there from Somersby but was prevented by his father, possibly because the father feared ill effects on his own social ambitions from the son's appearance at Grimsby where the family was so well known.

Of course there was no need for old George to disclose his intentions in regard to the division of his property until his death and the publication of his will, but it seems clear that he wished to make his preference plain during his lifetime – indeed immediately – for Hallam, Lord Tennyson records that a neighbouring squire (Heneage of Hainton) on being told by young George's father of his intention replied 'George, if you do this you will be damned, you will indeed'.

Heneage's reaction was not solely due to the sacred principle of primogeniture. No doubt young George had already made an impression in his own right. He was tall (over six feet) and strongly made, with rugged but pleasing features, swarthy complexion and black hair. His voice was remarkably strong and vibrant, his walk rapid and decisive. Not long after settling at Somersby he was appointed a Justice of the Peace and his attendance at Spilsby Sessions was always welcomed by the barristers' mess owing to the brilliance and geniality of his conversation. However much he disliked his profession, he seems to have taken its duties seriously, preaching the kind of elaborately dogmatic sermons (some of which can be seen at the Tennyson Research Centre, Lincoln) which were expected from a parson at that time, without much thought for their suitability to his rustic congregation, one of whom years afterwards told an enquirer ' 'E read 'em from a paäper and I didn't know what 'e meant.' But his methods were not wholly conventional. Tradition says that he would never read the Athanasian Creed, was stoutly opposed to the doctrine of eternal punishment and took a great deal of snuff in the pulpit.

It seems that at one time he contemplated publishing a collection of 'Select Miscellaneous Compositions' – probably after his appointment to Benniworth but before his institution to Somersby and Bag Enderby. He was an excellent Latin scholar with a fair knowledge of Greek and could read Syriac, Hebrew and several modern languages. He was also a good musician, playing excellently upon the harp, and was deeply interested in architecture and painting. As is well known, he designed the curious Gothic Hall, which he and his servant, Horlins, built at Somersby in 1819 to accommodate his increasing family, and executed many of the carvings on the mantelpiece and over the door himself.

He collected a considerable number of quite tolerable old masters and amongst his papers have been found a manuscript treatise on oil painting covering forty-four pages and followed by a list of famous painters of all countries including over 200 names, with the dates of their births and deaths and occasional notes. The same notebook (now at Lincoln) contains an elaborate treatise on bookbinding, illustrated with fine pen drawings by the Doctor himself, who used to bind with his own hands the manuscript books used by Alfred during his boyhood. There are also historical notes, one series being on Queen Mary, at the end of which is written in his hand the concise summary 'a sad, bloody devil'. Other pages contain mathematical problems, illustrations of such things as a new method of hanging curtains, drawings of figures and faces, some very well done, sketches of proposed buildings and so on.

His taste in books was that of a widely read scholar and connoisseur and in the early days of his married life he bought extensively, with an especial fondness for fine sixteenth- and seventeenth-century folio editions of classical authors, many of which he obtained at the sale of the library of Bennet Langton, of Langton Hall (two or three miles from Somersby), the friend of Dr Johnson, who had succeeded the Doctor as Professor of Ancient Literature to the Royal Academy and died in 1801. Considerable relics of the Somersby library are now in the Tennyson Collection at Lincoln, but the inventory taken at Dr Tennyson's death, in June 1831, of which what appears to be a very inaccurate copy remains, shows that the original collection was very much larger, amounting to not less than 1,300 titles and 2,500 volumes and covering a very wide range of subjects. The largest section is theological. This suggests that Dr Tennyson had a deeper interest in his profession than one would suppose from his unhappy life-story and the very secular tone of his correspondence. There are many editions of the Testaments, both old and new, in English, Greek, Latin, Hebrew and Syriac, while the inclusion of Hebrew and Syriac grammars and dictionaries shows that the Doctor's study of these languages was more than perfunctory. There are many works on ecclesiastical history and a large collection of sermons. Amongst general theological works the inclusion of such books as Priestley's *History of the Corruptions of Christianity*, Pastorel's *Zorcastré, Confucius et Mahomet* (1788), works by Eusebius, Gregory Nazianzen and Fénelon, Casaubon's *De Rebus Sacris*, Cudworth's *Morality* (1731), Condorcet's *Outlines* and a considerable number of volumes by Voltaire, suggests an unconventional approach for a country parson.

Ancient philosophy was well covered in the classical section and Dr Tennyson owned Locke's works in ten volumes, Descartes' *Meditations*, Garnett's *Philosophy* (2 vols 1801) and works by Paley, Whiston, Nieuwentydt and others. Godwin's *Political Justice*, Burke *On the Sublime*, and Ferguson's *Moral and Political Science* (2 vols 1792) touch on kindred subjects.

The classical collection is very comprehensive. The standard authors

are well represented, the great number of editions of Homer and
Cicero showing a special interest in these authors. In addition there is a
wide range of post-classical and secondary writers, such as (to quote
only a few examples) the *Satyricon* of Petronius (two editions) the
Eclogues of Stobaeus, Chariton's *Chaereas and Callirhoe*, Themistius'
Orations, Valerius' *Argonautica*, the poems of Prudentius, Lycophron's
Cassandra, and the histories of Quintus Curtius, Suetonius and L.
Annaeus Florus. A goodly array of dictionaries, grammars and
commentaries supports the main collection.

The largest section of all was probably the historical. Greece, Rome
(Gibbon in 12 vols), England, Scotland, France, Spain, America and
India are covered, the first five very fully, and there is a considerable
collection of memoirs, biographies (for instance, lives of Catherine the
Great and Genghis Khan), books of travel and 'antiquities', including
the well-known works of Gros and Brand. An interesting item in
view of Dr Tennyson's Russian adventure is a volume entitled *Secret
Memoirs of the Court of Petersburg* 1801.

The scientific collection was small but important. It included
Newton's *Principia*, the complete works of Euclid (Gregory, 1703),
McLaurin's *Algebra*, Stone on *The Construction and Use of Mathematical
Instruments*, Pliny's and Buffon's *Natural Histories*, Borelli *De Motu
Animalium*, two books on *Mechanics* (1807 and 1818), Vince on *The
Principles of Fluxions*, Priestley's *Electricity*, Adam Smith's *Wealth of
Nations*, Horne Tooke's *Diversions of Purley* (philological), Watt's
Logic, Winslow's *Anatomy*, the aphorisms of Boerhaave, Linnaeus'
introduction to the *Systema Naturae*, two volumes on astrology,
Marshall's *Gardening*, Hill's *British Herbal*, Rohault's *Physics* and several
books on chemistry.

A few standard books on law such as Bacon's *Abridgement*, Black-
stone's *Commentaries* and Cunningham's *Law Dictionary* are probably
due to Dr Tennyson's appointment as a magistrate.

The collection of belles-lettres is not as full as might have been
expected, though Inchbald's plays, fifty volumes of British novelists
and twelve of ancient romances make a good foundation. Among the
poets are volumes by Cowper, Hayley, Scott, Byron, Beattie, Rogers
and Cowley, Bloomfield's *Farmer's Boy*, Macpherson's *Ossian*, Spenser's

Faerie Queen (2nd edition), Milton, the complete works of Chaucer, Shakespeare and Beaumont and Fletcher, Butler's *Hudibras* and Percy's *Reliques*. Foster on *Accent and Quantity* is an intriguing entry and of special interest is that strange book Bryant's *Mythology* which may have had considerable influence on Alfred Tennyson's approach to the Arthurian legends. His university prize poem 'Timbuctoo' suggests that he was familiar with it at an early age. Also very influential for Alfred was the small collection of books on oriental subjects, which included Sir William Jones's works, Savary's *Letters from Egypt*, Jablonski's *Pantheon Egyptiorum* and Sale's *Koran*. In Italian Dr Tennyson had the works of Ariosto, *The Decameron*, *Orlando Furioso*, the complete works of Machiavelli and two English editions of *The Divine Comedy*. The French collection was inconsiderable and very unrepresentative, though it contained a very fine Montaigne's *Essays* of 1595 and Rabelais' works in five volumes, as well as the *Memoirs* of Madame de Maintenon and seven volumes of *Lettres Historiques et Galantes* dated 1733. In Spanish the Doctor had a *Don Quixote* (Madrid 1797) and the well-known *La Araucana*, which was quoted by Alfred in 'The High Priest of Alexander' *in Poems by Two Brothers*.

It is clear from the make-up of his library that Dr Tennyson had the instincts and, to some extent at least, the habits of a scholar. He also had considerable imagination and poetic power. Hallam Tennyson in his *Memoir* of his father (vol. I. p. 11) quotes him as saying 'my father was a poet and could write regular metre very skilfully'.

A few examples of his verse remain, some of which seem to shew personal feeling as well as technical ability. Hallam Tennyson quotes stanzas 7, 8 and 9 of the following poem which is entitled 'Verses addressed to a Lady on her Departure by G. C. Tennyson'. Nothing is known about the lady to whom the poem is said to be addressed.

I

> O I have passed a Southern summer's day,
> The dazzling landscape dim'd th'astonish'd sight,
> And in that overpowering blaze of light
> Entranc'd and lost I lay.

2

The sun is set, and indistinctly seen
The fading visions wear a graver hue,
And softer prospects open to the view
Less vivid, more serene.

3

Yes, from the memory of enjoyment past
A calm yet mingled feeling we derive,
Mournful tho' sweet, which in our hearts alive
Shall ever, ever last.

4

And who this pensive pleasure would resign,
This silent, tender luxury of thought,
For all the unideal transports bought
By revelry and wine.

5

Imagination fades, enjoyments pale,
But memory's pleasures never shall decay,
Shall shine tho' clouds of Age obscure our day,
Shall bloom tho' vigour fail.

6

Can I forget thee? while the purple tide
That warms this heart, shall bid its pulse to play,
That pulse shall beat for thee tho' far away
For thee and none besides.

7

Can I forget thee? In the festive hall
Where wit and beauty reign and minstrelsy

My heart still fondly shall recur to thee
Thy image still recall.

8

Can I forget thee? in the gloomy hour
When wave o'er wave, tempestuous passions roll,
Thy lov'd Idea still shall soothe my soul
And health and peace restore.

9

Farewell – may choicest blessings round thee wait
And kindred angels guard that angel's form,
Guide and protect thee in life's ruder storm
And every blast of fate.

10

Star of the North farewell – thy brilliant ray
Shall happier skies illumine – O restore
To us the lustre – visit us once more
Our life, our light, our day.

'The Wandering Jew' has a distinctly personal ring about it, although there is nothing to throw any light on the date of its composition.

I

O Stranger, why enquire the hapless fate
Of one most sorely scath'd by power supreme?

My guilt past utterance why should I relate
Or tale of Woe will bid thine eyes to stream,
With pity's kindly drops – my fortunes teem
With incidents so horrible and rare
That thou incredulous perchance may'st deem
Reason divested of her throne and care
And Age to have installed second childhood there.

2

And yet this stedfast eye no sign betrays
Of intellectual frenzy or decay,
My memory is firm and tells of days
In dark oblivion long pass'd away:
When Rome submitted to Augustus' sway
I first drew breath and oh! that in my spring
The bud of life had withered for aye
Oh! that e'en now at last oh heavenly king
Thou would'st in mercy deign to snap this vital string.

3

Ah! not thro' ignorance I sinn'd but pride;
I bow before thy righteous judgments, Lord!
I saw thy works and yet thy power denied,
Contemn'd thy threat'nings and despis'd thy word;
Thy lowly guise my carnal heart abhorr'd;
O yet at last revoke thy fearful doom
Let Mercy temper judgment, let thy sword
Of Vengeance slumber, and the silent tomb
This ever sleepless eye and withered heart enwomb.

4

How vain the prayer! I bear a charmed life,
I tarry till he comes; such the decree
Of him who sav'd the world, and neither knife
Rope, rack, nor pois'nous herb, nor malady
Fire, earth, nor air can ever set me free;

When blood and water issued from his side
'Twas I who pierc'd him on the fatal tree
And therefore now a wretched deicide
Deathless and vagabond I wander far and wide.

5

And on my brow an ever burning spear
Fed by the self renew'd and anguish'd brain
Adown these furrow'd cheeks the scalding tear
Compels, and bids me woefully complain;
Ah! who can live in never ending pain?
Yet till the great Archangel's trump shall call
The dead to judgment, must I still sustain
This fiery torment; till this earthly ball,
Enwrapt by flames shall shrivel like a parched scroll.

6

Ye mortals, insects of life's little day,
Of brief and puny sorrows why complain?
Awhile ye flutter in the solar sky
And die at eve – soon is your mingled skein
Unwound, and fate divides the thread in twain;
Ye deem your joys and woes shall ever last,
Your hopes are fruitless as yours fears are vain,
Ye burst like bubbles on the Ocean vast
Of dread Eternity – the dream of life is past.

or

Ye mortals, insects of life's little day
Your brief and puny sorrows why deplore?
Awhile ye wanton in the sultry ray
And die what time bright Hesper doth restore
The evening grey – soon is your mingled skein
Unwound by Destiny's resistless powers
And pitying Death divides the thread in twain –
But I in this dark world for ever must remain.

Very different in feeling are the stanzas which form Part II of 'a Sublime Ode', addressed 'to the illustrious sovereign who now sways the sceptre of these realms, King George the Third'. These relate to the doings of the Prince of Wales (afterwards George IV) and were no doubt written about 1805–6 when the first commission of inquiry into the conduct of his wife had been instituted, and the Prince, supported in some degree by his mother, was disputing with the King (George III) regarding the education of his unfortunate daughter and doing his best to have her removed from the state and public dignity which should have been accorded to his heiress-apparent.

PART II

15

On a broomstick or a fiddle
Hervey prates, why should not I
Prate of Winter, now i' th' middle?
Is it worse to prate than lye?

16

From all subjects grave deductions
Rise in good and pious mind,
Greasy thus or sour eructions
Rise in Throat from pent up wind.

17

From each theme 'tis poet's glory
To derive some moral good
Tho' as foreign to the story
As King George from old King Lud.

18

Young and old, robust and feeble
Learn to moralize apace
Ye whose bass is turned to treble
Ye whose squeak is not yet bass.

19

Dames desert your pins and laces
Ribbands, kerchiefs, capes and rings,
And deduce sententious phrases
E'en from mean and trivial things.

20

Girls, desert your childish gewgaws
Baby Houses, Dolls and Frocks,
Hearken to my weighty new saws
Moralize, nor care who mocks.

21

Men who dream of fame or riches
Ponder well the things I say
Youths who just are cloath'd in Breeches
Spurn your Tops nor heed your play.

22

Thou enthron'd in earthly splendor
George with Charlotte by thy side
Who, of faith August Defender
Rul'st o'er nations far and wide.

23

Prince, with regal robe invested
Hearken to my moral lay
Then of earthly power divested
Thou shalt reign in endless day.

24

What tho' giddy sons perplex thee
Shake their elbows drink and wh——
What tho' wanton Jersey vex thee
Veteran Fitzherbert more,

25

What tho' of his wife and daughter
England's hope forgetful prove
And by base contrivance sought her
Life, who ought to be his love,

26

What tho' Brunswick's Issue ducal
Be neglected and reviled
And thy Son, to make us puke all
Wish't to bastardize his child,

27

What tho' still the jaundiced Charlotte
Stimulate her impious son
Yet to stigmatise as harlot
One as spotless as the sun,

28

What tho' he in tricks detected
From Newmarket was kicked off
And unworthily rejected
Even of fools and knaves the scoff,

29

Yet come quickly, learn my Science
And though he be mad and vile
Thou to Grief shall bid defiance
And midst woes look up and smile.

The most interesting of all the poems amongst Dr Tennyson's papers is a 'Mad Tom' song, which was evidently composed in imitation of the popular 'Tom o' Bedlam' ballads of the seventeenth and eighteenth centuries.* The 'Song' cannot be traced to any other

---

* See article by F. Sidgwick on 'The Tom o' Bedlam Ballads', *London Mercury*, March 1923, vol. 7, p. 518.

source, and, as it appears in a notebook in which the remaining contents are all evidently Dr Tennyson's compositions, it appears to be an exercise by him in the traditional manner. It is interesting to note that a copy of the lines in Alfred Tennyson's hand (and apparently not in a very early hand) was sold at Sotheby's a few years ago, but there is nothing else to suggest that the song is Alfred's work.

SONG

I am mad Tom, I know it
And sometimes I am furious
But I am wise and rule the skies
    Orion, Sol, Arcturus.

What tho' Folks point I'm wiser
Than e'er was mortal found
I rule the moon in her high noon
    And whirl the planets round.

I'll climb those lofty mountains
And there I'll fight the gypsies
I'll play at bowls with the sun and moon
    And kick them to eclipses.**

I'll climb those lofty mountains
In spite of wind and weather
I'll tear the rainbow from the skies
    And splice both ends together.

What tho' I'm poor I'll marry
And then poor Tom will sing
For Saturn rolls by my command
    And I'll marry with his ring.

* This word should perhaps be 'ellipses'.

I have no dirty acres
To settle on my love
But the flaming fields of space are mine
And the canopy above.

With heaven's studded concave
I'll bind her forehead fair
Her eyes shall be the northern light
And a comet's tail her hair.

Oh then I'll breed a riot
And be a merry loon
With mountains I'll at ninepins play
And trundle with the moon.

CHAPTER FIVE

THE UNHAPPY DOCTOR

THE year 1820 was a turning point in the life of Dr Tennyson, for it was the year in which he removed Charles and Alfred, the third- and fourth-born of his twelve children, from Louth School, where they had spent four wretched and unprofitable years, and began to educate them himself, working hard to polish up his Greek for the purpose. He had always taken a keen interest in their education, making Alfred learn and repeat all the Odes of Horace before sending him to Louth at the age of seven with a copy of the second edition of *Paradise Lost* in his portmanteau. This volume is now in the Tennyson Room at the Usher Gallery, Lincoln, inscribed 'Alfred Tennyson Louth Oct. 7'. Now no doubt he hoped to find in the development of his children (Frederick had already gone from Louth to Eton) some compensation for the waste of his own abilities. 'Phoenix-like, I trust (though I don't think myself a Phoenix) they will spring from my ashes, in consequence of the exertions I have bestowed upon them,' he wrote to his brother.

In spite of his letter of 14th August 1820 (see pp. 39, 40) the Doctor's relations with Bayons had, on the whole, been reasonably good since he settled at Somersby. He had called his first child, who was born in 1806 and died in infancy, George, and his third (born in 1808) Charles. But his father had evidently been conscious of some adverse feeling on his eldest son's part, for on 20th June 1807 he wrote to Charles, 'Mary and George's conduct towards myself and your dear Mother have of late made both myself and her low and dispirited'. Two years later there was talk of Mary going to live with George, though no reason is stated. Charles had married in 1808 Fanny Hutton of Morton – a blameless and well-endowed bride – but only after exasperating delays while his father investigated her morals and haggled about the settlement. The progress of the courtship can still be traced in a diary kept by Charles where he recorded in the decent obscurity of the French language every occasion when he squeezed Fanny's hand under the dinner table or put his arm round her waist in the carriage on the way to the theatre. Soon after the marriage the bride-groom's health broke down and he and his Fanny came to live at Caenby only thirty miles or so from Somersby. Probably relations between the brothers had never been very close, as there was six years difference in age, but at first they and their families seem to have got on pretty well together – George's eldest child was born only two years or so before Charles', and the parents would dutifully attend the christening ceremonies which recurred so regularly in their respective families (Charles was to have seven children, George eleven). Two or three times the correspondence shews George's elder children staying at Bayons and the families liked to meet for holidays at the seaside though there were difficulties about location, as Charles preferred Cleethorpes, which George maintained was too expensive for 'a poor parson who could not be supposed to have any spare rhino [money] to sport away in extravagant expeditions'. On the other hand rooms at Mablethorpe, which George preferred, were difficult to secure, as is shewn by a letter written by the elder brother to the younger on 19th August 1813.

My Dear Charles,

I immediately began a most diligent inquiry with respect to lodgings . . . but to no avail. Every potbellied grocer and dirty linen draper bespeaks his lodgings from year to year, and they are therefore pre-engaged throughout the season. At last I got the refusal of a very comfortable house near the sea, upon the departure of the lodgers, and I was going to write to you when the man to whom the house belongs came and said that the Brackenburys who came to his house every year had written to him saying that they were coming and he could not disoblige them. This was very scurvy treatment. D—n the lousy race of Brackenbury through all its branches and from end to side. There are no lodgings to be had at Sutton, every dirty cottage runs over. At Trusthorpe, a small village near Mablethorpe, every miserable shed is occupied by the aforesaid greasy and potbellied grocers and linen drapers. As for the inns, you cannot be at all decently accommodated in them. They are stinking filthy places, not fit for a pig, and at Sutton a bedridden person has existed in the kitchen among the cooking for the last twenty years. They are, besides, hyper-extraordinarily dear, and according to my calculation had we gone there they would have cost a hundred pounds a month. So far for the black side.

About a mile from the sea at Mablethorpe there is a very nice cottage with a very comfortable parlour, also a good bedroom and good bed for yourselves with a fireplace, another good room with bed and fireplace for a nursery. There is another small bedroom in which the woman of the house and her servant sleep, and your man-servant, if you come, must have a bed made up for him in the kitchen. . . . There is a very good stable for four horses and an excellent carriage house. She (Mrs Scamblesby) can let you have hay for the horses and a close if you like to turn them out. You will be very comfortable in every other respect than the distance from the sea which is, as I said, about a mile.

Little George can bathe with our children, and I have a covered cart on purpose to take them to the sea and for them to dress in. You will have the house for 25/-. If you put your horses at the inn they would charge you beyond all bounds.

1813 was a good year for George Tennyson, for in it he took the degree of LLD at Cambridge, was appointed chaplain to the High Sheriff and preached the assize sermon, to which Charles had contributed 'a grand encomium on law' and which Fanny liked very much, though it was 'not admired by all at Lincoln'. George himself had not expected this, fearing that the subject which he had chosen, being 'a little intricate and certainly unhackneyed might well lead to misunderstanding.' Every now and then Charles would look in at Somersby or his way to Lincoln and George liked on such occasions to entertain parties of the neighbours in his honour. Moreover the brothers made a compact to visit Cambridge once a year together, an event to which George greatly looked forward, as involving 'fine music, fine sights and *alma mater*'. But the elder brother's grievance smouldered on, occasionally breaking out into moods of violent resentment – for example, Charles wrote to his father in April 1815: 'George seems to have forgotten me or to remember me with such bitterness he will not mention my name or family'. And the animosity was apparently

shared by George's wife Eliza, for we find Fanny writing to her
mother from Caenby on 11th July 1811 of her intention to ask Eliza to
stay in the shooting season 'for company for me when Charles is out,
you will know it is no use his being much at home when she is here
as she won't speak a word to him: if she knew her Father had made
him one of the Trustees in his will she would be more silent than ever.'

Dr Tennyson's feelings against his brother were no doubt intensified
by developments in the years immediately following. In 1817 Matthew
Russell inherited Brancepeth Castle and immediately set about restoring
it regardless of expense, with the skilled assistance of Charles, who was
a true son of the Gothic Revival and had become an enthusiastic
antiquarian. Matthew in return generously forwarded Charles's
nascent political ambitions, and with this backing and his father's
influence in Grimsby Charles was elected M.P. for Grimsby in 1818.
It was a tough fight, reviving all the old Tennyson–Pelham animosity,
and Charles's political naïvety nearly led to an early breach with his
agent, who severely criticised his unwillingness to begin his campaign
in Holy Week and some tactless remarks which he made about
electoral purity. However he sent a Christmas gift of coal to the voters
and a stone and a half of flour accompanied by the same amount of
beef, and celebrated his election to Parliament in the traditional manner
by standing godfather at ninety-two christenings in the parish church
and giving each child a bottle of wine. His father followed the course
of the election with feverish interest; the sudden intervention of a
strange baronet with a mysterious assistant, 'a black Boanerges kind
of man', caused him the gravest alarm, and the rumoured defection of
a committed freeman called Nell evoked a typical outburst: 'if he
deceives you he is not worthy to live and the honest freemen will not
let him live!' Dr Tennyson too supported and encouraged his brother
and was not a little distressed when, after Charles had been returned
head of the poll, the Tory candidate Fazackerley – 'that Yarborough
tool with the hard name I can't spell' – lodged a petition against Charles
alleging bribery and corruption, which fortunately was unsuccessful.
But Dr Tennyson disagreed with his brother on many points of principle
– especially in regard to Catholic Emancipation. This Charles was
thought to favour, against the view of most of his supporters, in-

cluding his elder brother, who feared it might lead to an alliance between the Catholics and the Methodists. If this got into power 'what a bigotted, hypocritical, fanatical, hypochondriacal set of fellows we should become – from a dominion of the saints Good Lord deliver us!' But Dr Tennyson also had his liberal principles which he expressed more bluntly than his brother. As a Justice of the Peace he was horrified by the Peterloo massacre which took place on 19th August of this year and on 2nd September we find him writing that the Manchester magistrates who had taken so prominent a part in the affair should be indicted for murder 'if they were hanged it would be of great use to the magistrates generally, but especially to the clergy.'

No doubt Dr Tennyson's resentment against his brother and father, so strikingly displayed in his letter of 14th August 1820, was intensified by Charles's success at a second election which took place early in 1820 and of which the successful candidate omitted to inform his brother.

The letter of 14th August 1820 undoubtedly disturbed George Tennyson the elder. He did not reply to it until 1st October and then only mentioned it in the concluding sentence of a business letter. But on 10th October he instructed his agent to tell Dr Tennyson that he was altering his will and settling £20,000 on the doctor's younger children in equal shares. This codicil was in fact executed on 15th December 1820.

Dr Tennyson's health, both mental and physical, deteriorated steadily during the 1820s. His family and friends thought that the intense effort which he devoted to the education of his children was largely responsible. There may well have been other causes. His condition at the beginning of 1822 was so bad that he went to Cheltenham for a cure. On 15th April he wrote to his mother that the doctor was satisfied that a cirrhus had not yet formed on his liver, which suggests the possibility that he may already have been drinking to excess. Elizabeth Russell was already at Cheltenham, and Charles, with whom George was again on very bad terms, had only just gone, leaving his wife Fanny behind. Before the end of the month news was received that Matthew Russell, the jovial giant, had suddenly been struck down by serious illness. A few days later he was dead. The shock to his wife was terrible, but George, freed from the cares and embarrassments of

Somersby, rose splendidly to the occasion. 'He is all kindness and feeling on this unfortunate subject,' wrote Fanny to her husband, 'and I know not what we should have done had he not been there'.

Unfortunately George's health did not improve. On 7th November his father wrote to John Fytche, Elizabeth's brother, offering to allow sixty pounds a year each for all or as many of the five elder boys as George might choose to send to Louth or any school of the same kind. He also offered to pay off George's debts, if he owed any, and to pay his expenses for a further visit to Cheltenham. The approach through John Fytche was apparently necessary because George was obstinately refusing all material assistance. Two days later his mother wrote to Charles, whose wife Fanny was at Cheltenham, referring to Doctor Tennyson's 'dreadful disease', though there is no indication of the nature of this. Apparently the Doctor did go to Cheltenham before the end of the year. There he found his sister-in-law Fanny and seems quickly to have recovered health and spirits, for Fanny writes on 6th January 1823 after he had returned to Somersby:

You cannot think how much I miss your brother. I really think my spirits have drooped ever since; he was so droll and agreeable, kind and obliging. We used to take long walks together, in short he became at last quite a Beau, but I had much difficulty in making him so. You will be surprised to hear he has a new suit of clothes, Hat and Boots which I vowed to buy him myself rather than he should appear in his nasty old schoolmaster's shoes. He promised to write, but I have not yet heard; I hope he keeps well.

But any improvement of relations was short-lived and the unhappy events of 1822 at Cheltenham even became a cause of resentment against Elizabeth Russell. In January 1824 the Doctor writes to Charles, declining an invitation to visit him in town: 'I am best here and have neither strength nor spirits to go from home. . . . I never set myself about anything that I can possibly avoid.' He then launched into a tirade against his sister:

I hear that Mrs Russell is very gay at Brighton; her gaiety is no business of mine. When I last saw her, I requested she would write to me but I suppose she is so utterly absorbed by amusements and the things of this world and its pomps and vanities that she either does not care or does not deign to take any notice of my wish. I think it is not the way I ought to be treated – I, who gave up the express purpose for which I went to Cheltenham, the recruiting of my health, to administer to her solace and support, might reasonably have a line from her when I requested it. I say that I devoted my health and time and money to her (the time that I was with her cost me £30 at Cheltenham) and she little recollects when in a bad state of health (as indeed I now am) how she trespassed upon that health by being almost the whole night in my room for a series of nights. This I vow to God in the most solemn manner I have never recovered. My wife knows it as well as myself. I did not think that Mrs Russell had been so ungrateful and so callous. But money, I am well persuaded, deadens the feelings, and I suppose Mrs Russell is not so superior to the rest of mankind as not to feel its paralysing influence. You would scarcely believe that she told me, a little time before her husband died, that my family could live well and be educated genteely for £800 a year!!! She would put out my children to school when in *distress*! This of course I refused. Her indifference, and I must say ingratitude, has nettled me to the quick. The only reason which she can alledge for this conduct is that when lately she offered to come and see us we had not accommodation.

This I suppose is to cancel all former benefits. We are three and twenty in family and sleep five or six in a room. Truly we have great accommodation for Mrs Russell and her suite. We have not the house at Brighton nor the castle at Brancepeth. . . .

Poor Mrs Russell, it is to her credit that she did not visit the sins of the unhappy Doctor on his children, for when he was dead and the family were living together on their small annuities, she was always ready to help with money and was regarded with great affection by her nephews and nieces. Indeed, the Doctor himself seems to have realised that the fault may not have been all on one side, for two months later he wrote to Charles that he had had a letter from his sister and admitted that he might have been a little too hasty about her.

During the next year poor Dr Tennyson began to suffer from some kind of seizures thought to be epileptic. This affliction may have developed earlier, but mention of it first appears in the correspondence at the beginning of March. The family doctor was called in and sent an alarming account to Bayons which old George forwarded to

Charles. Charles replied suggesting that his brother should be got away to Cheltenham or some other place where his mind could disengage itself from the harassing occupation to which he was daily devoting himself and get it into new channels of thought and his body into more active habits of exercise. On 21st March old George wrote again to Charles:

I understand your brother is in his usual state of health and spirits. You may write to him if you think proper, he will not consent to see us! but we have and always will do our Duty to him and all our children as well as we can yet we cannot but feel his condition of mind and more on his account than on our own. I believe he is in a very bad state of health, and you too our dutiful Charles are a great invalid and sufferer. Eliza and Mary also. You may be sure we cannot be happy. God be thank'd your dear Mother is in as good health as she commonly is.

But the fits continued. Dr Bousfield called again at the end of April or beginning of May and was told that Dr Tennyson had had two more, but he could not see him as Eliza did not dare to tell the Doctor of his visit.

Early in July Eliza at her husband's request sent for old George to come over from Bayons. He found George just recovered from a fit, weak and feeble and was forced to the conclusion that he could never recover his strength.

A few days later Eliza wrote from Somersby to Charles:

I received your letter last night and which I answer without delay and read it to poor George as he was too ill to see what it contained himself. He has never been free from disorder since your Father left us, he could not perform the service at his Churches last Sunday nor attend the Bishop's visitation on the Friday following. He had a violent Paroxysm yesterday in the afternoon and greatly alarmed us all as we really thought he would have lost his senses but thank God it abated in a few hours and though he continued exceedingly ill until 12 o'clock at night he then got a little rest which enabled him to read prayers today and tho' he was scarcely able to walk to church he got through the service better than I could have expected. He is indeed a severe sufferer and has such frequent returns of this complaint that I fear ultimately (if he lives) it will deprive him of his intellect. He was pleased with your letter my dear Charles and bids me say he shall be happy to see you next month when you are in Lincolnshire and hopes dear Fanny will accompany you. We shall be much gratified to see you both and thank you for all your kindness to ourselves.

On 28th July Elizabeth Russell wrote to Charles:

I fear our poor dear brother is a pitiable sufferer but I think and hope his sufferings not of a nature to destroy him prematurely. It is painful indeed to take a view either a home or perspective one of all the branches as well as the stems of our family. . . . locomotion is the only thing I believe for spirits like ours when depressed and fixing exclusively on one subject.

Before the end of the month, however, Dr Tennyson was well enough to take Frederick to Cambridge to enter him for St John's. On his return he had another fit. His father came over immediately to see him and was pleased that he more than once mentioned his brother with affection. A letter from his sixteen-year-old son Alfred, franked 2nd August 1825, carries on the story:

My dear Uncle

It is with great sorrow that I inform you that my poor Father is not any better than before. He had another violent attack of the same nature yesterday. Indeed no one but those who are continually with him can conceive what he suffers, as he is never entirely free from this alarming illness. He is reduced to such a degree of weakness from these repeated attacks, that the slightest shock is sufficient to bring them on again. Perhaps if he could summon resolution enough to get out more, he would be relieved, but the lassitude which the fits leave incapacitates him from undergoing any exertion. He has already had two of these since my Grandfather was here which is not much more than a week ago and sometimes previous to that had three each night successively. He was not able to attend The Bishop's Visitation on Friday.

With Kindest Remembrance to my Aunt and Cousins
Believe me, my dear Uncle,
Yrs Affectionately
A. TENNYSON

Little correspondence survives from the months following Alfred's letter. Perhaps the death of Mary Tennyson, mother of George and Charles, in the late summer of 1825 shocked the contending elements of the family into silence. It may even have revived old springs of affection. She had suffered for many months uncomplainingly and even cheerfully, as a letter written to Charles on 7th July 1825 touchingly shews.

Gratitude and thanks to God for giving me so affectionate a child. What to tell you of my disorder, I know not how to convey, my asthma and short breathing – you will be sorry to hear I am perpetually combating. I cannot move even from chair to chair without hurry or rather palpitations of the heart yet by slow movements I can get out not only from room to room, but an airing every day.

Dr Tennyson looking thin but in tolerable spirits brought his wife and two eldest daughters to Bayons in March 1826. Unfortunately the family physician soon after this put the Doctor on a course of laudanum, which he took in large quantities, and calomel, the results of which can hardly have been beneficial. Charles was at this time on the point of retiring from Parliament and handing the seat over to George Heneage of Hainton. Dr Tennyson's apparent improvement in health set his indomitable father thinking of the possibility of securing for him in exchange some advantage from Mr Heneage's great command of church patronage. The old man also agreed to pay Frederick's expenses at Cambridge, where he had gone into residence in the autumn of 1826. Soon after this there had been talk of Dr Tennyson visiting Bayons again, but once more the father's irritability, or the son's unjustified suspicions, inflamed perhaps by laudanum and calomel, intervened. The very letter, dated 22nd January 1827, in which Dr Tennyson sent Frederick's Cambridge bill to his father, ended with the following paragraph.

I have here to regret the reason of my not visiting you as I had intended with some part of my family. I have been credibly informed that you make it your business to speak in the most disrespectful terms of me to everyone and to one person you represented me as 'the greatest liar that ever spoke' and this you said immediately prior to writing me a very affectionate invitation. How you can think so ill of me and yet write so kindly is more than I can comprehend. I regret exceedingly you should continue to speak of me in so injurious and unkind a manner as it absolutely precludes me from visiting you, when I know you harbour so unjust and unfavourable an opinion of me, neither can it be pleasant for you to receive me, a person, according to your description, of so despicable a character – I am my dear father your affect. son.

G. C. TENNYSON

This was more than the old man could stand and indeed one finds it hard to believe that, at this particular moment when there seemed at last some chance of reducing the tensions which had for so long distracted the family, he could have been guilty of so lamentable an indiscretion. His reply of 27th January was uncompromising:

I have as I purposed reflected upon your letter of the 22nd Jan. . . .
I have decided upon allowing you £1,000 instead of £700, with which you must be content, and, as I do, consider it to be ample and sufficient provision from me to you for the general good of your family, premising that you will pursue proper plans of education for your children and that I shall be precluded from further applications.
The concluding paragraph of your letter forbids all comments, your experience and your knowledge of me as a Father and a friend ought to have furnished a ready contradiction to him, who could so slander me. . . .

By now it is probable that Dr Tennyson had been for some time trying to find escape from his troubles in drink. Charles and Alfred were now in their nineteenth and eighteenth years. They had been mainly responsible for the volume *Poems by Two Brothers*, published in March 1827 by Jacksons of Louth, Frederick only contributing four pieces.

The metrical skill of the verses, the wide range of subjects (a large proportion of them academic) and the wealth of quotation in a variety of languages with which the volume is garnished shew how thorough the Doctor's educational methods had been. All seven of the boys were of unusual intelligence and their father's desire to make the most of their abilities was fanatical. To keep up with their needs he had to drive

C

himself harder and harder. The strain became too great and during
the rest of the year his condition rapidly deteriorated.

On 10th October 1827 the Reverend William Chaplin, an old
friend of the family, wrote to Charles from Thorpe Hall, Louth, the
home of Eliza Tennyson's brother, John Fytche. The style of the letter
is peculiar and may suggest some lack of balance in the writer, but one
must surely accept it as generally reliable:

I know not how to express my sorrow and to feel it my duty to call
your attention to your afflicted brother. You must know that he has
long been most singular in conduct. I am sorry to add is now dangerously disposed to his wife and children: I dread the fatal effects towards
some of them, which would consign him to perpetual confinement for
his life – A coroner's verdict would declare him under the influence of
insanity, should such a horrid death be perpetrated by him, this excessive
habit of drinking brings on such repeated fits, that he is as deranged as
madness can be described – However dreadful to meditate, the requisite means to curb these horrid paroxysms must arise with his own
friends and the sooner they place him out of reach of such bad effects
to his wife and children the better. The children are alarmed at him and
the wife in the greatest fright both in day and night. I may in truth say
in daily danger of her life – I think he might be reclaimed and his
health restored if under the care of Dr Willis – but as long as he is under
the uncontroll'd power of liquors daily dangers await him and he may
be under the influence of insanity. I think his Physician Dr Bousfield of
Horncastle (a clever man and late pupil of Dr Harrison) would have no
difficulty in giving a Certificate that he is in such a state, that he is not
responsible for any act he may commit. The more I consider his dreadful state the more I am alarmed for him and his family – He will not
allow them to go to school and he will not clothe them, what must be
the end of all this for he cannot educate them himself.

I am confident that the greatest necessity now exists that his own
friends must come forward, stop so much evil and impending dangers.
It would be cruel to expect your Father to undertake such measures as
are now requisite but I hope you can discover some friend able to take
the arduous task and let prompt steps become prevalent. His duty is
sadly neglected, and his fits have come on in the church – so everyone is
afraid of him, and the church neglected.

The only person having influence with him is a faithful servant, a
coachman. He can stop some violent paroxysms but that cannot last
long. He will not pay any household bills nor allow necessary food for

his family – I am sorry poor Fytche by long bad health is unequal to such a scene as that at Somersby – he has been at Harrogate and Buxton and is the worse for both. Nobody knows where George hoards up his money – he pays nobody. I shall be glad to hear that you devise some plan of study to all, and believe me yrs truly,

W. CHAPLIN

Charles immediately wrote to Dr Bousfield to go over to Somersby from Horncastle. Bousfield reported the result of this visit on 17th October.

In consequence of your letter, I yesterday rode over to Somersby – I found Mr Tennyson as well as I have usually seen him of late and in an argument after dinner displaying the same acuteness of mind and playfulness of manner as when I first met him 13 years ago.

I found that Mrs Tennyson really does labour under the apprehensions at which your letter hinted, from the violent state of nervous irritation which breaks out occasionally in her husband. It is more however on her children's account than her own that her placid disposition appears so greatly unhinged – He habitually indulges too much in strong liquor, to which he has gradually been led by its soporific quality, having been always tormented by sleepless nights – I need not urge that the most gentle and delicate means only could have any favourable effect on Dr T's unfortunate malady – All reasoning, I fear, would be inefficient. . . .

He suggests a Continental tour of a few months to restore mental and bodily health and continues:

This would I hope return him to the bosom of his family restored in a great measure to both bodily and mental health, and capable of enjoying that happiness which a most promising and highly gifted set of children would naturally provide.

This was to some extent reassuring and on receipt of it Charles was able to write to a friend who had been inquiring about George's condition:

I do not believe that my brother's health is at all worse in any respect than it was a year ago. What I am most anxious about, after my brother's comfort and that of his family, is that Mr Chaplin, Mr B and others should not retain such impressions as they seem to have formed.

But a letter which Eliza Tennyson wrote on 30th October shews that Chaplin had not exaggerated the dangers of her position. In this she describes the terrible evening which the family had endured on Sunday. Her husband had refused to allow her to take any of the children to see her father at Louth and would not let her take the carriage there unless she would stay away for half a year. This of course she could not do, having regard to his condition. Indeed it seems like the idea of a madman. He now turned again to his father, offering to leave everything in his hands and to follow any course of action he might recommend.

The first thing to be done was to get Dr Tennyson out of the country as soon as possible, and arrangements were made for him to visit Paris where some French friends of the family, called Marthion, undertook to look after him. He refused to go unless Charles would go with him, which Charles reluctantly agreed to do. By the end of the month they were in Paris. The effect of the change was magical. The Doctor wrote to Alfred expressing his delight with the city and 'its many noble edifices'. He wrote restrained and sensible letters to his father cordially approving the suggestions for dealing with his children. These involved one very momentous decision. Frederick was already at Cambridge and their father's growing instability made it desirable that Charles and Alfred should follow him there and so be got away from the Somersby atmosphere. There was an additional reason for getting Charles out of the Rectory. It was feared that he had fallen in love with his sisters' music mistress, Miss Watson, a young woman of considerable charm and vivacity. Old Mr Tennyson intervened with a letter of inquiry to Frederick, and was not convinced by Frederick's opinion that Charles was not of a very ardent temperament, or at all events had too much sense, or at least prudence, to make a sacrifice of his more vital interests to the gratification of any passion whatsoever. 'Don't you think too', he asked, 'that if my mother had supposed that any danger was likely to arise she would have exerted her authority, however ineffectual on most occasions, to allow a timely check upon the enterprising spirit of Miss Watson.'

Ultimately, Miss Watson solved the problem by getting arrested for debt – apparently she had been in the habit of buying goods without paying for them and selling them for ready money – and retiring to nurse an invalid father in Cheltenham. The fact that Charles does not seem to have displayed any interest in this denouement suggests that Frederick's diagnosis was justified. Charles's only reference to Miss Watson that survives is in a letter to his grandfather, which crossed the latter's letter to Frederick, and described her as a lively woman, who would amuse the house-party 'during these drowsy, hazy, obnubilated, gloomy, wet, blue-devil begetting, sunless, hopeless, joyless days of November'.

Cambridge was obviously the best solution for both brothers. Charles in due course secured a Bell Scholarship, which helped towards the payment of his expenses; Elizabeth Russell contributed £100 to Alfred's. A letter to her from old George dated 23rd November contains a curious reference to Alfred. 'The day his father came here, Alfred set out for Cambridge, not wishing to meet him, where he proposes to stay till the £100 you kindly promised him is exhausted and what is to be done with him, I don't know.' Alfred himself had no difficulty in securing admission to Trinity, for on 5th December he wrote to his grandfather that he had been examined by the tutor, Mr Whewell, and the Dean who both said that he was fully competent.

It was now proposed that Edward should be kept at Bayons for six months copying deeds and preparing himself to go as clerk to a solicitor; Arthur was, if possible, to go into the Navy; fortunately for his mother, who was much distressed by the proposal, this proved impossible owing to his age; Septimus and Horatio were to continue at school at Louth, as in fact did Arthur when the Navy scheme failed. There was a general lightening of the atmosphere and his father wrote to Charles almost gleefully of conditions at Somersby. 'Eliza speaks most affectionately of her husband and she and her children are looking forward with delight at the prospect of his return home with improved health and spirits. His is a fine family and fervently do I hope they will prove blessings.' The old man actually took Edward and Septimus back with him to Bayons and was evidently not disturbed by Eliza's suspicion that Septimus was suffering from worms because he had been grating his teeth in his sleep!

CHAPTER SIX

THE 'MAN OF SORROW'

D R Tennyson appears only to have stayed in Paris for a few weeks and not to have derived much benefit from the visit, for his son Charles, writing to old Mr Tennyson from Somersby during the Christmas vacation, gives a melancholy picture:

My father, at this moment excessively ill from spasms of the chest, desires me to say that he feels utterly unable to meet you and will be much obliged if you will come over here, as the exertion would be too much for him. Last night he suffered very much for the same cause. Tonight it has returned with great violence. My father is lying for ease on the floor and it is now midnight.

At the end of March occurred a wretched tragedy which further injured Dr Tennyson's health and nervous stability. The cook set fire to her dress and was so seriously burned that she died a few days later. The Doctor himself was badly burned in trying to help her. The entire burden of looking after the poor woman and arranging for her funeral and other consequences of her death fell on Dr Tennyson, for his wife had no ability to deal with such situations, and the resulting pressures were increased by malicious gossip in the neighbourhood, where the Doctor's growing eccentricity had made him a target for ridicule. Now a tale went round that he had given orders for a butt of water to be kept in future by the kitchen door, so that any cook who caught fire could jump in and extinguish herself without troubling her master. The effect on the unfortunate Dr Tennyson was disastrous. His health rapidly deteriorated and the old resentment against his father and brother flared up again. There were more ill-tempered letters to Bayons and he began to be obsessed with the fear that his three eldest sons were wasting their time and his money at Cambridge. In December of 1828 came the climax. Frederick, in spite of having won the University Prize for a Greek ode in his first year, had declined to take any interest in the normal studies of the time, which were almost entirely mathematical and linguistic, and devoted himself instead to poetry and philosophy. Moreover he had consistently omitted to attend the compulsory chapel services or to do the exercises set him as punishments. He was summoned to appear before the Dean, and instead of attempting to justify himself asked why young Wordsworth, the son of the Master, had received a much smaller imposition than himself for the same offence. The Dean thereupon passed him on to the Master and he was summoned to appear before the convention of the Fellows. To this reverend body, according to the account which Charles Tennyson's eldest son, who was now at Trinity, sent home to his father, Frederick behaved with smiling and satirical impertinence, with the result that he was rusticated for a year. Immediately Dr Tennyson heard the news he very sensibly set off for Brighton to consult the Reverend Edward Maltby, a distinguished churchman and scholar who was to be appointed Bishop of Chichester in 1831 and transferred to Durham five years later, and whose wife was a cousin of Frederick's mother. On Dr Maltby's advice he then went to Cambridge and brought Frederick to Brighton. Dr Maltby summed up Dr Tennyson's tragedy with remarkable accuracy – his sense of wasted ability and dislike of the profession into which he had been forced by his father; his gradually increasing eccentricity; his moroseness and strangeness in the family circle; his avoidance of society with his neighbours. Frederick he had met before at Cambridge. He began the interview with considerable prejudice against the young man, but this quickly vanished. He soon saw that Frederick shared the eccentricity and, more largely, the talent of his father (himself a scholar and a clever man), and he came to the conclusion that there had been no intentional violation of the college rules by Frederick and that the adverse reaction of the college authorities had been due to the unhappy impression made upon them by his manner, which was 'always *distrait* and more like an inhabitant of Laputa than of England' – a contemporary of Frederick's at the University described him as 'sinister in aspect and terrific in manner, even to the discomfiture of elderly dons'. Dr Maltby no doubt gave Dr Tennyson excellent advice, but when the Doctor and Frederick returned to Somersby the situation rapidly deteriorated. The Doctor began to drink again. Drink exacerbated his feelings against Frederick. Frederick's violent temper exploded and made matters worse. The Doctor appealed to his father whom he persuaded to make Frederick take his name off the books of his college, thus making it impossible for him to take a degree. The Doctor also persuaded his father to interview Charles and Alfred before they went back to Cambridge at the end of the vacation. He was afraid, with some justice, that they were running into debt and doing little work. The result was unfortunate. 'They did not act disrespectfully to me,' wrote the old man to his son Charles on 26th January 1829, 'but they are so untoward and disorderly, and so unlike other people I don't know what can be done with them. . . . these three boys so far from having improved in manner or manners are worse since they went to Cambridge.' The Doctor's suspicions were also aroused against his wife and elder daughters. He wrote to his father accusing them of driving about the county during his absence and running up bills, and he sent the ponies, which the girls used to ride and drive, to Bayons asking his father to accept them as a present. Eliza wrote urgently for their return as Mary and Emily badly needed horse exercise. But the old man was obdurate. By the middle of February the position at the Rectory had become disastrous. One night the Doctor was found with a large knife and a loaded gun in his room. He was with difficulty restrained from firing the gun through the kitchen window and threatened to kill Frederick and others with the knife. On other occasions there were violent quarrels between father and son, and the Doctor would heap on his wife and children 'such degrading epithets . . . as a husband and a father and above all a person of his sacred profession ought particularly to avoid'. After one of these terrible evenings the Doctor sent for the village constable and asked him to turn Frederick out of the house. The constable very sensibly asked Frederick to stay at his cottage and after three days his father sent for him and undertook to make him an allowance of a hundred a year if he would go to London to study for the Bar, which Frederick agreed to do. Dr Tennyson and his wife wrote dramatically opposed descriptions of these distressing events to Bayons, the Doctor on 25th February saying that the children should on no account be left under his wife's charge and that he proposed to send all except the two eldest daughters 'from under her superintendence'. On Friday, 27th February, Eliza wrote to her father-in-law telling him that, owing to her husband's violence, she felt it unsafe either for herself or for her children to remain any longer in the house with him and that she was going to leave him and take rooms in Louth.

Dr Tennyson wrote to his father the same day saying that he would come to Bayons on the following Monday (2nd March) with Edward, who was now sixteen years old and already shewing signs of mental instability the seriousness of which his father was in no condition to realize – 'a very awkward unlicked fellow who fancies himself to be a superior genius and who scarcely knows that 2 and 2 make 4. In short he is ruined here and must go from home.' However when his wife and family (presumably including Edward) left for Louth the Doctor changed his mind and stayed on at the Rectory, gradually reducing himself to such a state of misery and degradation that his neighbours sent for his close friend Mr Rawnsley, Vicar of Halton Holgate less than ten miles away, to come and look after him. Rawnsley came on Monday 9th March, fearing that his old friend would 'sink under his depression and epileptic tendencies'. He found him 'most miserable and feeding upon himself' and persuaded him to return with him to Halton. Rawnsley wrote on 12th March to Charles in London telling him of the Doctor's unhappy plight and strongly urging that he should be got away from his family, perhaps on another visit to France. 'I need not add', he concluded, 'how deeply I regret the loss of such a neighbour, and sorrow over the decay of such a powerful intellect, brought on by whatever cause it may be.' The Doctor talked of going to visit his brother in London, but instead he returned to Somersby on the eighteenth (Friday) on which day Frederick and his sister Emily walked the twelve miles from Louth to Somersby, wishing to see him 'and submit themselves'. They went to the constable's cottage and Emily sent in a 'humble note' begging her father to see them, but he refused and they walked back to Louth. On the fourteenth the Doctor wrote to his father saying that he would come to Bayons as soon as he could and apologizing for his bad handwriting as being due to his 'nervous and tremulous' condition – the letter is however beautifully written and entirely legible. On the nineteenth he actually went to Bayons. His father and brother quickly decided that he should be got over to Paris as soon as possible to stay once more with the Marthions. Meanwhile the Doctor's carriage horses were sold at Horncastle Fair, his bills were got in and steps taken to deal with them, and his family returned to Somersby where, however, Bayons tried to exercise strict control over expenditure, taking strenuous objection to poor Eliza's decision to engage a governess for her daughters – with a special objection to a certain Miss Eccles 'for very particular reasons'. In due course the Doctor went up to London to stay with Charles in the hope that he might be quickly got away to Paris. But this proved no easy matter, for the unfortunate man was unable for some days to take the necessary steps to obtain a passport and licence. It was 14th May before he left London for Paris via Brighton and Dieppe. Before he left he had a letter from his wife which he did not answer because, he complained, she put all the blame for what had happened on him and none on herself.

At home there was a lightening of the atmosphere once Dr Tennyson had left England. Dr Maltby, having no doubt heard from Trinity that Frederick had taken his name off the books, approached Charles through a common friend with a strong appeal that he should persuade his father to have Frederick reinstated. 'I do assure you', he wrote, 'that of all the numerous cases that have come before me in my experience, I never knew a young man, whose views and conduct appear to me to have been more completely and more injuriously misconceived. . . . Indeed there is no saying to what height talents such as his, kindly fostered and wisely directed, might not attain.' Meanwhile Frederick had on 24th June seen his Uncle Charles in London and offered to write a suitable letter to his father. He followed this up by getting a job to take a young man to France as tutor. There he saw and was reconciled to his father. This greatly pleased old George Tennyson whose irritation had already been mollified by the news that on 6th June Alfred had been awarded the Chancellor's Gold Medal for a poem 'Timbuctoo' – the first time the prize had ever been given for a poem in blank verse. The old man now yielded to Dr Maltby's appeal and shortly afterwards Frederick's name was restored to the books at Trinity and in fact he took his degree in 1832 with his brother Charles.

For Dr Tennyson the change of scene and company acted like a charm. He wrote enthusiastically of the drive through Normandy and the Île de France to Paris and of his cordial reception by the Marthions, nor was he unduly depressed by the knowledge that Elizabeth Russell and her married daughter Mrs Hamilton were in Paris, though he took care to avoid them as he dared not trust himself 'in slanderous company'. But after a few weeks he began to fret. He complained of spitting of blood and of neglect by his family (against whose past treatment of him he continued to fulminate) and by the end of June he was writing aggrieved letters to Charles whom he pressed to join him in Paris for a tour to Switzerland. But Charles was deeply engaged in the House of Commons where the proposals for Catholic Emancipation were at a crucial stage. Early in July the Doctor set off on a whirlwind tour by himself – first to Geneva via Lyons, thence by steamer to Lausanne and round to Geneva by way of Chillon, Villeneuve, Neuchâtel, Neuville and Brienz (to visit the Isle of Rousseau).

I will not attempt [he wrote to his father on 31st July] to describe the beauty and sublimity of some of the scenery. It would beggar all descriptions and neither Painter nor Poet could do a thousandth part of justice to it. You will, I hope, excuse me for not having written before. I have been up occasionally four nights without intermission, frequently two. When the body is very much fatigued the mind cannot act. But I have endeavoured to dissipate all mental feeling by violent exertion and the inspection of foreign manners and scenery. It will not do. I feel here as an isolated being, an outcast from England and my family. I am very uncertain in my movements and a mind ill at ease is generally so. I will write again in the course of a few days, and then I shall be able to determine where I shall go.
P.S. I keep a journal and some of my observations on the manners and costume of the people where I have occasionally sojourned may perhaps amuse you on my return. I am very desirous of doing so but it will be of no avail as Mr Fytche and Mary Anne Fytche have encouraged my family to act in open rebellion against me. Mr Fytche may perhaps have some time or other rebellious children himself and

he will then be able justly to appreciate his own infamous conduct towards me.

The correspondence gives no further information about his movements till late in December, when he was in Italy. But family tradition has preserved a characteristic story. It seems that when crossing the Italian frontier he was unable to produce his passport. The Austrian customs official asked him fiercely: 'What business have you here without a passport?' 'What business have you here at all?' replied the Doctor in his most majestic manner, and was allowed to pass without further hindrance. On 18th December he wrote a long letter from Naples, Part of this is taken up with lamentations about the lack of news regarding his family. Charles's silence on the subject in his last letter 'gives rise to the greatest uneasiness and the most distressing apprehensions.' The rest of the letter (about two thousand words) is occupied with elaborate descriptions of an eruption of Vesuvius and the ruins of Pompeii, and of visits to the cave of the Sybil, the labyrinth of Daedalus, the Elysian Fields, the rivers Styx and Acheron, and Pozzuoli 'where is the lake Avernus or the mouth of Hell.'

The energy of these descriptions, which are written regularly and carefully in a fine small hand, suggests that the Doctor's mind was no longer monopolised by his worries and anxieties. However, at the end he relapses – perhaps rather perfunctorily – into his old mood.

Adieu, my dearest Father and Brother, may God bless you both and preserve you and all that are dear to you, and bestow upon you every happiness and comfort. As for myself I feel that I have but little happiness to expect in this world and hope sheds but a feeble ray.

Dr Tennyson seems to have got back to England in May or June of 1830. The last weeks of his stay in Italy and his journey home had, by his own account, been marked by violent adventures, reported by his son Charles in a letter written just after his father's return. At Rome, during the Carnival, a man had been stilettoed in his arms. Once he had been almost buried alive by an avalanche, once he had been seized with giddiness on the edge of a precipice and only saved from death by the presence of mind of a companion. Finally, when driving over a high pass, the horses, frightened by a dog, had run away and hurled the carriage over a sheer rock, dashing themselves and their driver to death a thousand feet below and leaving the Doctor himself clinging to a pine which he had clutched convulsively on the descent. Bearing in mind his accounts of his Russian adventures twenty-nine years before, it is hard to take these stories literally, though it may be that he believed them, just as he no doubt believed in the picture of himself as the blameless and persecuted father which he presented so convincingly to his own father and his brother Charles.

His return set his family anxious problems. His father invited him urgently to Bayons, offering very considerately to go with him from there to Somersby, where only his wife, his son Charles and the younger children were in residence, Frederick fortunately being away on the Continent and Alfred on his way to the Pyrenees with Arthur Hallam to meet the Spanish revolutionaries.

The Doctor at once began to busy himself about the future of the three younger boys, Edward now nearly seventeen, Arthur just over sixteen and Septimus sixteen months younger. Edward and Arthur were packed off to Bayons for examination by their grandfather, who found the elder boy amiable and desirous of being instructed and proposed that he should be sent to a coach to be prepared for Cambridge. His view of Arthur was less favourable: 'it is high time he should get some further information before he goes into training for any profession'.

Early in the New Year 1831 Dr Tennyson fell into his last illness. The doctors diagnosed it as a 'low typhus' and it seems to have lasted several days. The only description of it which survives is in the following letter from Alfred to his Uncle Charles.

March 15th, 1831

My dear Uncle,

All shadow of hope with respect to my poor Father's ultimate recovery has vanished. Yesterday he lost the use of one side. It is evident that he cannot last many hours longer. It is a great consolation to us, however, that he is free from all suffering and perfectly mild and tranquil, seeming not to interest himself in anything that passes, which is the effect of pressure on the brain: the strength of his constitution has enabled him to resist his complaint a fortnight longer than his physician expected, during which period we have had many fluctuations of hope and fear: at one time we almost ventured to be confident that he would be restored to us: but that is all over now. We *must* lose him. May my end be as calm as his.

Your ever affectionate Nephew
ALFRED TENNYSON

If the physician's diagnosis was correct it would seem that the Doctor's final illness had no connexion with the epileptic seizures, the spasms in the chest, the spitting of blood, and the suspected cirrhosis of the liver mentioned in earlier references. On 16th March he died.

It was characteristic of those he left behind that even the arrangements for his funeral were to cause fuss, frustration and argument. Old George Tennyson was too unwell to be present at the funeral and Charles pleaded an attack of sciatica and the necessity of attending the House of Commons on 22nd March when the second reading of Lord John Russell's Reform Bill, of which he was a strong supporter, would take place. His eldest son George – third of the name – therefore represented Bayons on the occasion. Poor Eliza wanted to have the ceremony at Tealby, as befitted the eldest son of the Squire of Bayons, but the old man objected on the ground of expense. The service therefore took place in the Doctor's little crumbling church at Somersby, which has undergone at least two major restorations since that date. Six neighbouring clergymen carried the coffin and Mary Bourne came over from Dalby and was visibly affected. For the poor Doctor's epitaph let us quote from a letter which his second son wrote to his uncle Charles to announce his death:

My poor father, all his life a man of sorrow and acquainted with grief, has gone to that bourne from which no traveller returns. . . . He suffered little and after death his countenance, which was strikingly lofty and peaceful, was, I trust, an image of the condition of his soul, which on earth was daily racked by bitter fancies and tossed about by strong troubles.

CHAPTER SEVEN

BAYONS AND
ARTHUR HALLAM

I T might have been hoped that the unhappy Doctor's death would
have relaxed tension at Somersby and Bayons. This however was
by no means the result. As soon as decency permitted, Mr Rawnsley
and Charles (the elder) who were the Doctor's executors, with his
father, now in his eighty-first year, set about planning the careers of
his children and winding up his affairs. Frederick was out of the
country. The church and a tutorship were proposed for him. Charles
was on the point of being ordained and it was known that his Uncle
Sam Turner intended to leave him property near Caistor in the north
of the county with the advowson of Grasby. Alfred was brought
back from Cambridge, without taking his degree, to look after the
family, as his mother was considered wholly unpractical. His uncle
pressed him also to go into the church and reported his agreement
'though I do not think he much liked it'. In fact of course Alfred never
did take orders and his grandfather soon ceased to press the point, as he
became apprehensive of disestablishment, which he thought might
make the Church less lucrative as a profession. Septimus, now fifteen
years old, was thought to be a clever, sharp fellow, suitable to be
articled immediately to a solicitor. His uncle Charles suggested that he
should try to get Horatio, still at Louth School and only eleven years
old, into the Navy. To his mother's great relief the boy was found to
be too young for this. Edward's mental health was still too unstable for
any profession. His grandfather once more formed a very poor
opinion of Arthur who was seventeen:

He even does not know the multiplication table or anything useful.
He could learn if he would but is as idle as a foal. He must be instructed

before he can be fit for anything. His gestures and twitchings are ridiculous and he would be a subject of ridicule anywhere. They are all strangely brought up.

Before the year ended the case of poor Edward became critical, his depression growing so severe that all concerned felt it absolutely essential that he should be removed from home and placed under skilled medical supervision. At first his grandfather and uncle, with his mother's entire concurrence, arranged for him to be moved to the house of the Horncastle doctor, nominally as a pupil – but this soon proved to be impracticable and the poor boy, still only in his nineteenth year, had to be removed to Lincoln Asylum, which he never left until his death in 1890.

By this time the estimate of Septimus' capacities was beginning to prove over-optimistic. He soon became acutely miserable at the solicitor's office and by the end of 1833 was back at home. How unfortunate the effect of this move was may be seen from a letter which Alfred wrote to his uncle on 13th January 1834.

I think it my duty to inform you of Septimus's state of mind. My grandfather talks of letting him stop at home 2 or 3 months longer – if this is acted upon I have very little doubt but that his mind will prove as deranged as Edward's, altho' I trust his intellect may yet be preserved by getting him out into some bustling active line of life remote from the scene of his early connexions. I have studied the minds of my own family, I know how delicately they are organised and how much might be done in this instance by suddenly removing Septimus from all those objects and subjects with which he has been familiar and upon which he has been accustomed to brood, into some situation where he might be enabled to form his own friendships with those of his own age and to feel there is something to live and care for – but this, if done, should be done immediately, because every hour which he wastes at home tends to increase his malady. At present his symptoms are not unlike those with which poor Edward's unhappy derangement began. He is subject to fits of the most gloomy despondency accompanied with tears – or rather he spends whole days in that manner, complaining that he is neglected by all his relations, and blindly resigning himself to every morbid influence. For God's sake do not consider these as idle words but use whatever influence you have with my grandfather to prevent so miserable a termination. I am sure you will feel for us in this matter. No half measures will do nor ought the savings of a few pounds to be an object here. I repeat it, he should be removed as far as possible from home and into some place where new objects and the example of others might rouse him to energy. Believe me my dear uncle yours very affectionately.

A. TENNYSON

As a result arrangements were made for Septimus to leave home and study medicine under the doctor at Horncastle.

To the old man the most distressing feature of the position was that, although Dr Tennyson's affairs were not in such a mess as might have been expected (there was in fact almost enough cash and easily disposable personalty to cover his debts), Frederick, Charles and Alfred had, as their father feared, incurred substantial debts at Cambridge, about £330 owing by Frederick, £320 by Charles and £170 by Alfred. It was unfortunate that Frederick, as the eldest of the three brothers and the most heavily indebted, had to play a leading part in the resulting discussions and inquiries at Bayons. As always, this led to violent altercations between him and his grandfather. 'On his leaving me', the old man reported to his son Charles after one of these encounters, 'I said he would kill me by his conduct. His answer was "you will live long enough".' Ultimately the old man devised an ingenious plan to cover both the boys' debts and the sum which would have to be advanced to clear Dr Tennyson's liabilities. He took two bonds for the total amount of the debts involved, one from Frederick, Charles and their mother and one from Frederick, Charles and Alfred. The interest on these he proposed to deduct from the allowance which he would make to the Doctor's widow. After his death he bequeathed the bonds to his trustees for the Doctor's younger children.

In June young Charles was ordained and appointed to the curacy of Tealby by his grandfather, who allowed him accommodation in a house in the park at Bayons. Unfortunately at about this time Charles began to suffer from some complaint which caused severe neuralgic pains. Still more unfortunately, the doctor whom he consulted prescribed laudanum. Before long poor Charles had become an addict – 'making no use of body or soul' as Frederick described him. In April 1834 his cousin Clara wrote of him as 'almost killing himself' with laudanum, and a few months later her youngest brother Eustace wrote: 'I cannot help pitying him, poor fellow, for he is the most good-natured fellow in the world and I think he will kill himself soon. I have a great regard for him and always shall have.' Others of the family however disliked poor Charles's untidiness and unconventional habits. His grandfather disapproved of his 'hubble-bubble method' of conducting the service in the parish church and his naval cousin Edwin described him as 'going about in a rabbit skin and looking like the dog's-meat man.' As a result poor Charles's presence became a cause of continual annoyance at Bayons. Old Mr Tennyson began to regret the liberal arrangements which he had discussed with him in 1832, and when Charles proposed taking over the Grove House so that he might have his sister Mary to stay with him and look after him his grandfather peremptorily refused permission. Perhaps in this he was to some extent influenced by his Bayons' grand-daughters, who thought that 'it would be disagreeable to have a tribe of Somersby people so near us, as of course Mary would expect to go everywhere we did', which would not do, for both Mary and Cecilia, who came to visit Charles, were, in spite of their strange beauty, 'shy and awkward, like the rest of the family'. Charles bitterly resented his grandfather's change of attitude and freely expressed this resentment in letters which increased the old man's annoyance.

But beyond all these minor harassments there was one overriding factor which embittered the relations of Somersby with Bayons. The Doctor's death had removed the one obstacle to old George Tennyson's open avowal of his preference for his younger son, who had by now made quite a name for himself in national politics. He had for ten years or more been an ardent supporter of, and indeed a leader in, the struggle for Parliamentary Reform. In 1827 he had been entrusted by a committee of Birmingham politicians, the secretary of whom was the well known reformer Joseph Parkes, with the introduction of the bill to disfranchise East Retford for corruption, and transfer its electoral rights to the City of Birmingham, which at that time had no representation in Parliament. Though the bill never became law it was without doubt an important step towards the ultimate triumph of the Reform agitation and Charles's promotion of it in the House made a considerable impression. Then in 1831 he had successfully challenged the Cecil interests at Stamford in an election which caused intense national excitement and led to a duel at Wormwood Scrubs between the rival candidates, Charles himself and Lord Thomas Cecil, brother of the Marquess of Exeter at which fortunately no one was injured.

When in the summer of 1832 the fight was over and the bill passed, Charles, who had secured appointment to the Privy Council, felt himself to be on the crest of the political wave. This brought the possibility of a peerage into view. The prospect fired his social ambition and antiquarian zeal. He began to think of reviving the ancient name of d'Eyncourt, and in due course, should fortune prove kind, the barony. As a first step he proposed that his father should petition for leave to adopt the name in place of his own. To this the old man expressed strong antipathy:

It would hurt my feelings to lay aside the name of Tennyson for this Frenchified name, and should we not be laughed at and held in derision for so doing? Besides I consider that all our ancestors in the Tennyson line have been by professions and otherwise gentlemen, that the females of the family have done nothing discreditable, that the family have always paid their debts and none died insolvent.

In short, the name of Tennyson was one he could not be 'ashamed of or out of.' Finally, however, after much discussion as to the use or elimination of an apostrophe after the 'd' and as to the merits of various alternative signatures – such as 'Geo. Tennyson d'Eyncourt,' 'G.T. d'Eyncourt,' or even (on the analogy of 'Lord Brougham and Vaux') 'George Tennyson and d'Eyncourt,' and many protestations of his wish in all things to fall in with Charles's view and not in any way to influence him with his own feelings and prejudices, he agreed to sign the petition. But he tried to the last to keep open the question whether he might not himself retain the old name during his lifetime and let it continue in the Somersby family. Failing this, he even expressed the hope that the application which had been prepared and launched with such care might be refused, as in fact it ultimately was, for the time being.

Charles now began to press his father to rebuild Bayons Manor, which was in considerable need of repair, in the Gothic manner; but this the old man entirely refused to countenance. Even Brancepeth, with its combination of luxury and antiquity, he had found uncongenial and depressing, and he wished the old house to retain its comfortable domestic character, to which he had been so long accustomed.

All these discussions made old Mr Tennyson rather uneasy at Bayons and his uneasiness was increased by the doubts which, in spite of Charles's optimism, he had begun to entertain about his son's political future. Charles had not been included by Grey in his first Reform Government in 1832 and he began to drift into opposition to Grey's Government which his father considered 'the best that was ever constituted and likely to stand'. The old man also realised with considerable astuteness that the 'Liberals', amongst whom Charles ranked himself, were being beaten out and out by the 'Tory-Whigs and Whig-Tories' and had no political future. He himself had always remained a Tory at heart, though Matthew Russell had in 1818 induced him to be elected for his pocket borough of Bletchingley to fill a gap for a few months – one suspects as very much a 'Tory-Whig'. But, however much he may have disliked Charles's radical tendencies, he had from the beginning been almost pathetically anxious to leave him free and not to endeavour to 'influence' him. Now there was a new element and he began to fear that continuance in the House of Commons would wear out his favourite son's health and purse and lead to no tangible result. Charles's daughter Julia, upon whom care of her grandfather chiefly devolved, did her best to fight her father's battles with him, but she found the old man 'cranky and crooked', unable to 'correct that innate propensity and pleasure of his life of finding fault with everything he sees' – yet feeling deeply for his beloved son even while continuing to find fault with his every action. By degrees he became convinced that the only thing to be done was for him to give Bayons up to Charles, in the hope that this would make him abandon London and Parliament altogether and settle down as a county magnate. The decision was a hard one for him, but after some months of fret and vacillation he at last made up his mind and, by the end of 1833, had moved to a house which he owned at Usselby, a few miles to the west, leaving Charles in possession of his old home and openly adopted as his successor. At Usselby his granddaughter Julia lived with him and acted as housekeeper, while the other Bayons grandchildren and of course Charles himself were frequent visitors. The result was to intensify Somersby's feelings of humiliation and resentment.

But there was one sequence of events which more than anything else embittered the relations between Somersby and Bayons. In the spring of 1829 Alfred had begun the friendship with Arthur Henry Hallam which was to lead twenty-one years later to the publication of *In Memoriam*. In the Christmas vacation of 1829 Arthur had visited the old Rectory at Somersby, where he became deeply impressed with the beauty and romantic idealism of Emily, the fifth of Dr Tennyson's children. A year later he was there again and now definitely proposed marriage to her and was accepted. His father Henry Hallam, the famous and influential historian and jurist, had apparently had no prior knowledge of his son's attachment. He accepted the position without enthusiasm, and on condition that Arthur and Emily should not see each other or correspond before 11th February 1832, when Arthur would be twenty-one years old. This decision he had communicated to Dr Tennyson, who had, only a few weeks before his death, accepted it in one of his most massively sensible letters. In February of 1832 Henry Hallam's ban expired and Arthur came again to Somersby and announced his engagement. The question then arose as to what money each family would put into the marriage settlement, for Arthur was still reading for the Bar and had no income with which to support a wife. Henry Hallam, who was not very keen on the connexion though he felt that he must accept Arthur's decision, offered to allow his son £600 a year and to settle a jointure of £500 a year on Emily. He urged George Tennyson to settle £4,000 on his granddaughter after his own death, reserving the income from this to himself during his lifetime, but the old man stubbornly refused to make any change from the arrangements which he had already laid down in his will. He would allow Emily £70 a year during his life and after his death would leave her one seventh share in an estate which should be worth about £3,000 to her. He declined to add anything to the provision which he had already made for Dr Tennyson's daughters or to make any distinction between them. As John Bourne, who was with him at Bayons when he dealt with Henry Hallam's appeal, reported, 'he seems to care nothing about the persons whom either the boys or girls choose to marry – Miss Bellingham, Kitty Burton or Kitty the cook-maid are equally the same to him – he totally declines interfering with any of them.'

He would have taken more interest in the subject had he realised that Frederick was falling in love with his favourite granddaughter Julia. But for Arthur and Emily there was deadlock. Henry Hallam felt unable to go beyond what he had offered. George Tennyson was immovable. But worse was to come. Ten months later Arthur Hallam died suddenly at a hotel in Vienna where he was staying on a holiday tour with his father. The effect on Alfred and Emily Tennyson and their brothers and sisters was crushing. In four short years Arthur had become their sheet anchor. 'Never', wrote Frederick, 'was there a human being better calculated to sympathise with and make allowances for those peculiarities of temperament and those feelings to which we are liable.' The blow seemed irremediable.

CHAPTER EIGHT

BAYONS MANOR AND HIGH BEECH

THE affairs of the Tennyson family were destined to undergo great changes during the year 1835. Early in March old Sam Turner died and left his estates at Grasby and Caistor to Charles, who now changed his name to Turner. He was nominated to the Grasby living and straightway moved from Tealby to Caistor. There he took up his abode in the fine old house in the market place, in which his grandfather had courted Mary Turner sixty years before. Then in July old George himself, after a series of grim delaying actions, in the intervals of which his powerful will and fierce intelligence seemed to regain almost their full strength, died at the age of eighty-five, grasping the hand of his favourite son and gasping out 'I am dying – help me!'

The funeral was a notable ceremony, attended by two thousand people, and Bayons Manor was filled from morning till night with crowds of neighbours paying their respects to the old gentleman and taking refreshment. Elizabeth Tennyson declined her brother-in-law's letter of invitation in a very formal note, which incensed him greatly. No doubt the prospect of seeing him, as the new squire, doing the honours and receiving the homage of the county was too much for her. Charles was ill and Frederick still absent in Corfu, where he had gone from Italy to stay, at his own invitation, with his cousin George, in the hope of getting some paid employment at the Residency.

The contents of old Mr Tennyson's will, which would no doubt have been generous by contemporary standards if Dr Tennyson had been the younger son, served only to increase the resentment of the Somersby family. The Grimsby property went to Frederick, charged with an annuity of £200 to his mother. Three thousand pounds were left in trust for Edward. Alfred received a small property at Grasby, worth about the same amount, and an estate at Scartho worth fifteen or twenty thousand pounds was directed to be sold for the benefit of the seven younger brothers and sisters, Charles being already provided for. The remainder of his father's landed estates and all his personalty were left to the elder Charles. To the estate of Usselby, which Elizabeth had hoped would be devised to her and her family, Charles had induced his father to attach a condition that he should take the name of d'Eyncourt. The King's licence permitting this arrived within a few weeks of the old man's death and there was much jubilation at Bayons over the prospect of the change and the splendid pedigree, prepared by Bernard Burke, which accompanied it. This, it was felt, would give them an eminent position in the county and keep them well clear of the erratic and Bohemian cousins. As a final blow to Somersby, there was no relaxation of the old gentleman's fiat that the bonds exacted from Elizabeth Tennyson and the three elder sons should be realised for the benefit of the younger brothers and sisters.

All this unfortunately increased the resentment of the Somersby family, and reports of Alfred's attitude sent to Charles by Mrs Bourne, with whom he was staying at Dalby in August, caused great indignation at Bayons, though Fanny maintained stoutly that he was quite incapable of the remarks attributed to him. His sailor cousin Edwin's comment was nautically concise: 'What can you expect from a hog but a grunt?' He added – curiously – that he had never seen Alfred but twice in his life, and then by accident. Matters were not improved by the return of Frederick, who came with all speed from Corfu to look after his affairs. George, who had a large share of the Tennyson temperament and irritability, was not sorry to see the last of him, and wrote with some heat that he had had enough of being browbeaten by a northern bear. Frederick himself was quite unconscious of any lack of harmony in his relations with his cousin; but unfortunately it was reported to his uncle soon after his return that he was commenting with his usual ferocity on the change of name and sarcastically announcing his intention of changing his own to Clayton.

At Bayons the months succeeding the old man's death were a stirring time. Charles d'Eyncourt, as he was now called, began immediately the rebuilding of the old house. The first step was a modest one, merely involving the addition of a mediaeval dining hall. This was, however, only a beginning. During the next two years, the old building was entirely reconstructed in the Gothic manner, or rather entirely buried in a new and splendid Gothic edifice, for old George had been very insistent that the little seventeenth-century manor house should on no account be pulled down.

Month after month a perpetual stream of letters in Charles's hurried, sprawling handwriting poured from Westminster to his steward at Bayons, with rough drawings of arch mouldings and armorial emblems, numbered paragraphs of detailed instructions for masons and foremen, and laments for mistakes committed and orders ignored. As Fanny wrote in November 1836, the continual blunders and botherations and vexations attending on the building harassed and irritated Charles to such a degree as to produce a wish that it had never been begun. He became quite ill with pains about the heart and spasmodic pains in his limbs, but still the work went on. A skilled craftsman was employed for many months carving decorations at suitable points in the façade and elaborate chimney-pieces within. Everywhere there were to be seen badges and coats-of-arms of the d'Eyncourts, Lovels, Beaumonts, Marmions, Greys, Plantagenets, Lancasters, Bardolphs and others, through whom Charles claimed descent.

Out of doors cottages were pulled down and roads sunk and diverted to form a fine rolling park, which was populated with deer and horned sheep. A moat was made along the western front and the lake below stocked with curious aquatic birds. Stained glass, tapestry, armour and old pictures were purchased for the interior and a special wallpaper for the state rooms copied from one in the palace at Blois. Special portraits were commissioned of Edward III and other royal personages who figured in the new pedigree. As for the general plan, Charles had endeavoured to give the impression of an ancient manor house, which had gradually evolved out of a feudal castle. Accordingly, the architecture was of several different periods, the ruined keep on the rocky eminence behind the house being Anglo-Saxon or Early Norman; the eastern towers, the curtain, the large central flag-tower and two of the gates of a period ending about the accession of Edward III, the great hall and its oak fittings in the style of Richard II and the more decorated portion towards the west representing for the most part the period between Henry V and Henry VII.

Antique statues of English Kings adorned the walls. Two of these were bought from the old Houses of Parliament which had been burned down in 1834. They have now been returned to Westminster Hall. There were concealed staircases and secret rooms; the great hall and great library occupied the whole height of the building and were covered with fine open roofs; and the great curtain wall, with machicolations and angle towers, ran from the back of the house up to the slope behind to enclose the outhouses and domestic offices, the whole circuit of curtain and moat containing an area of about six and a half acres.

Finally Charles diverted the drive, which used to run straight from the park gates south-west of the mansion to the front door on its southern side, now flanked by the great hall. The new approach was so arranged that to reach the entrance the visitor must drive right round the entire building, passing beside the moat, which extended along the western front, turning due east over the wooden drawbridge (often dangerously slippery for horses in wet weather), under the great gate and portcullis, across the barbican, then through a postern gate in the western side of the curtain wall, then past the back premises of the mansion, under another great archway and portcullis, through yet a third gateway in the southern side of the curtain, and so round the south-east corner of the house under the shadow of the great hall to the front door.

Such an arrangement made every visitor drive about a quarter of a mile further than was necessary and compelled the unfortunate châtelaine of Bayons to keep every yard of the great building's exterior perpetually swept and garnished. But such mundane considerations were not allowed to interfere with Charles's great idea. And indeed the grand tour was worth making. The new mansion was beautifully designed, both in mass and profile. The detail was graceful and accurate and the whole charmingly placed in the wooded landscape of Tealby Vale, one of the most agreeable sites in Lincolnshire. Charles, who was the directing architect, had indeed profited by his experience at Brancepeth.

The county however did not take his achievement quite so seriously as he did himself, and many stories about him and his aspirations were soon current in Lincolnshire. For example, it was told that one neighbour, calling to see him and ringing the portcullis bell, was received by the butler with the statement, delivered in all solemnity, 'The Right Honourable Gentleman is walking on the barbican'; and one of the Lincolnshire papers published a story that he had called at a hotel in Harrogate for dinner and put his card at the head of the table to reserve the principal place, which he claimed as Privy Councillor, thereby becoming embroiled with a local pundit who had occupied the seat from time immemorial. This story was copied in the London *Times* and *Observer*, and poor Charles spent many feverish hours trying to stop its circulation and obtain public apologies. Another malicious rumour was that young George d'Eyncourt had published a notice in the papers that he would not be responsible for his father's debts.

Charles was particularly susceptible about such *canards*, as he was at this time more than ever hopeful of political preferment. However Melbourne, who should have been favourable, proved the opposite and poor Charles's hopes gradually faded away, though he stuck to his seat in Parliament until 1852 and found little leisure to enjoy the romantic retreat which he had created at such heavy cost.

A rather touching story is preserved in the family that one day not long before his death in 1861, as he was driving away from home through the park followed by the respectful gaze of the herds of deer, the horned sheep and the curious aquatic birds, he put his head out of the carriage window, looked back at the house, then sank down again on to his seat, sighing 'I must have been mad'.

In 1837 however disenchantment was still many years ahead. As yet Charles had no misgivings. He still had political hopes – even beyond his Privy Councillorship. He had converted the modest 'Beacons Manor', which his father had purchased with such foresight, into an antiquarian's dream, a home fit for any noble family in the land; he had by the change of name staked his claim to noble – even Royal – ancestry; and he had surely more than realised his father's ambition of elevating the Tennysons to the status of a county family.

It was far otherwise with the Somersby Tennysons. The Doctor's

widow and nine of the children stayed on at the Rectory for just over
two years after his father's death. Frederick, whose inheritance of the
Grimsby property made him independent, left home for Italy some
time in 1835 after dashing off a fine flowing letter of proposal to his
cousin Julia, saying that he had loved her devotedly and her only ever
since he had first seen her as a boy twenty years before. Of course there
could, having regard to the relation between the two branches of the
family, only be one reply to such a letter, whatever Julia's feelings may
have been, and there is no reason to think that she reciprocated
Frederick's. Poor Julia, for all her charm and sweetness of nature, was
not destined for happiness. Family tradition says that she fell in love
with her father's friend Edward Bulwer Lytton, who had been living
apart from his wife, Rosina, since 1836, and, not being able to marry
him, became a Roman Catholic, took the veil and died after many
years of seclusion in a convent at Coventry.

Charles, the Doctor's second son, succeeded during 1835 in freeing
himself from the opium habit and in May 1836 married Louisa Sellwood of Horncastle, daughter of an old friend of the family, whose
sister Emily Alfred was to marry fourteen years later.

Alfred, evading all efforts to force him into a profession, stayed on at
the Rectory, looking after the family – a task which his mother gladly
surrendered to him. Septimus seems to have left the solicitor's office
and come back to live with his mother once more, and his Uncle
Charles had apparently given up the effort to equip Arthur for any
profession. Horatio, after being for a time at a school kept by a friend
of Alfred's at Blackheath, seems to have come back to live with his
mother. The girls of course never left home and the whole family with
the exception of Frederick and Charles passed two years, as Mr
Rawnsley described them, 'leading a harmless and quiet life, and that
is what the ancient poets and philosophers say is after all the highest
state of permanent enjoyment', although, he added, 'I wish they would
earn more either of fame or profit.'

No doubt Rawnsley exaggerated the conventional quietude of the
Somersby household. Tennyson households were never very quiet or
conventional, and during these years there were special elements of
disquiet. The rebuilding of Bayons and the social advance of Uncle

Charles were no doubt a constant irritant. The death of Arthur Hallam
hung like a cloud over the brothers and sisters for many years. Frederick's unreturned love for his cousin Julia must have increased his
natural turbulence as long as he remained in England, while Alfred,
during a large part of the years 1834, –5, and –6 suffered from a
frustrated love affair with Rosa Baring, niece of Lord Ashburton and
step-daughter of Arthur Eden, the tenant of Harrington Hall, about
two miles from Somersby Rectory. The progress of this love affair
and the deep wounds which its frustration – no doubt chiefly for social
and mercenary reasons – inflicted on his sensitive spirit are convincingly
described by Professor R. W. Rader in *Tennyson's Maud: The Biographical Genesis* (University of California Press, 1963). The wounds
left scars which marked, some think marred, his poetry in such works
as *Locksley Hall* (1842), *Maud* (1855) and *Sixty Years After* (1886).

It must have been a relief to the whole family when, in 1837, they
learned that the new Rector wished to take over the Rectory, and they
decided to move to High Beech in Epping Forest (near Waltham
Abbey), on the estate of Sergeant Arabin whose wife was a friend of
Elizabeth Tennyson's. Oddly enough Bayons seems to have regarded
the move with some disquiet, for Eustace d'Eyncourt, Charles's
youngest and favourite son, wrote on 27th February 1837 to his father
'I am sorry to hear that the Somersby people think of moving into the
south for they almost lived unheard of and unthought of in Lincolnshire. I am sure wherever they go they will not bring any credit upon
us'.

The migration from Somersby of Elizabeth Tennyson and her
children brought to an end a period of intense suffering and (for the
children at least) intense happiness. The children were all blest – or
cursed – with extreme sensibility, and the scandal arising from conditions in the Rectory drove them closer together and, to some extent,
cut them off from the outside world. Being sensitive and imaginative
they created a world of their own in which their imaginations and
affections were forced into an intense but confined development. The
eleven brothers and sisters were born over a period stretching from
1807 to 1819 and the intensity of their exposure to the tragic conditions
of life at the Rectory varied with their age. Frederick, Charles and

Alfred (born in 1807, –8 and –9) felt the full impact of the worst years of their father's instability, which began with their return from Louth in 1819–20, though Frederick escaped much of the calamity by going to Eton. On the other hand they had, when they came home from Louth, attained a degree of development which, while it gave them some power of resistance, led to varying degrees of temperamental violence – most marked in the case of Frederick, but breaking out occasionally in Alfred and even in the good-natured Charles, as for example over his grandfather's treatment when he was curate at Tealby. Edward, Arthur and Septimus, born respectively in 1813, –14 and –15, were mere children in the years when their father's instability was reaching its most disastrous phase. Their power of resistance was no doubt weak, and they suffered accordingly. Horatio, born in 1819, was too young to feel the full pressure of home life in the early 1820s and during the years when he might have suffered most, 1827–30, his father was absent for long periods on the Continent. The girls seem to have felt the effect of domestic troubles less acutely than the boys; perhaps they suffered less from divided loyalties and were more protected by their mother. But they grew up decidedly eccentric and married late – Matilda not at all, Cecilia at twenty-five, Emily at over thirty, Mary at nearly forty-one.

Undoubtedly a considerable part of the ill effects on the children of conditions at the Rectory was due to division of loyalties. All the evidence suggests that the boys, particularly, were fond of their father – some of Alfred's books are inscribed by him *Ex dono patris amicissimi.* Though he was a hard taskmaster, they respected his love of learning and interest in the arts and welcomed the discerning encouragement which he gave to their early efforts at poetry, though, if he thought that they were allowing these efforts to interfere with their educational work, he would tell them that 'they would never get bread by such stuff'. Moreover in his lucid intervals his unconventionality and wide interests must have made him a delightful companion.

The children all adored their mother, a woman of exceptional simplicity and charm and of a profound, instinctive and unquestioning Evangelical pietism, which contrasted strongly with the more matter-of-fact attitude of her husband, to whom any excess of emotion or pietism in religion was distasteful. Edward FitzGerald wrote of her years afterwards as 'one of the most innocent and tenderhearted ladies I ever saw,' and this view of her is confirmed by a Somersby tradition which tells how the country lads used to bring their dogs and beat them beneath her window, in the certain hope that she would bribe them with money to desist. To Alfred she was 'one of the most angelick natures on God's earth, always doing good as it were by a sort of intuition.' His love and admiration for her are recorded in many of his poems and remained a powerful influence throughout his life.

For the rest, we read of her being pulled about the Somersby country-side in a basket chair by her tall sons, or by a huge dog, which village gossip in after years credited with hooves, and which, when the weather was hot, would lie down in the road refusing to proceed until the spirit moved him. On these expeditions she would read aloud from Mrs Hemans and Beattie's *Calendar*, and her sons owed much to her encouragement and enthusiastic belief in their powers. When in 1850 Alfred had after a long and painful struggle at last achieved success and his mother was living in Cheltenham with Mary and Matilda, her pride and joy in her Ally's triumph were delightful to see. Cheltenham, where he had been a frequent visitor and where his romantic figure and unusual habits were well known, naturally took a keen interest in his success, and for a time his name was on everyone's lips. When Elizabeth heard strangers speaking of Alfred Tennyson and *In Memoriam* in shop or omnibus, she would interject with a charming complacency: 'It may interest you to know that *I* am the *mother* of the Laureate.' And sometimes she would add, with a mother's care for her less-favoured offspring: 'My sons, Frederick and Charles, also have written some very beautiful verses.'

When in 1865 Elizabeth died at Hampstead in her eighty-sixth year, Alfred's last words to the clergyman who had conducted the service were 'I hope you will not think that I have spoken in exaggerated terms of my beloved mother, but indeed she was the beautifulest thing God Almighty ever did make'.

All her three eldest sons wrote poems about her, of which the earliest seems to be that by Charles – probably written during the tragic years through which he passed between 1832 and 1836.

MY MOTHER

Think'st thou if spirits pure as thine
   Through life might be for ever near,
I should not every fear resign,
   As from my boyhood's home I steer?

A mother heard our infant cries,
   And folded us with fond embrace,
And when we woke, our infant eyes
   Were opened on a mother's face.

Our wishes she did make her own,
   Her bosom fed and pillow'd too,
Answering each start or fitful moan
   With trembling pulses fond and true.

Then knowledge was a thing untaught;
   Heaven's charity, a daily dole,
Stole in inaudibly, and wrought
   Its gentle bonds about the soul.

And oh! if spirits pure as thine
   Through life might be for ever near,
There would be scantier chance that mine
   Would sink beneath the doom I fear!

Alfred's verses from *The Princess* (1847) are well known.

Not learned, save in gracious household ways,
Not perfect, nay, but full of tender wants,
No Angel, but a dearer being, all dipt
In Angel instincts, breathing Paradise,
Interpreter between the Gods and men,
Who look'd all native to her place, and yet
On tiptoe seem'd to touch upon a sphere
Too gross to tread, and all male minds perforce
Sway'd to her from their orbits as they moved,
And girdled her with music. Happy he
With such a mother! faith in womankind

Beats with his blood, and trust in all things high
Comes easy to him, and tho' he trip and fall
He shall not blind his soul with clay.

Perhaps the most appealing of all is by Frederick, who no doubt had given her the most trouble and therefore had the most reason to appreciate her qualities. The poem, cannot have been written long before Frederick's death – at nearly ninety years of age.

A HELIOGRAPH

No earthly touch of mortal Art
  Hath shaped this magic counterpart,
  That lovely aspect, soft and bright,
  Was drawn with pencils of the light.

One moment – and the hand divine
  Had wrought thine image perfect-fine,
  The Shaper of the substance, He
  Could trace the shadow, only He.

Though I was young when thou wert old,
  Young is the face that I behold,
  And now my days outnumber thine
  When lengthen'd to their last decline.

Thy truth with the same truth is given –
  Clearly, as tho' the arch of Heaven
  Were shadow'd in a waveless sea,
  Thy faith, thy love, thy life I see.

Mother, it is thyself, the same:
  Should Death, who took thee, take our name,
  Whoever looks on this may see
  All thou hast been, all they should be.

If in those eyes some clouds o'ertake
  The laughing lights that from them break,
  Thro' them more clearly didst thou see
  The true shape of humanity.

D

If round that mouth, whose peaceful gate
Was ne'er unclosed to scorn or hate,
Earth's ills have tortured to the earth
The Heavenward-winged curves of mirth,

More mercifully from it came
The low sweet voice that could not blame,
The tearful smile that most endears
More tenderly dried up our tears.

Ev'n as I gaze, mine ear down-dips
To catch the breathing of those lips,
Where the last blessed words, that fell
In blessing from them, seem to dwell.

My days roll back, I dream no more,
Thy very self I stand before,
And thou art showing me again
How women serve to make us men.

I hear thee say – 'When it shall be
That years have sunder'd thee and me,
And care and space shall hold apart
Hand from hand, and heart from heart;

'Oft as thou seest the moon-lit night
Like blessed memories, calm and bright,
Oh! know, I send o'er Land and Sea
On its hush'd wheels a love to thee.'

The lamp wanes dim, and dimmer now,
I feel thy lips upon my brow,
And now I sleep, and dream – of things
Ah! not like my rememberings!

Thou mayst be Queen of some soft star
  Far off, immeasurably far,
  And strong in godlike thoughts and deeds,
  And mindless of thy mortal weeds;

Thou mayst be close beside me here;
  But could I bid Thyself appear,
  And live – I should be half afraid
  To choose between thee and thy shade.

How oft the Flatterer's art hath drest
  Weak Vanity in Falsehood's vest;
  Here in this sun-drawn image see
  The very Self of Charity!

Elizabeth Tennyson remained the central point of the family until her death, both sons and daughters continuing to live with her until they married, or left England. The family stayed at High Beech until early in 1840, when they moved to Tunbridge Wells. This they none of them liked and in the autumn of 1841 they settled at Boxley near Maidstone in order to be near Alfred's Cambridge friend Edmund Lushington. Emily and Cecilia both married in 1842 and at the end of 1848 Arthur and Septimus went off to Italy with Frederick. The house at Boxley now became too big and Elizabeth moved with Mary and Matilda to Cheltenham in December. Alfred, who lived a wandering life during most of the 1840s, made his mother's home his central point until he married in 1850, and Charles was a frequent visitor. Then in 1853 Alfred handed over to her the remainder of the lease of the house at Chapel Row, Twickenham, which he had rented for himself and his wife and when the lease came to an end in 1855 he bought a house in Flask Walk, Hampstead, where she lived with Matilda next to Emily, who occupied the larger house next door (now number 75) with her husband Richard Jesse. There Elizabeth Tennyson died in 1865.

CHAPTER NINE

'THIS EXTRAORDINARY BROOD'

I FREDERICK, CHARLES AND ALFRED

WHEN the George Tennysons left Somersby in 1837, the two eldest sons, Frederick and Charles, had already parted from the family group. Both however continued to keep in close touch with mother, brothers and sisters, and both bore through life the scars of their distressful upbringing.

Frederick, like Alfred, eluded all efforts to make him adopt a profession after his father's death, and soon after his grandfather died, in 1835, he set off for Italy where he was to make his home for the next twenty-three years. At first he seems to have travelled about Europe and the Near East – 'Travel', he said, in a typically resounding phrase, 'makes pleasure solemn and pain sweet.' Then, in 1839 he married Maria Giuliotti, daughter of the chief magistrate of Siena, and settled in Florence. It was characteristic of Frederick that he omitted to ascertain the legal position of a British subject living abroad and to go through the form of marriage before the British Consul which was necessary to validate his union with Maria. Consequently his eldest son was illegitimate by English law, which caused a good deal of trouble in dealing with the English real estate. His choice of Florence was determined by the great passion of his life – music; he had found no other place where music could be had so good and at so low a price. He first rented a villa – the Villa Torregiani – on the Fiesole road, just outside the city; supposedly, the house had been planned by Michelangelo. Here, though according to his own account he had at that time an income of only four hundred pounds a year from the Grimsby property, he could arrange for a complete opera orchestra to come out and play to him of an evening as he sat alone in his armchair. Later he moved to a city palazzo with a fine garden; and, as his family increased, found it necessary to reduce expenditure, only having a company of fourteen players to make music for him and a few chosen friends.

Sometime in the 1840s he seems to have experienced some kind of religious conversion. Hearing that his sister Mary had become a member of Swedenborg's Church of the New Jerusalem, he began to study Swedenborg's writings and became deeply impressed by them. 'After this,' he wrote many years later, 'I never ceased to feel, yea to know, that I am ever in the presence of God' and 'to realise the warning of St Paul – Pray without ceasing.' At about the same time he became a fervent British Israelite and a believer in spiritualism. However, his more youthful ways were not wholly eradicated. One day early in 1851 he went out for an evening stroll, forgot the time, and got back to find the Porta Romagna closed for the night. When the porter refused to unlock for him, pleading government orders, Frederick retaliated with a torrent of abuse, in the course of which he characterised the government as *porcelli*. This was too much. The civic guard was summoned and he was marched off to prison, to be released next day at the intercession of the Irish dramatist and politician, Richard Lalor Sheil, who had just been appointed British Minister to the court of Tuscany.

Very soon after this, Frederick made the acquaintance of Robert and Elizabeth Browning. As the Brownings had lived in Florence on and off since 1846, their late meeting shows how secluded Frederick's life had been. He quickly became an immense favourite with both Robert and Elizabeth, who were deeply impressed by his earnestness, truthfulness, and simplicity. 'Selfhood – the *proprium* – is not in him,' wrote Elizabeth. They were impressed, too, with his many remarkable talents and acquirements, which only his extreme shyness prevented him from putting to some striking use. Robert found his conversation very rich and suggestive, and summed him up very acutely when he said that he seemed to possess all the qualities of his brother Alfred – only in solution. 'One was always expecting them to crystallise but they never did.'

Frederick did, however, crystallise to some extent in an unending flow of long, exquisitely written and beautifully expressed – if prolix – letters to chosen friends. There is a large collection of Frederick's papers and correspondence at the Lilly Library of Indiana University. At the same time he maintained a poetic output of considerable volume, which fully bore out Browning's acute criticism. His verse is always sincere, fluent, and melodious, with an ingenuous largeness of vision, which is at once grand and childish. 'Organ tones rolling among the mountains,' Alfred called them, and the description is a just one. The poems roll grandly along, but they are too often mere *tones* – inexpressively melodious. In Robert Browning's phrase, they seldom crystallise. In 1853, he had a bulky volume of lyrics privately printed, and in the following year, 1854, under pressure from his friends, including Edward FitzGerald, he published, through John W. Parker of West Strand, a volume, entitled *Ways and Hours*, containing about sixty-five lyrics of varying lengths. But though he continued to write as freely as ever he did not publish again for thirty-six years.

All the brothers and sisters were in some degree valetudinarians in spite of their longevity. 'All we Tennysons have weak health but strong constitutions,' so one of them ingeniously expressed this paradox. Frederick was no exception. He would carry chestnut twigs in his pocket as a cure for rheumatism, and by 1856 he had begun to find Florence too exciting for his nerves. He tried Pisa and Genoa, but without success. Then in 1859 he settled in Jersey where he was to make his home for the next thirty-seven years.

In Jersey his eccentricities increased. Spiritualism and Swedenborgianism became obsessions. At first he had not taken the spirit-science quite seriously. For instance in a letter to Alfred of 1852 he had written of the 'unfortunate ghosts' who 'either drivel like schoolgirls or bounce out at once into the most shameful falsehoods', and in another letter of the same time he speaks contemptuously of 'Owen the Socialist and a host of infidels' who 'by a peculiar logical process of their own, after seeing a table in motion, instantly believe in the immortality of the soul!' But Frederick, in spite of a determined antagonism to the leading sects of the Christian Church (he loved to inveigh against 'the frowzy diatribes of black men with white ties – too often the only white thing about them'), was at heart of a profoundly religious and mystical temperament. He hated materialism and agnosticism in any form, and craved for some creed which might express and justify his unshakable belief in the immortality of the soul and the existence of an omnipotent moral law. Such a creed the philosophy of Swedenborg seemed to offer him and the phenomena of spiritualism fell naturally into place as illustrations and evidence of the master's doctrine. He even came to believe that he himself held communication with the spirits of the departed by means of a kind of electrical ticking heard in his room at night, and for some time he would execute automatic writing under spirit dictation, but the results were so trivial that he gave up the practice and confined himself to the theoretical aspects of the subject. At the same time he grew intensely interested in Free-masonry and for a time was deeply influenced by Henry Melville, a neighbour in the island, who claimed to have discovered a long forgotten science of astrology in which the true explanation of Masonic Symbol-ism was to be found.* He even travelled to London with Melville in 1874 and spent several disheartening months in an endeavour to impress the importance of the discovery on the Duke of Leinster, then Grand Master of Ireland. During this visit Edward FitzGerald saw Frederick for the last time and described him as 'quite grand and sincere' in his enthusiasm for Melville's scheme 'as in all else; with the faith of a gigantic child – pathetic and yet humorous to consort with.'

Frederick seems to have lived in even greater seclusion in Jersey than at Florence. The supernatural and the future life now occupied his whole soul 'to the exclusion of almost every subject which the gorillas of this world most delight in, whether scientific, political or literary'. Alfred and Charles visited him from time to time, and in 1885 Robert Browning called on him. Browning was delighted to find him just as of old, pleasant and genial to the last degree, but felt sadly his growing eccentricity and the seclusion in which he lived. 'I groan over such a noble and accomplished man being as good as lost to us all,' he wrote.

But notwithstanding these vagaries, Frederick's interests remained extraordinarily varied and his mind extraordinarily active. In Italy he had been a keen student of painting, buying with discretion, and also attaining considerable proficiency in the art himself. The University of Indiana possesses one excellent example of his work, an Italian landscape painted in half an hour on the back of his plate after breakfast, and the manuscripts of the Jersey period are often covered with spirited pen and pencil sketches, which shew that he had not entirely abandoned his former hobby. But it was to literature and philosophy that his mind

* Melville's theories are set out in a singular publication, *Veritas: the Meridian and Persian Laws* by Henry Melville, ed. F. Tennyson and A. Tudor, London, 1874.

was now principally devoted, and he continued to read voraciously on every kind of subject. In an old notebook, the contents of which obviously cover a very short space of time, there are entries in his handwriting which give some idea of the scope of his interests. There are scraps of English and Latin verse, several rough drafts of an Essay on Figurative Language, notes on various books such as Scott's *Napoleon*, *She Stoops to Conquer*, Gray's *Letters*, *Tristram Shandy*, Æsop. *Humphry Clinker*, and the Koran; the beginning of a disquisition on Gothic poetry, with references to Saxo Grammaticus and Blair's *Ossian*, some very technical notes on the distribution and variation of biological species, long lists of rhymes and military terms, an elaborate analysis of the Evidences of Christianity, besides a sketch of the Peninsular War and fragmentary discussions on such subjects as Greek History, the Origin of the Art of Writing, the Exploits of the Buccaneers, and the Philosophy of Sterne.

Other glimpses of Frederick's life in Jersey suggest that the old Adam kept very much alive in him. One shews him raging up and down the stairs shouting out, 'where are my trousers, where are my trousers? I have forty pairs and I can only find thirty-five!' It seems that his eldest son, Julius, who was reputed the strongest man in the British Army, inherited the paternal temper and tendency to fits of violence. When the storm raged too heavily, Frederick would emerge from his study (which he seldom left); his tall stooping figure would loom through the doorway for a moment, his long white hair hanging almost to his shoulders – 'Enough! to your room,' and Julius would quickly and silently withdraw.

Frederick retained, up to extreme old age, his mental as well as his physical vigour. Until well into his eighties he continued to play and improvise on the piano and on a small organ, and he went on writing verse, though he did not publish again until 1890, thirty-six years after the issue of his first volume. He then brought out *The Isles of Greece*, a collection of blank verse poems based mainly on the story of the poetess Sappho. In 1891 he followed this up with a volume entitled *Daphne and Other Poems*, another collection of blank verse adaptations from Greek mythology. Four years later (in 1895) he published *Poems of the Day and Year*, a selection from his volumes of 1853 and 1854 with a few additional poems. About this time his sight began to fail and in 1896 he left

Jersey to live with his son Julius in London, where he died in 1898 in his ninety-first year.

Frederick's poetry, in spite of its weaknesses, has its charm and occasional splendours and we must not take leave of him without a few quotations. These are taken from *Shorter Poems of Frederick Tennyson* (London, 1911).

First a few lines of Aristophanic quality from a long and rambling poem which he never printed:

> *I had a vision very late*
> *After a dinner of white-bait;*
> *Methought I saw the Himalaya*
> *Peak on Peak to heaven aspire*
> *Higher still and ever higher.*
> *But when my sight grew somewhat clearer*
> *And the Himalayas nearer,*
> *They changed to dunghills, only think*
> *What magic in a fortieth wink!*
> *Alas to dunghills! What a change*
> *From that stupendous snowy range!*
> *To dunghills, dirty slope on slope*
> *Of dunghills, and a cock atop*
> *Of each one, with disdainful crow*
> *Dumfoundering the cock below.*
> *The first with awful Majesty*
> *Pealing his early Kickerykee*
> *Silenced the second, who was heard*
> *Cock-a-doodling down the third.*
> *Between the first heap and the last*
> *Continuous chanticleering passed*
> *And the lowest was the loudest*
> *And the last little cock the proudest.*
> *Each one like a human swell*
> *Had his little tale to tell*
> *Of how he had a grain or two*
> *More than his neighbour. . . .*

More characteristic are some stanzas entitled 'The Glory of Nature'.

> If only once the chariot of the morn
>   Had scatter'd from its wheels the twilight dun,
>   But once the unimaginable sun
>   Flash'd godlike thro' perennial clouds forlorn,
>   And shown us Beauty for a moment born;
>
> If only once blind eyes had seen the Spring,
>   Waking amid the triumphs of midnoon;
>   But once had seen the lovely summer boon
>   Pass by in state like a full-robed King,
>   What time the enamour'd woodlands laugh and sing;
>
> If only once deaf ears had heard the joy
>   Of the wild birds, or morning breezes blowing,
>   Or silver fountains from their caverns flowing,
>   Or the deep-voiced rivers rolling by,
>   Then night eternal fallen from the sky;
>
> If only once weird Time had rent asunder
>   The curtain of the clouds, and shown us night
>   Climbing into the awful Infinite
>   Those stairs whose steps are worlds, above and under,
>   Glory on glory, wonder upon wonder!
>
> The Lightnings lit the Earthquake on his way:
>   The sovran Thunder spoken to the World;
>   The realm-wide banners of the wind unfurl'd;
>   Earth-prison'd fires broke loose into the day;
>   Or the great seas awoke – then slept for aye!
>
> Ah! sure the heart of Man, too strongly tried
>   By Godlike Presences so vast and fair,
>   Withering with dread, or sick with love's despair
>   Had wept for ever, and to Heaven cried,
>   Or struck with lightnings of delight had died!

> But He, though heir of Immortality,
>   With mortal dust too feeble for the sight,
>   Draws through a veil God's overwhelming light.
>   Use arms the Soul – anon there moveth by
>   A more majestic Angel – and we die!

'A Dream of Autumn' has a naïve charm.

> It is a golden morning of the spring,
>   My cheek is pale, and hers is warm with bloom,
>   And we are left in that old carven room,
>   And she begins to sing;
>
> The open casement quivers in the breeze,
>   And one large musk-rose leans its dewy grace
>   Into the chamber, like a happy face,
>   And round it swim the bees;
>
> She stays her song – I linger idly by –
>   She lifts her head, and then she casts it down,
>   One small, fair hand is o'er the other thrown,
>   With a low, broken sigh;
>
> I know not what I said – what she replied
>   Lives like eternal sunshine in my heart;
>   And then I murmur'd, 'Oh! we never part,
>   My love, my life, my bride!'
>
> And then, as if to crown that first of hours,
>   That hour that ne'er was mated by another –
>   Into the open casement her young brother
>   Threw a fresh wreath of flowers!
>
> And silence o'er us, after that great bliss,
>   Fell, like a welcome shadow – and I heard
>   The far woods sighing, and a summer bird
>   Singing amid the trees;

The sweet bird's happy song, that stream'd around,
The murmur of the woods, the azure skies,
Were graven on my heart, though ears and eyes
Mark'd neither sight nor sound.

She sleeps in peace beneath the chancel stone,
But ah! so clearly is the vision seen,
The dead seem raised, or Death had never been,
Were I not here alone.

To conclude, here is a sonnet which shews Frederick's, perhaps un-expected, skill in this difficult form:

THE POET AND THE FOUNT OF HAPPINESS

There is a fountain to whose flowery side
By divers ways the children of the earth
Come day and night athirst, to measure forth
Its living waters – Health and Wealth and Pride,
Power clad in arms and Wisdom argus-eyed:
But one apart from all is seen to stand,
And take up in the hollow of his hand
What to their golden vessels is denied,
Baffling their utmost reach. He, born and nurst
In the glad sound and freshness of that place,
Drinks momently its dews, and feels no thirst;
While, from his bowered grot or sunny space,
He sorrows for that troop, as it returns
Thro' the waste wilderness with empty urns.

Both in character and in the circumstances of his life, Charles, the brother next in age, presents an extraordinary contrast to Frederick. He was the closest in spirit of all the brothers to Alfred, and the most generally beloved for his frank and genial disposition, winning manners, and friendly sense of humour. Like Alfred, though perhaps not so extravagantly, he was capable of moods of extreme lethargy and outbursts of ridiculous fun. One of the few points of resemblance between Charles and Frederick was in the timing of their literary output. Frederick published nothing between 1854 and 1890 – an interval of 36 years; Charles published in 1830 a slim volume of sonnets greatly admired at Cambridge and praised by Samuel Taylor Coleridge, and then maintained a silence of thirty-four years between 1830 and 1864. Moreover, both brothers followed up their second publications with two subsequent volumes, Frederick in 1891 and 1895, Charles in 1868 and 1873. In Charles's case the primary cause of this intermission was the tragic opium addiction which overshadowed the whole middle period of his life.

Soon after his marriage Charles again succumbed to the opium habit. His wife Louisa struggled devotedly to free him. She succeeded, but at the cost of her own mental health. As a result she had, late in 1839 or early in 1840, to be placed under medical care and it was not until 1849 that she and her husband could resume their life together, and settle down in his vicarage at Grasby which they never left except for short holiday visits until Charles died in 1879. It is surely significant that within a month of his death Louisa also was carried to the grave.

Charles's neurosis never made him egotistical. Except for the un-settled early years of his marriage, he gave up his whole life to the care of his remote rural parish. When, for example, in 1864 his cousin Lewis Fytche offered him the shrieval chaplaincy he refused it as being 'too public and prominent for my rural habits'. His devotion was complete. The last thing he ever considered was his own interest. Not long after he returned to the parish in 1850, he found that he had been robbed of a large sum of money by a fraudulent agent. He was with great difficulty persuaded to take proceedings against the man. These were successful and he recovered a considerable sum of money. The whole of this he expended in rebuilding the church and the school, and his friends noticed that he always afterwards spoke of the fraudulent agent as though *he* had been the ill-used person. Indeed Charles's charity was all embracing. He loved his parishioners, most of whom were rough and illiterate almost to brutality, and his sensibilities always remained open to the pathos and humour of their lives, as was his purse to their often unprincipled importunity. He was tireless and fearless in visiting them even when infectious disease was rampant in the village. His favourite expression when things went wrong was 'I wish we were all in Heaven'.

Grasby was a somewhat barbarous village when he obtained the living. The villagers still believed in witchcraft, a popular countercharm being to cut a sheep in half, lay it on a scarlet cloth and walk between the pieces. The climate was harsh and friends remembered Louisa Turner going about her business in clogs, and during one particularly sharp winter 'in a castle . . . of double cotton-wool petticoat and thick baize drawers and waistcoat'. The Turners soon found the big house in Caistor too remote from the parish and Charles built a new vicarage on the small estate at Grasby which his Uncle Turner had left him. He also bought the inn and put it in charge of a reliable servant, which, for a time at least, had an excellent effect on the temperance of the village.

There were no children of the marriage, but Charles and Louisa adopted the whole village, opening their house and garden for Christmas parties and summer festivals. Animals were as dear to them as children, for Charles was, as the villagers noticed, 'strangen gone upon birds and things.' He never shot after the murder of the swallow (see p. 113) and birds of every kind flocked to him as he fed them on the vicarage lawn. Flowers and trees he loved as dearly as birds and he quarrelled almost fiercely with one of his curates whom he found exorcising, by means of the service in the *Directorium Anglicanum*, the flowers provided for church decoration.

During the early and latter years of his manhood poetry meant much to him and occupied much of his time. Poetry for Charles meant sonnets, and each sonnet meant a great deal of work and a great deal of time, for each would go through a long succession of forms. He would work on the lines morning after morning and read the results to Louisa in the evening after dinner. Moreover most of the sonnets were the result of keen observation or study. In consequence, the 342 published in the collected edition issued by Kegan Paul after his death (1880) are all sincerely felt and sensitively finished and a third of them, at least, reach a high poetic standard. In fact they convey a picture of their author more vital and more complete than any outsider's description can hope to do. Here are a few examples to complete our portrait.

THE LITTLE HEIR OF SHAME
He was a little heir of shame – his birth
Announced by peevish voices, and his death
Welcomed by all; he staid not long on earth,
Nor vex'd them long with his fast-fleeting breath;
He felt their blows, too young to feel their scorn;
How that poor babe was beaten and reviled,
Because, albeit so mischievously born,
He wail'd as loudly as a lawful child!
They hurried to the goal his faltering pace;
Full soon they bore him to his mother's grave;
No more for other's sin accounted base,
In Paradise he shows his harmless face;
The Saviour flinches not from his embrace,
But gives him all his infant-heart can crave.

TO A SCARECROW, OR MALKIN, LEFT LONG AFTER HARVEST
Poor malkin, why hast thou been left behind?
The wains long since have carted off the sheaves,
And keen October, with his whistling wind,
Snaps all the footstalks of the crisping leaves;
Methinks thou art not wholly make-believe;
Thy posture, hat, and coat, are human still;
Could'st thou but push a hand from out thy sleeve!
Or smile on me! but ah! thy face is nil!
The stubbles darken round thee, lonely one!
And man has left thee, all this dreary term,
No mate beside thee – far from social joy;
As some poor clerk survives his ruin'd firm,
And, in a napless hat, without employ,
Stands, in the autumn of his life, alone.

AFTER THE SCHOOL-FEAST

The Feast is o'er – the music and the stir –
The sound of bat and ball, the mimic gun;
The lawn grows darker, and the setting sun
Has stolen the flash from off the gossamer,
And drawn the midges westward; youth's glad cry –
The smaller children's fun-exacting claims,
Their merry raids across the graver games,
Their ever-crossing paths of restless joy,
Have ceased – And, ere a new Feast-day shall shine,
Perchance my soul to other worlds may pass;
Another head in childhood's cause may plot,
Another Pastor muse in this same spot,
And the fresh dews, that gather on the grass
Next morn, may gleam in every track but mine!

TO A 'TENTING' BOY

Early thou goest forth, to put to rout
The thievish rooks, that all about thee sail;
While thy tin tube, and monitory shout
Report thy lonely function to the vale;
From spot to spot thou rovest far and near,
While the sick ewe in the next pasture ground
Lifts her white eyelash, points her languid ear,
And turns her pensive face towards the sound;
All day thy little trumpet wails about
The great brown field, and whilst I slowly climb
The grassy slope, with ready watch drawn out,
To meet thy constant question of the time,
Methinks I owe thee much, my little boy,
For this new duty, and its quiet joy.

THE FLOCK FOR THE MARKET:
Or, Hope and Despondency

Two hundred strong they pour'd into the field,
A gentle host, for one brief night's repose
Before the market, for their doom was seal'd;

They left their pasture ere the morn arose.
I listen'd, while that multitudinous sound
Peal'd from the highway through the twilight air,
A cry for light, while all was dark around,
A throng of voices like a people's prayer;
Slow broke the dawn; the flock went plodding on
Into the distance, some at once to bleed,
Some to be scatter'd wide on moor and mead.
But while I sigh'd to think that all were gone,
A little lark, their field-mate of the night,
Saw them from heaven and sang them out of sight.

ON SHOOTING A SWALLOW IN EARLY YOUTH

I hoard a little spring of secret tears,
For thee, poor bird; thy death-blow was my crime:
From the far past it has flow'd on for years;
It never dries; it brims at swallow-time.
No kindly voice within me took thy part,
Till I stood o'er thy last faint flutterings;
Since then, methinks, I have a gentler heart,
And gaze with pity on all wounded wings.
Full oft the vision of thy fallen head,
Twittering in highway dust, appeals to me;
Thy helpless form, as when I struck thee dead,
Drops out from every swallow-flight I see.
I would not have thine airy spirit laid,
I seem to love the little ghost I made.

CALVUS TO A FLY

Ah! little fly, alighting fitfully
In the dim dawn on this bare head of mine,
Which spreads a white and gleaming track for thee,
When chairs and dusky wardrobes cease to shine.
Though thou art irksome, let me not complain,
Thy foolish passion for my hairless head
Will spend itself, when these dark hours are sped,
And thou shalt seek the sunlight on the pane.

But still beware! thou art on dangerous ground:
An angry sonnet, or a hasty hand,
May slander thee, or crush thee: thy shrill sound
And constant touch may shake my self-command:
And thou mayst perish in that moment's spite,
And die a martyr to thy love of light.

(*A Hundred Sonnets* by Charles Tennyson Turner was published in 1960 by Rupert Hart-Davis, London.)

In the absence of Frederick and Charles the superintendence of the migration from Somersby to High Beech devolved on Alfred. It was a crucial moment in his career. He had, with his extreme sensibility, suffered more than any of his brothers from the distresses of life at the Rectory. To this had been added the calamitous reception by the critics of his volume of 1833. Then had come the terrible shock of Arthur's death and the humiliating rejection of his suit by Rosa Baring's family. To these misfortunes may be attributed the morbid shyness, the recurrent fits of psychopathic depression and the extreme susceptibility to criticism, even, as he once said, when directed 'against the straightness of his toe-nail,' which were to afflict him until the end of his long life.

But he had one source of strength not shared by any of his brothers. He had made up his mind while still a boy that he would become a great national poet and from this determination he never deviated, rejecting all other ways of making a living even when this threatened the continuance of the engagement to Emily Sellwood. The extraordinary precocity of his childhood had given him confidence in his own power and this, reinforced by the no doubt sometimes exaggerated encouragement of his Cambridge friends, had carried him through the first distressful Somersby years and was to carry him on to the *annus mirabilis* of 1850, which saw his ambition realised. One can see from *Locksley Hall* and from section CIII of *In Memoriam* that on leaving Lincolnshire in 1837 he felt, however obscurely, that he was taking an important step on his chosen road, though he could not foresee the trials which still awaited him. These were, no doubt, largely due to his own weaknesses. During the first year at High Beech he became engaged to Emily Sellwood, but at the end of 1839 through what the only contemporary witness calls, 'an overstrained morbid scrupulousness', he broke off the engagement though not the correspondence with Emily. Probably this was due, in part at least, to his own morbid diffidence, in part to his fear of alienating her from her father to whom she was devoted and who, he felt, did not trust or understand him. In the following year her father forbade further communication between the two. The whole, very obscure, episode is fully and understanding discussed by Professor Rader in his *Tennyson's Maud*. Whatever its exact causes may have been there is no doubt that it had a disastrous effect on Alfred. The moderate success of his two volumes of 1842 was restorative, but in 1843 came the loss of the whole of his small capital in the wood-carving speculation (see pp. 152–9). In 1845–6 his friends secured a pension of £200 a year on the Civil List for him, but it was not until 1850 that the great popular success of *In Memoriam* enabled him to marry and secured his appointment as Poet Laureate. From this point he became a national and even an international figure and so passes beyond the scope of this book – though he was never to feel that he had passed beyond the scope of his family.

Before taking leave of him, however, we will quote a few contemporary descriptions which seem to us to throw a sharper light on his singular personality than any description of our own could do.

AT SOMERSBY

'Here's a leg for a babe of a week!' says doctor; and he would be bound,
  'There was not his like that year in twenty parishes round.'
          —Said by the Somersby doctor of Alfred.
          Memoir vol. 1, p. 2.

'If Alfred die one of our greatest poets will have gone.'
          —Dr G. C. Tennyson, about 1821.
          Memoir vol. 1, p. 22.

'I remember as if it wur nobbut yistuday, my man, as was a fiddler bit of a fellow, was off to Hildred's theer at Skegsnesh, to play fur quality at a dance, and he was cooming hoam in the morning early, and bedashed, who should he light on but Mr Alfred, a-raävin and taävin upon the sand-hills in his shirtsleeves an' all; and Mr Alfred said, saäys he, "Good morning" saäys he; and my man saäys, "Thou poor fool, thou doesn't know morning from night," for you know,

Sir, in them daays we all thowt he was craäzed.'
—H. D. Rawnsley quoting an old Somersby resident
Memories of the Tennysons (Glasgow, 1900).

'As for Mr Halfred he was a 'dacious one. He used to be walking up and down the carriage drive hundreds of times a day, shouting and holloaing and preaching, with a book always in his hand and such a lad for making sad work of his clothes ... down on his heels and his coat unlaced and his hair anyhow. He was a rough 'un was Mister Halfred and no mistake.'
—H. D. Rawnsley quoting an old servant
at Somersby Rectory.

'Alfred could hurl the crow-bar further than any of the neighbouring clowns.'
—Edward FitzGerald.

'That bloated ploughman.'
—Edwin Tennyson (afterward d'Eyncourt).

'In proof of his strong muscular power, when showing us a little pet pony on the lawn at Somersby one day he surprised us by taking it up and carrying it.'
—Mrs Lloyd of Louth, Lincs.

'As he was when I first saw him I cannot imagine anything more beautiful in human form.'
—Emily, Lady Tennyson.

CAMBRIDGE

'That man there must be a poet'.
—W. H. Thompson, Tutor, Trinity College, 1827.

'Charles and Alfred left me on Friday. They did not act disrespectfully to me, but they are so untoward and disorderly and so unlike other people that I don't know what will become of them. ... So far from having improved in manner or manners [they] are worse since they went to Cambridge.'
—George Tennyson, Jan. 26th 1829.

'I remember him well, a sort of Hyperion.'
—Edward FitzGerald.

'Alfred, it isn't fair that you should be both Hercules and Apollo.'
—W. H. Brookfield.

'In Alfred's mind the materials of the very greatest works are heaped in an abundance which is almost confusion.'
—J. M. Kemble.

'I could not be mistaken in the universality of his mind.'
Edward FitzGerald, 1835.

'. . . . His almost personal dislike of the present, whatever it may be.'

—James Spedding, 1835.

'The more I see of him the more I have cause to think him great. His little humours and grumpinesses were so droll that I was always laughing.'

Edward FitzGerald, 1835.

'He seeks for strength, not within but without, accusing the baseness of his lot in life and looking to outward circumstances far more than a great man ought to want of them.'

—James Spedding, 1835.

IN LATER LIFE

'You do not know Alfred? A massive, irregular, dusty, brown-complexioned man; a large rough-hewn face full of darkness, yet of kindness, even of good-humor; large, gloomy-kindly, Indian eyes, an immense shock of dusty black hair; and one of the best *smokers* now living! Right well do I like a pipe beside Alfred; his speech in that deep, clear metallic voice, is right pleasant to me; his very silence, amid the tobacco clouds, eloquent enough.'

—Thomas Carlyle, 1842.

'A Life-guardsman spoiled by making poetry.'

—Thomas Carlyle.

'Really ill in a nervous way, what with an hereditary tenderness of nerve and having spoiled what strength he had by excessive smoking. . . . poor fellow, he is quite magnanimous and noble-minded, with no meanness or vanity or affectation whatever, but very perverse according to the nature of his illness.'

—Edward FitzGerald, 1840 (at the time of the breaking off of the engagement with Emily Sellwood).

'A man solitary and sad, as certain men are, dwelling in an element of gloom, carrying a bit of chaos about him, in short, which he is manufacturing into cosmos.'

—Thomas Carlyle, 1842.

'He looked and said he was ill: I have never seen him so hopeless.'

—Edward FitzGerald, 1844.

'A valetudinarian almost: not in the effeminate way, but yet in as bad a man's way. . . . Alas, for it that great thoughts should be lapped in such weakness . . . alas that one cannot put a dram of a mean man's prudence into that great soul of his, hang him.'

—Edward FitzGerald, 1845.

'He was in a rickety state, brought on wholly by neglect but in fair spirits and one had the comfort of seeing the Great Man.'

—Edward FitzGerald, 1846.

'He seems. . . . in truth but a *long*, lazy kind of man, at least just after dinner – Yet there is something naive about him – the genius you see too.'

—Robert Browning 1846. After seeing Tennyson
for the first time – at a public dinner.

'Oh Alfred could you but have the luck to be put to such employment [Thucydides's command of a naval squadron in the campaign for the relief of Amphipolis, 423 B.C.] no man could do it better: a more heroic figure to head the defenders of his country could not be.'

Edward FitzGerald, 1847.

'He has indeed a most noble countenance, so full of power, passion and intellect – so strong, dark and impressive. He is as simple as a child and not less interesting for his infirmities.'

Aubrey de Vere, 1848 (after the grant of
the pension and the success of *The Princess*).

To give a picture of Tennyson in later life we have included an appendix founded on notes made by Hallam Lord Tennyson, his eldest son, of conversations with his father in about 1867–70 (see pages 197–208).

II EDWARD, SEPTIMUS, ARTHUR AND HORATIO

Of the four younger brothers (Edward, Septimus, Arthur and Horatio), very much less is known. As has already been told, Edward, who was born in 1813, succumbed on the verge of manhood to the neurosis which haunted all the brothers in different degrees. At a comparatively early age, he began to show some poetic talent and a high degree of sensibility. This developed into a nervous state so acute that it became necessary to place him under restraint from which he could never be released. In 1890, at seventy-seven, he died in an asylum.

Two sonnets by Edward which were published in an article on 'J. M. Heath's "Commonplace Book" ' in *The Cornhill Magazine* (CLIII (1936), 430–32), suggest a genuine poetic gift, and this is confirmed by some lines recently discovered in a manuscript book of Mary Tennyson's (now in the Tennyson Collection, at the Usher Gallery, Lincoln). These lines are fragmentary and disconnected and seem clearly to have been written in a condition of considerable mental

excitement. They are not signed but they occur in the middle of a series
of Edward's poems and no doubt are by him:

> The Sun's rosy laugh met the faint white half
>   Of the young moon in the West,
> And ducklings crouch on their grassy couch
>   Beside their mother's breast.
>
> Alone I rove, alone I prove
>   All human pleasure vain,
> I sigh for change, there is nothing strange
>   In this wide world of pain.
>
> Forlorn I pass by the smoking mass
>   Of chalk and arid clay,
> . . . .
>   Drifts gustily over my way.
>
> The loaded wain o'er the sandy plain
>   Grates harshly on the wind,
> On the causeway near and the thorny [briar?]
>   Leaves wisps of straw behind.
>
> There drovers urge with painful scourge
>   A litter of helpless swine,
> The loud whip cracks on their galled backs,
>   Loud bellow the rushing kine.
>
> They toss and rear through excess of fear
>   And lash their tails around,
> The flesh flies cling with their maddening sting,
>   And rankle the fresh-made wound.
>
> And still the more they plunge and roar
>   The flesh flies rend their prey
> And . . . bees smell the tainted breeze
>   From . . . borne away.

In proud disdain of his griping chain
   With sullen step and slow,
With heavy tread is a strong bull led
   Where the valley waters flow.

His heavy tread and his bulky head,
   His ample swelling chest,
His strong set neck and his fetlock thick
   No trifler dare molest.

The fate of Septimus was hardly less tragic than that of Edward. His youth gave promise of a brilliant future. He was tall, strong, handsome, with great personal charm, and undeniable poetic talent. The elder brothers loved and admired him, and Arthur, his senior by a year, remembered all his life a summer morning when Frederick and Alfred, after bathing in the brook behind the old rectory at Somersby, had raced about the meadow 'chairing' little Septimus between them and 'admiring his fair proportions' – little thinking that the child, so beautiful and vital, would be the shortest-lived and the most unhappy of the whole brotherhood. Septimus' neurosis took the form of acute hypochondria and extreme indolence. Many stories of this, half comic, half tragic, were current in the family, and one was repeated with gusto by D. G. Rossetti, who would tell how once, when calling at the Henry Hallams' house in Wimpole Street, he was ushered into the drawing room which he thought was empty, until a huge, untidy, shaggy figure rose from the hearth rug on which it had been lying at full length, and advanced towards him with outstretched hand, saying, 'I am Septimus, the most morbid of the Tennysons.'

When his father died in 1831, Septimus, then sixteen years old, and apparently regarded by his father's trustees as a sharp, clever fellow, was apprenticed to a local land agent. Before long however the 'black bloodedness of the Tennysons' began to assert itself and as a result of Alfred's letter of 13th January 1834 to his uncle Charles (see p. 80) arrangements were made for Septimus to leave home and study medicine under a doctor in another part of the county. When his grandfather died a year later he became entitled under his will to about three thousand pounds. It seems that he then gave up his apprenticeship to live with his mother. In 1843 he and Arthur went to live with Frederick in Florence. For a time the plan seemed to be successful and on 24th February 1844, Edward FitzGerald wrote to Frederick 'I am glad to hear Septimus is so improved – I beg you will felicitate him from me. I have a tacit regard of the true sort for him as I think I must have for all of the Tennyson build. I see so many little natures that I must draw to the large even if their faults be on the same scale as their virtues.'

But Septimus only remained with Frederick for two or three years. From that time onwards inertia gained more and more hold on him. His small capital dwindled away; he ceased to write even to his mother, to whom all the family were so passionately devoted, and in 1866 he died, at fifty-one, with nothing to show for the brilliant promise of his youth.

Mary Tennyson's manuscript book has a number of sonnets by Septimus. We will quote two to show the scope of his talent. The first, which is dated 13th November 1832 and was therefore written soon after his seventeenth birthday, has a genuine, if rather callow, grandeur, and in the last two lines something more. The second was evidently written not long after Septimus had gone to Italy with Frederick, and reflects the intense love of home, which was shared by all the brothers and sisters and is also evident in some of the other poems by Septimus quoted in the article on 'J. M. Heath's "Commonplace Book"' (*Cornhill*, CLIII (1936), 426–49).

SONNET

Thou Mighty Being! to whose works the earth
And all that it contains is as a grain
Of sand on the seashore, or drops of rain
Added unto the ocean; ample birth
Of high and holy thought have I, when e'er
I strive to see (what thou wilt not disclose)
In every glowing star that shines more fair
The mystic fountain whence his lustre flows!
What art thou? and who are we that thy Sun

Of righteousness should so distinctly shine
Upon our little world as He hath shone?
Bountiful effluence of love divine!
Perhaps even now (or have we sinn'd alone?)
In that same dewy star thy brow sharp thorns entwine.

SONNET

I am in the land of beauty and the vine,
Olive and glowing light encircle me,
All that should glad the heart of man is mine
Yet am I not from vain repinings free;
But, longing for my native Isle, would be
Amidst its lowing vales, its bleating hills;
The cold gray slopes, the fertile vales and rills
That run rejoicing to a well-known Sea!
What aileth me? I languish: I am dull:
It vexes me that I may not employ
My pen less feebly on such forms sublime,
Vast forms and vivid colours beautiful,
That should possess my soul with song and joy –
Yet all my heart turns to that colder clime.

Arthur, who was born in 1814 and lived until 1899, narrowly escaped an equally tragic fate. He seems to have been from the first a highly imaginative and nervous boy. When quite a small child he was once discovered groping about under the dining table, and, on being questioned, explained that he was trying to find God's legs. He seems very early to have become the confidant of Alfred, his senior by four years, and, like all the brotherhood, he adored Charles. Writing on a nostalgic visit to Somersby when he was seventy, he recalled a morning spent perhaps sixty years before with Charles (then a stout fellow 'in the hay-day [sic] of existence'), leaping backwards and forwards over the brook. An 'encouraging shilling' held out by the elder brother stimulated the little boy to an especially broad jump. This shilling he straightaway changed into twelve coppers, and sitting on the top of the church bank above the lane opposite the rectory, 'sported and

threw these about him, wondering that one little silver shilling should
be the father of such a large rolling copper family.' Though he never
published, it is believed he wrote verse intermittently and some lines
discovered in Lord Ravensworth's visitors' book over what appears to
be his signature, suggest that he had a real poetic talent. The lines
relate to an engraving by Bewick:

> *A gate and a field half ploughed,*
> *A solitary cow,*
> *A child with a broken slate,*
> *A titmouse on the bough,*
> *But where, alas, is Bewick*
> *To tell the meaning now?*

He had a very genuine artistic gift also and spent some time as a boy
studying under Espin, a well known Lincolnshire artist, at Louth. All
the brothers were great doodlers, Alfred and Frederick specialising in
romantic buildings and female heads, Arthur and Horatio in grotesque
male heads. There is in the Tennyson Collection at the Usher Gallery,
Lincoln, an album filled with drawings and doodles, chiefly we think
by Arthur, a feature of which is the great number of comic devils,
reminding one of Alfred's *Devil and the Lady*.

Arthur must have been a singular boy. When he was summoned for
inspection by his grandfather after his father's death, the old man
described him as 'idle as a foal,' with gestures and twitchings which
would make him a subject of ridicule anywhere, and ignorant even of
the multiplication table. If Arthur attempted to get into any profession
he, like Septimus, seems to have given it up after his grandfather's death
and to have gone on living with his mother, first at Somersby and then
at High Beech near Epping. According to the reminiscences of Henry
Evan Smith (1828–1908) who knew them in Lincolnshire, the elder
Tennyson boys had for many years a close connection with Caistor,
which they would visit from time to time, taking rooms in an old
house opposite the present Red Lion Hotel. Arthur appears to have
gone there a good deal during the later 1830s. Evan Smith described
the brothers as keeping aloof from intimate acquaintance and com-

panionship, less from pride than shyness. It was obvious, he says, that, although delightful companions for cultured people and scholars, they were unable, through what was probably an inherited form of indolence, to put forth half their strength, physical or mental, and none of them had the nerve or resolute will required for winning distinction in any profession or competitive form of enterprise. Evan Smith was especially friendly with Arthur Tennyson, who would often have small parties in his rooms, entertaining them with *extempore* verses and with his skill at acrostics. No doubt the indulgence of their mother was far from beneficial to her unbalanced and erratic offspring. A friend described her sitting in her drawing room at High Beech, after the family had left Somersby, surrounded by her tall sons, all drinking pots of beer. When one of them blew the froth from his brimming pot on to the carpet, she only smiled benignly – 'The exuberance of youth.'

Such indulgence was particularly bad for poor Arthur, who about this time took seriously to drink. In 1842 he agreed to go for a cure to the Crichton Institution at Dumfries, which seems to have been half lunatic asylum, half hospital for the treatment of nervous diseases. He stayed at the Crichton nearly a year, then, in September of 1843, it was arranged that Frederick, who was on a visit to England, should take him and Septimus back with him to Italy – no doubt in the hope that a change of scene might steady the precarious mental balance of the two younger men. This was a generous act, but it is doubtful whether, with his violent temper and reserved habits, Frederick was well suited to so difficult a situation. The little that is known about Arthur's condition during the thirteen years of his stay with Frederick, suggests that the experiment was not altogether a happy one. Robert, afterwards first Earl of Lytton, who came to Florence in 1852 as attaché to his Uncle Henry Bulwer, the British Minister, evidently soon began to hear strange rumours about Arthur. Frederick he no doubt knew through the Brownings, but he failed for a long time to meet the younger brother. On 7th January 1854, he wrote to Mrs Browning, who was staying in Rome:

I have made the acquaintance of Arthur T [ennyson] at last, he is not the genius we expected, but in all other respects has fulfilled our

wildest anticipations; for he dined with me one evening, got! [*sic*] and his brother has since requested that he never come up here again. I indeed have a sneaking sympathy for this reprobate, who complains that he is chilled and stunted through the whole nature of him by the frosty atmosphere and Tenarian gloom of his elder brother, whose exhortations, little conciliatory and perhaps somewhat pompous, only exasperate and bewilder, missing altogether their honest aim.
(*Letters from 'Owen Meredith' to Robert and Elizabeth Barrett Browning*, Waco, Texas, 1936, p. 57)

When Frederick left Italy, Arthur returned to England. There is some doubt as to the actual date of his return. He himself wrote thirty years later that he had lived with Frederick in Italy for eighteen years. But we are inclined to think this mistaken and to put his return not later than 1859. Whatever the actual date may have been, it seems probable that he went before long to stay with Charles at Grasby and that Charles's influence proved more beneficial than Frederick's. It seems also that soon after his return from Italy he experienced the religious conversion that came to Frederick and the other members of the family at some time in their lives. In June 1860, he married Harriet West, sister of the vicar of the adjacent parish of Wrawby, and it is clear that he had for some time past been working devotedly among the sick and poor of the parish.

Arthur's marriage was to bring him into close relations with Horatio, who had been a young man of eighteen when the family left Somersby (and who was to marry Harriet's sister Catherine in 1870). Horatio displayed in an extreme degree the other-worldliness of the Tennysons. When the family left Somersby in 1837, there was talk of his going with Septimus to Demerara in search of fortune, but this idea had been given up and some time afterwards Horatio took his small capital to farm in Tasmania. He soon found that he was not cut out for a farmer and in the middle of June 1843 he was back in England seeming, as FitzGerald observed after meeting him in London, 'rather unused to the planet'. 'One day,' writes Fitz, 'he was to go to Cheltenham, another to Plymouth; then he waited for an umbrella he thought he had left somewhere. So where he is now I have no notion.'

The next fourteen years Horatio appears to have spent chiefly at his mother's home at Cheltenham, with occasional visits to Alfred and Charles. During these visits he became attached to Charlotte Elwes, sister-in-law of the vicar of Bigby and Wrawby, near Grasby, and member of a family which owned a house at St Lawrence, Isle of Wight, and were on friendly terms with Alfred and Emily Tennyson. Horatio married Charlotte Elwes at St Lawrence in 1857, just before Arthur returned from Italy. From then onwards Arthur and Horatio were often in the Grasby district where their strange personalities became legendary. The visits grew more frequent after the death of their mother in 1865, for her house in Hampstead continued until the end of her life the chief centre and meeting-place of the family.

The two brothers were alike in many ways and they had much in common with Frederick, Charles and Alfred. Like them, they both, as a friend once observed, combined an extraordinary childlikeness with an intense realisation of the verities of the spiritual world and a consequently slight hold on what the majority of men think important. They had also, both of them, Alfred's keen eye for, and deep appreciation of, natural beauty. Physically their resemblance to him was remarkable: they were both dark, tall, aquiline, with a fine growth of hair and beard, Arthur having the closest resemblance in feature, but being shorter and slighter than Alfred, while Horatio was well over six feet in height. The late Mrs Gould of Hitchin, Hertfordshire, whose father was Rector of Owmby-cum-Searby in those days, and who remembered Charles, Arthur and Horatio, wrote down, before her death about twenty years ago, some memories of them. So far as possible, we give her description in her own words:

Tennysons are not easy to describe. There was both a natural grandeur and simplicity about them; a streak of impish mischief and a love of the gruesome. Delightfully unconventional, they were never like ordinary people; even their dress and their walk seemed 'different'. They might ramble, stalk, saunter or stride over the country-side and be sure of a warm welcome wherever they went, for their genuine friendliness made them universally liked.

Sometimes their remarks were not complimentary; as long as it was a Tennyson who said it, all was well, for they never intentionally hurt anyone's feelings. A Tennyson could 'steal the horse'.

I well remember Mr Turner, who was often seen in his parish; often hatless, wrapped in a big cloak and enveloped too in a sort of scholarly benevolence. When talking to my mother there was often a sprinkling of laughter which was good to hear. When 3 years old I was taken to a Grasby farm. Out came a gobbling turkey and I thought it was bleeding when I saw its red feathers. I screamed with fright and dear Mr Turner hoisted me up in his arms and hugging me tight against his *unshaved chin*, carried me all the way back to the vicarage. The great events in the summer were the Village School Treats. The one at Grasby was the most popular, because Mr Turner always took such an active interest in all the activities of the young people.

In the winter 'spelling bees' brought the neighbours together; but Mr Turner was more ambitious and started poetical 'bees'. There was a final competion, judged by Mr Turner, and he awarded the first prize to my mother, much to our delight.

In the early days of photography my brother Charles longed to take a photograph of Charles Turner. To his surprise he readily agreed and brought a chair out into the garden, quite ready to pose. At the last, most critical, moment he made a comical and hideous grimace, and though Charles was disappointed he enjoyed the fun and thought it 'so like Mr Turner'.

When the Turners went away for a change, Horatio and his family stayed in Grasby vicarage. He had been at school at Louth with my father and he used to stride over to Searby church on week days to read the lesson. I thought he was the most beautiful man I had ever seen: he must have been well over 6 feet and very distinguished looking.

Mr Arthur Tennyson I remember very vividly. My brother and I looking out of the schoolroom window would sometimes see him floating down the garden path, his picturesque figure clothed in an ample cloak with a large collar open at the neck and a wide artistic hat over his somewhat unkempt locks. He helped himself along with a tall clothes prop, or so we thought. Once when we were racing round the house at top speed we came hurtling into the large porch, there to find Arthur quite at home placidly smoking his pipe, and not at all perturbed by our boisterous entrance. He would never knock or ring but just wander in, for he knew he was always welcome and would join us in any meal that was going. My sister Emily had golden hair and blue eyes; when he went up to her he asked her quite sternly, 'Emily, what are you doing here? You ought to be in heaven.'

One warm summer day, hearing that the famous strawberry bed at

Bigby rectory was ripe, Mr Arthur strode over to investigate. No one saw him come and he made straight for the strawberry bed. He was never given to exerting himself very much and he found it far too exhausting to stoop down to get a strawberry and then to straighten himself up and eat it, so he just lay full length on the strawberry bed and propelled himself along biting strawberries as he went. This was too much for young Arthur Field, the Rector's schoolboy son and Arthur's godson, who saw him from a window. He ran out and got the large strawberry net and pegged the big bird firmly down under the net.

By supper time all seemed forgiven and Arthur Field was chattering happily about his day in Brigg and how he had seen the pretty Miss Cotterell. 'Is she really pretty?' Mr Tennyson asked. 'Why yes,' said Arthur, 'she is called the Belle of Brigg.' 'I would like to see for myself', he said, 'and go to Brigg tomorrow.' So he stayed the night at Bigby rectory and in the cool of the evening he stalked down the road to Brigg. Coming down to breakfast next morning Arthur Tennyson said 'Good morning' to Miss Cotterell, and after closer scrutiny, 'You are not so pretty as I thought you were last night.'

Horatio seems, like Arthur, to have undergone some kind of religious conversion in middle life. Like Arthur, he devoted much time and emotional energy to visiting the sick and unfortunate, often to the serious detriment of his own health, and it was characteristic that at lunch and dinner he would stow away in his pockets generous portions of any dish which he particularly fancied, for distribution in due course to his less fortunate friends. Sometimes he would forget to distribute his bounty and would go cheerfully about his business radiating a powerful odour of fish. He had what Arthur sometimes lost through the stress of his struggle with an unhappy temperament, a keen sense of humour and a happy knack of description – as, for example, when he described some children singing carols in a poor street as 'gutter cherubim', and said of the harsh voice of a preacher 'that it was like a tiger licking a sore place.' The artist friend who asked his opinion of two panels which she was painting for a reredos, must have been rather disconcerted at his reply. He looked at the panels silently for quite a long time and then said dreamily, 'After all, angels are only a clumsy form of poultry.'

He was never happier than when writing long hieroglyphic letters to his children (one of these contains over fifty tiny and very skilful drawings on three small pages of script) or making puns and riddles with Alfred's two small boys (born in 1852 and 1854). Occasionally an outrageous example would creep into a letter, as in the following postscript to the massively built Frederick, 'I gave you a dirty riddle in my last; here is another from the same manufactory – "why should your *podex* [behind] rank among aerial phenomena rather than mine?" Answer: "Because it is a meteor" (*Sc.*meatier).'

Horatio's letters, serious and otherwise, admirably reflect his personality. They are all dashed off on the spur of the moment, without pause for choice of phrase or self-conscious adaptation. Here is a vivid and powerful bit of description, written while he was staying with his sister Cecilia Lushington at Glasgow in December 1854:

You would have been amazed had you witnessed a quarrel here t'other day between an old scotch hag, blind with wrath and drink, a mere compound of clouts and curses, and a policeman, but the combat was very unequal and the latter utterly discomfited made a hasty retreat, thoroughly bespattered with abuse, and, to the great amusement of the bystanders, as the old beldame withdrew, she shot at him over her shoulder a gleam of murderous hate as tho' to have set her teeth in his heart and taken a long pull at his life's blood would have afforded her a keener relish than anything that could have been offered her in the whole compass of heaven and earth.

Thirty years later comes a lively description of a dull sojourn at Weston-super-Mare:

My dear
. . . . How Maud and you will revel in this place! a fine stretch of mud for a mile or more when the tide is out with a narrow riband of water much of the same complexion representing the sea. High and inspiriting! I go daily and wallop myself in the mud, and sit in my coat of mud at meals exhaling ozone, to the benefit of myself and the house in general. As you walk along the road bordering the sea, you catch the pipe of wild birds who run about making a peripatetic sea lunch meal then by way of set off against this solitude, you have the native band every other day wh. takes its stand nearly opposite and this with the rapid transit of butchers' and bakers' carts is quite exciting and raises quite a little effervescence of the spirits, then lest this should

E

prove too much for the nerves we have a sedative every now and then, in a low-church clergyman or two who pass just under our windows or a hooded crow or so, a feathered parallel, who wings his slow way across the mudfield just opposite, then lest this should not be quite sufficient to quiet the mind thrown into rather too wild excitement by the music, butcher, bakers and grocers, a trio of old cats get together, now and then, to overhaul its neighbours; judging by the lovely smiles that pass over the cats' faces, the neighbours have no reason to think their affairs are in any wise a matter of indifference. I'm sure now after this glowing description of the physical and moral aspect of the place you will feel yourself compelled to take the next train and come down at once. . . .

Of about the same date is this description of a rough day at Tetford near Somersby where Horatio and Arthur were making a nostalgic visit:

The cottage stands on the Horncastle and Salmonby side of the little hill leading down in to Tetford, and so, being on highish ground, comes in for a full share of the equinoxes at this present flinging about the pendent tresses of a weeping ash in the corner of the damp little parallelogram called a garden in front of the house; there is also a single standard rose just opposite the window waggling its head at me with the same sort of paralytic motion as used to affect the head of Mrs John Fytche not quite so sweet and now gathered.

Here is another vivid Somersby reminiscence, written in 1885 – this time personal: 'I am 66 next September – what a distance from the time when Mrs ——— twitched up her lip in a tearful spasm by the old pig stye when I was some 10 or at most 12 years old, on hearing that I was likely to go to sea. "It's a' vara sad," as Carlyle once remarked to Alfred with face upturned to the deep starlit sky.'

Now and then there is a flash of sarcasm – very seldom, however. Horatio was too kindly, except where pretentiousness and insincerity stirred his bile:

What fine fun Val's letter is. How exactly it seems to jump with what I had conceived of the man. I think I see him bending his weak profile over the paper as he writes and thinking he has done it! 'from thence you must go to Venice – yes, beautiful Venice.' O, Lord save us! what a trashy, thin, sky blue, butter-milk style is this. 'Then you come on to Rome and there I leave you.' 'Sir, you cannot take from me anything that I would more willingly part withal' (see Hamlet in one of his interviews with Polonius).'

Usually Horatio was too much alive to his own shortcomings to be other than sympathetic to the faults of others. Now and then there is a flash of that fear of 'the something after death' which bedevilled so much of nineteenth-century religious feeling:

That terror of the next world takes hold of me at times and the thought that all that seems so fair here will look so black there, and the dread possibility of deceiving one's own heart here. I cannot, as some do, look exclusively at the mercy of God: surely he is just also, or how could he be God? Surely tho' beyond his mercy, whether seen of us or not, there rises with ever more and more threatening aspect, his tremendous justice ready to fall upon such as have rejected HIS LOVE.

These fears were no doubt based on Horatio's consciousness of the weaknesses of the Tennysonian temperament, to which he felt that he himself had too often succumbed before his 'conversion.' This comes out clearly in the many letters which he addressed to Frederick's second son Alfred, the scapegrace of the family. Here are two examples:

Yours is a nature, as once was my own, very prone to self indulgence, and every gratification of the senses nails a man down to the earth more and more, till he lies prostrate and utterly incapable of raising himself to higher things, as complete a captive as Gulliver who fell asleep and so suffered himself to be chained down by the pygmies. Giants as we all of us are by virtue of our spiritual endowments, yet if we allow these to slumber, the small pigmy passions, the little self indulgences, will render us utterly incapable of rising to our full spiritual stature.

There are certain natures whose upward development is sadly hindered by a certain indolence, and, what so often accompanies indolence, a softness too apt to slide into sensuality. Don't take offence at the word, a man's own self love would rather have the word modified into sensuosity, a word there is no need to say I have coined for the occasion – but it is better to give things their true names.

Horatio was deeply disturbed by Frederick's attitude towards the Christian faith and in several letters he urges the elder brother to think

deeply of the real meaning of the great Christian festivals and dogmas –
particularly those connected with the birth of Christ, his resurrection
and atonement. Here are two examples:

The most astounding fact that history has ever recorded GOD
INCARNATE, to a great percentage probably a mere myth, to
many more only a pleasant song, to some a mockery, to the few a
FACT, and the few are chiefly those who in the place of criticising
have learnt to *do* the WILL OF GOD. For I believe it is only for such
that God vouchsafes light.

Christmas is hardly a time to enter upon controversies of this kind;
the atmosphere at this most sacred season should be absorbed in the
stupendous FACT at this time announced by angels and believed in by
the faithful; no wonder a weak runner should stagger under such a
tremendous miracle of LOVE and it seems to me it is chiefly the love-
less hearts that find a difficulty in believing; for faith is the legitimate
child of love.

But in spite of their religious differences, Horatio had a deep affection
for Frederick which comes out touchingly in a letter written to him
not long after the death of Frederick's wife in 1884: 'now goodbye my
dear Fred and God bless you. As the stream of time floats you away
from your great loss it will open out to you more and more its actual
extent, suffused however with that tender colouring which takes away
all harshness of outline and lends even to keenest griefs an aspect of
loveliness.'
Now a last quotation from a letter, which shows that Horatio had
his full share of that mystic quality with which all the brothers and
sisters were endowed in different degrees:

How do you account for the following? I was travelling not long
since by railway, when the rough rhythm produced by the movement
of the train gradually evolved itself into the very sublimest music, I
think, that ear of man had ever heard: this kept growing in volume
and grandeur till at length the whole being was born upon the bosom
of the mighty melody: once or twice I noticed a passage out of some of
our best composers, but this, like some small effluence, was almost
immediately taken up and absorbed into the main melody, which
ever rising and deafening in its course bore grandly onwards, a solemn
and awful chant yet jubilant and triumphant to a degree and in a

combination never expressed before by any mere human composition. Surely if then and there I could have brought this inspiration (for what else was it), within the confines of bars and notes, all earthly harmony would have appeared as nothing in comparison. My spirit is yet lifted up at the mere memory of it. How and when it came or went I know not. All I do know – it is a rapture such as I never before experienced nor am likely to experience again – great wonderful and holy!!!

Perhaps it was due to this mystic quality in Horatio that his mind seemed to move slowly and that there seemed to be a strongly bucolic flavour in his personality. Henry James noted the same element in Alfred.

Horatio and Charlotte had four children, Cecilia, Maud, Violet and Bertram. Cecilia married Mr Pope, who became Censor of the non-Collegiates at Oxford, and had no children. Maud and Violet died unmarried. Bertram, of whom a short account will be found in *Glimpses of Tennyson*, by Agnes Grace Weld (London, 1903), led a very un-Tennysonian life of adventure. After a short service in the Navy, which he did not like, he went out to Manitoba to farm. Finding this impossible, owing to lack of capital, he spent some time driving a coach, breaking horses, and pioneering in the Far West. Then he studied law, was called to the bar and became a Queen's Counsel, taking up residence at Moosomin in the North-West Territories with a view to practising there. This proved a disappointment, owing to the slow development of the township. After a short and not wholly unsuccessful spell of gold-digging in the then exciting new field of Klondike, he came back to England where he died in September 1900, in his early forties. Bertram Tennyson had a considerable literary gift. According to Agnes Weld, his love of adventure was stimulated by an early passion for Scott's novels, and wherever he went he always carried with him his Bible and the works of Shakespeare. In 1896 he issued through the Spectator Printing and Publishing Company, Moosomin, N. W.T., a small paper-bound volume entitled *The Land of Napoia and other essays in prose and verse* most of the contents of which had been published in various periodicals, e.g. *Bailey's Magazine*, *The Toronto Week*, *The Quest* and the *Moosomin Spectator*. The few poems included in this volume shew that Bertram Tennyson had genuine poetic power and we include here three examples, an extract from 'The Seasons', 'Cumbrian Dales and Fells' and 'Plebeian and Patrician'. The third is of particular interest since it contains an echo from one of Alfred's best-known poems, which indeed it seems to criticise on social-ethical grounds.

From 'The Seasons' (*N.W. Territories*)

For all her beauty in the passing time
Is marked with beauty's breath
And like a beauty dying in her prime,
She robes herself for death.

A wild white land, that like a troubled sea
Runs into bitter ridges, where the snow
High heaped in pallid billows silently
Breaks into soundless surf when tempests blow;
Where the soft-footed wolf slides sidelong by,
Gaunt ribbed and lank with care,
Watching the passer with suspicious eye
Before he seeks his lair;
A wild clear sky, wherein the jewelled stars,
In frosty radiance gleaming,
Pale into milder splendours where the bars
Of Northern Lights are streaming. . . .

CUMBRIAN DALES AND FELLS
To William Watson, on reading 'Lakeland Once More'

On these plains where the brooding silence
Is broken only by wail of hawk
Or sound of the wind in the secret grasses,
That tell a tale for the breeze to bear
To the aspen poplars which quake and tremble,
Astir with the secret nature holds:
Here, in this lonely land of silence,
I read your chant of the English hills
And my heart went back to the meres and mountains
I knew of old in the dear home land,

For I heard the echo from high Helvellyn
    Flung back in challenge from bold Ned Scaur,
And saw through the mist the peaks sun-smitten
    Rise to a height before unknown,
Where the Langdale Pikes stand up to heaven
    Like giants watching the vale below,
And the insect creatures toiling slowly
    With blast of powder and swing of pick,
Delving the hills that have stood for ages,
    And still will stand when our race is done
And the sound of the greatest name among us
    Has gone as a breath of wind goes past;
Land of valley, and pass, and mountain;
    Of brook, and river, and falling spray,
Thunder of surf on your seaward bases,
    Ripple of beck in your inland green.
Here it is winter, keen and starlit,
    Ablaze aloft with the northern lights
That spring like spears of a charging army
    Loosed from the land of the polar star,
Or spread abroad like an angel's pinions
    Flung from the east to the western rim
Of the dim horizon blank and boundless,
    With only the drift of the snow between.
I heard your song, and the west, in answer,
    Faintly echoes a far reply:
We have not forgotten our northern country,
    Force, and torrent, and mountain tarn,
The grey and purple of crag and heather,
    And flying shadow on mountain side,
The Rotha sings in its rocky channel,
    We hear its voice in a song that's borne
From the north land with its mountain passes,
    Scree and echo, and ghyll, and scaur;
The years of exile are clean forgotten;
    The sunlight glints on Solvar's How.

PLEBEIAN AND PATRICIAN

Blind fools of fate who idly happy stray,
 Life's pathway through,
Content if but the passing summer day
 Be fair and blue;
Peals there no warning from the cloud-capped peak,
Where the great goddess whom we all must seek,
 Doth still remain,
Fair Freedom? while the multitudes forlorn,
Gaze with sad eyes at summits far withdrawn
 Above their pain.

Comes there no wail from famine-haunted slum,
 And crowded court,
Half smothered by the city's busy hum,
 And noisy sport?
Hark! to that sad, exceeding bitter cry:
Help us, oh! Father, for we slowly die
 Beneath the rod
Of grinding want, and social laws which clasp
The poor forever in their ruthless grasp.
 Help us, oh! God.

What help to us that Freedom broadens down
 With steady pace,
And somewhat smooths the fierceness of that frown
 On her fair face?
Are not our children dying at our knees,
While you lie softly upon beds of ease,
 Though we have none?
Some day shall freedom smile on all around,
But we shall lie unwept beneath the ground,
 Our troubles done.

Winter is gone but in the noisome lairs –
 Where we lie pent –

We cannot know the touch of sweeter airs
*   That spring has lent.*
Are we not freemen, can we not go too,
And walk at last beneath that arch of blue,
*   O'er field and fell?*
Yes, we are free – you raise the canting cry –
Yes, we are free – to rot and starve and die –
.   You know it well.

You know it well; if once we dare to pause,
*   Our loved ones fade,*
It is the fruit of those much vaunted laws,
*   The rich have made.*
God! there are children in this man-made hell
Who know the sound of curses passing well,
*   But never yet*
Have heard the skylark carol overhead,
Or plucked the wild flower from its grassy bed,
*   When dews were wet.*

Though you dream on, the night is almost spent
*   And dawn is near;*
The heavy cloud of misery is rent,
*   And hope is here;*
Say – for the issue rests within your hands –
Shall the day dawning the opposing bands
*   In battle view?*
Or shall the day-star in a sky serene
Beam from the heavens on a fairer scene?
*   It rests with you!*

In October 1868, when Horatio's eldest child was under ten years old, his wife died. Alfred immediately had a house made ready for him on the Farringford estate, but in December 1870 he married again – Catherine West, sister of Arthur's first wife. This marriage brought the two brothers even closer together. Judging by the great number of different addresses from which Horatio wrote during the remaining years of his life, he seems never to have had a settled home. He was often with Charles, with Alfred, and at Park House near Maidstone, the home of Cecilia and her husband Edmund Lushington. The quotations from his letters which we have given sufficiently describe his spiritual progress, marked by an enjoyment of life which never wholly failed him even in sickness and old age (he died in 1899 at the age of eighty), and an intense religious sense which never became morbid or egotistical.

Arthur's temperament was not so happy. His long struggle with the temptation to drink had weakened his spirit and driven his thoughts inward. His religious feeling was intense but egocentric. He corresponded regularly with Frederick, but nursed a subconscious resentment of what he considered Frederick's unsympathetic treatment in Italy, and he tormented himself with the feeling that Frederick's response to his advances was grudging and reluctant. Though Alfred was always ready (as was Frederick) to help him in his chronic financial difficulties, he felt that Alfred, who never answered letters if he could possibly avoid it, was becoming too grand and successful to care for him. Harriet, I believe, understood him and handled him with true affection and sympathy, but they had no children and on 17th June 1881 she died. For days he was inconsolable, walking about with one of her gloves or handkerchiefs in his hand, and with tears streaming down his face. A letter which he wrote to Frederick at the end of July shows the depths of his feeling:

We know not what health is until we miss it is an old truth, and I knew not while living with my gentle amiable darling how I loved her. You must forgive a wild letter, for while finding no voice of hers around me now, and chilled at times almost to the extreme of despair until my horrible feelings pass away and that is while finding myself at church and welcomed there by God who never fails upon my entering there to give me one of his short but strong embraces, which shows me at once that HE has not left me; and sure am I if I am sure of anything, that to compensate for the loss of her society on earth I am now blessed with a double portion of her spirit upon me from where she is – and if I am at times strained to the utmost by unhappy feelings some sweet voice every now and then tells me that God is on my side. I saw the dear little thing die the refined and beautiful death of one who has borne so much suffering (which has all been blessed to her as she went through life) from the cough and a weak heart for years and heard the death rattle of my best of friends save God, for she was sister, brother, wife and mother to me altogether may eternal blessings light upon the heads of all those dear souls who knew her and whom God has raised up to comfort me.

His friends were fearful that the shock of his loss would drive him to drink again. If this happened they felt it must end in death or the madhouse. But Horatio and his wife took him to live with them. Then on 7th December 1882 he married Emma Louisa Maynard. His Lincolnshire friends thought his new wife much too conventional and dominating. Spruce, smart, and very capable herself, she evidently tried to make him the same, and they missed the untidy, shaggy, abstracted Arthur whom they had known and loved. It may well be, however, that the discipline was good for him.

On 4th February 1884 he writes to Frederick a letter which shows that the spirit of Harriet was still very near to him:

When my blessed Harriet who had lived with me in England for so many years passed away from me one awful and never to be forgotten morning now going on fast to three years since, if not entirely three, never to be spoken to by me again in this life, but betwixt that sad morning and my now writing to you – for if ever a man felt helpless and surrounded by the most dismal darkness, I was that sad man, when I became fully conscious what a loving companion had left me – she who prayed so powerfully for me when on earth has most spiritually comforted me from where she is, and how often when I have been in keen distress has a voice soft and soothing and firm and decided spoken to me saying, 'I am not the less with thee in this great suffering of thine the greatest suffering thou has ever known in thy life, but more than I ever was' – what intense comfort this has been to me God only knows. One morning when in a state of all but maddening distress I cried – for a plain tale is soon told and without any ornament – 'O God I am going mad, save me' when the same soft kind firm voice spoke to me and said, 'Be still and know that I am God,' and then the high fever of anxiety and suffering fell instantly, and many other instances of the Almighty's supporting power could I give you, for I have learnt in suffering what I could never have learnt without it.

In 1883 Arthur and Emma began going to Malvern, where they

soon made their home. Here, as years before at Wrawby, he devoted much time to visiting the sick and poor. His methods must have been a welcome change from the normal routine of district visitation. 'Stop a bit, Betty,' he would say to an old woman who always greeted him with a torrential catalogue of her ailments, 'stop a bit, and let me tuck in a text.' The old lady would stop, the text was 'tucked in,' and off she would go again as merrily as ever.

At Malvern Arthur made friends with Eliza Stephenson, wife of the Chaplain at Allahabad (afterwards vicar of Boston in Lincolnshire). Mrs Stephenson was a novelist who used to have musical parties and 'Ruskin' and poetry evenings, which are described in *Pastel for Eliza* by Marjorie Broughall (London, 1961). Arthur liked to come to these parties and sometimes would read, generally from Alfred's poems: 'Morte d'Arthur', 'Guinevere', 'The Two Voices', and the dialect poems were favourites. He read in a magnificent voice and 'with all his heart.' Mrs Stephenson found something pleasant and tender and humorous about him. He seemed a man of a fine mind which he had never been able to turn to much account – a really good man, but nervous and broken down. He suffered much from depression and liked to come and unburden himself to one of the ladies whom he found congenial. Sometimes he would wander into the garden to pick and eat the ripe fruit, saying, 'God helps those who help themselves.' Once at a supper party he startled the company by pointing to a dish of trifle and asking for 'some more of that angel's vomit.' Another evening after a late picnic he pointed to the full moon, which was just rising, with the words, 'look at that great golden guinea which is going to buy us a beautiful night.' He was very High Church, while his wife was evangelical. Mrs Stephenson described her rather ominously as a bright, sensible, healthy woman, full of energy, who did all the organising, contriving, and acting while her husband just read and wandered about.

It is clear that even in Harriet's lifetime Arthur derived strength and solace from his religion, which had a markedly mystical quality. In February 1878 he wrote to Frederick:

In your letter you speak of what I may truly call the great sweet and peace-giving voice which answers your prayer and similar instances of encouragement to pray for what I most stand in need of are also thank God given to me, for instance, some time before going up to the altar, the dejecting consciousness of what I am would fain do its awfully overwhelming best to keep me from going there, but as prayer makes the darkest cloud withdraw, mixed with confession of what I am and how little I deserve this blessed body and blood refreshment, a happy change if I will but be patient comes at last, my gloominess falls from me and well it may for (and a plain tale is soon told) a most unmistakable and comforting voice and similar to the voice which I think speaks to you, pours into my ears these welcome sounds, Thou shalt go up, Thou shalt go up, and to make it all the more sweetly and affectingly welcome and to put it in my own rough language, that voice seems to [be] made up of mother's and the Almighty's together. This is an innocent way of telling it, is it not? I am fully aware of it, nevertheless it is not an inch less true for that, and I become painfully aware of this, namely that if I attempt to describe my state of mind during these God-comforting occasions (while encouraged to go up to the altar) in loftier language that I get entangled in such a web of difficulties as to make me very glad when I am once fairly out of it.

Arthur often had to fight hard against fits of depression which assailed him particularly in the early mornings. In 1884 he writes to Frederick from Malvern:

How little one knows what a moment may bring forth. In the early morning, and some hour or so before going down to breakfast, I was saying to myself, what more exaltingly, more hopefully cheering than sacred songs, while doing my best to cheer myself by singing them, for I am in the habit when waking in the early morning of doing my best to sing myself out of very dark and dismal states of mind indeed, similar to those painful thoughts upon awaking, which you at one time said belonged to you also when you awoke, but which you afterwards told me, by letter, had ceased altogether, or something like it. . . . I remember your remark well during those days when you told me that you suffered in this way, and that when they waylaid you in the early morning the anguish was intolerable.

Four years later he returns to the subject again in a letter which begins gloomily, 'At our great ages the great change may come at any moment, for are we not both of us undressing for the grave as rapidly as we can?' He asks again for Frederick's experience, having forgotten what answer he received to his earlier letter, 'for my sunstroke at Malvern coupled with so many things that have taken place betwixt then and now, quite dims my memory at times.' But the old resentment against Frederick smouldered on, now and then breaking into flame. In July 1889 he writes, rebuking Frederick for never initiating correspondence. 'You would be cunning, I think, to give me any exquisite reason why I should always be the first to write . . . you grieve me I must say much that since you took me for my soul's good you have been so little anxious to know how my soul fared since we lived together in Italy.'

Five years later he writes to Frederick's daughter-in-law Sophia:

Since I heard from you a remark of Frederick's to you to the effect – and I think it was this – 'who says I have been unkind to my brother or brothers?' I have pondered much upon it and prayed much about it and I cannot help thinking that if my brother Frederick could realise how much suffering he had caused me during the time I was with him in Italy and could send me a message that he was grieved at having caused me such pain, he would lift a heavy load from my heart and I believe would be a happier man himself. His last few lines touched me greatly and I think by his writing them to me (as the last letter *he says* he shall ever write on earth) that there was a hidden feeling in his heart that all had not been well betwixt us when we lived together. . . .

I consider you my dear Sophy as a woman of good judgement and kindness and therefore I leave this letter in your hands greatly wishing that Frederick might see it, as I believe with God's blessing which I have warmly and with all my heart prayed for, that it may be the means of healing a wound in both our hearts.

But Frederick was now eighty-seven; his memory had begun to fail, and Sophia could only reply that he had no recollection of Arthur's ever having lived with him at all.

Arthur now began to feel Malvern too cold in winter. He began to suffer from asthma and to 'find with dear old Job that it is with more or less difficulty that during the tight frosty atmospheres we draw in our breath and swallow our spittles.' He, therefore, moved in 1893, the year after Alfred's death, to a house (then called Belle Vue) near the

railway station at Freshwater and found the milder climate helpful;
but it was not long before cataract attacked his eyes and he became
almost blind. Yet he could find a charming phrase even for this
affliction. 'You see,' he would say, 'God has sent me to his night school.'

His sensibilities remained as keen as ever. He loved to sit on the
beach at Freshwater Bay. 'There is absolution in the sea,' he would say,
and to a friend who met him wandering about the Freshwater lanes one
May morning, and asked how he was, he replied with evident emotion,
'I cannot help being troubled by the terrible excitement of the spring.'

In June 1899, a month after his eighty-fifth birthday, Arthur
Tennyson's troubled life came to an end. Troubled it had certainly been,
but there had been consolations, and one must not paint too gloomy a
picture. The Lincoln Tennyson collection possesses several of Arthur's
sketchbooks which suggest that his art must have been a lifelong
pleasure and solace to him. The books cover travels in Italy, France,
England, Wales, Scotland and Ireland and contain a great number of
sketches in pencil, pen and ink, and wash, which shew a keen eye, a
skilful hand, a fine sense of composition and a remarkable power of
reducing grandiose and romantic scenes to a small scale without losing
their essential character. They also contain a number of delightful
caricatures of himself, his beloved Harriet, her sister Catherine, who
was to become Horatio's second wife, and Horatio's first wife Charlotte
(known in the family as 'Charlie'). These throw a pleasing light on
Arthur's capacity for simple fun and on his relations with his Harriet and
other members of his intimate circle. Yet here again one must speak
with reservations. On one of his caricatures there is scrawled in his
handwriting, 'Oh the pleasures of the imagination, how sweet they
are, but it is a dangerous sea to embark on without the pilot religion.'

III   THE SOMERSBY SISTERS AND MATTHEW ALLEN

The Somersby sisters were just as other-worldly as their brothers,
though it seems that on the whole their temperaments were happier.
Physically as well as mentally they strangely resembled their brothers.
Though Mary was lame from childhood, owing to some accident,

she and Cecilia as young women always produced an extraordinary impression by their dark, aquiline beauty, and Emilia (Emily as she was called in the family), though her head seemed rather large for her body, had singularly expressive eyes and a profile like that on a coin – *Testa Romana*, as an Italian friend of the family said of her.

From childhood the sisters were all omnivorous readers and three of them at least (Mary, Cecilia and Emily) wrote verse. Sewing, knitting and sampling they would have nothing to do with. They adored their brothers and, as far as possible, shared in their pursuits, especially story telling and play acting. According to Henry Evan Smith, 'The formation of a chivalrous manliness in the boys was greatly aided by the constant companionship and influence of the girls. Each sister selected a true knight or esquire from amongst the brothers, with whom their words of encouragement and smiles of approval were always high reward.' This sounds like a specimen of romantic Victorian fiction, but it probably derives from a true estimate of the relation between the brothers and sisters, who were essentially children of the Gothic Revival, like their uncle Charles. Their mother's family seems to have felt the same influence in some degree, for her eldest nephew changed his name from Fytche to ffytche, no doubt to give it a flavour of antiquity, and his younger brother always pronounced his name with a long 'y', presumably with the same object, while May ffytche, a member of the third generation, was consumed by a lifelong passion to act in Shakespeare's historical dramas, and did in fact appear with Irving in *King John* at Oxford in 1891 or 1892.

The intense and intimate family life at Somersby inevitably exaggerated singularities of character – particularly in the two elder sisters: Mary, only one year younger than Alfred, and Emily, one year younger than Mary. When Emily became engaged to Arthur Hallam, no doubt the pressure increased. Echoes of it still sigh through the stanzas of *In Memoriam:*

> *O bliss, when all in circle drawn*
> *About him, heart and ear were fed*
> *To hear him, as he lay and read*
> *The Tuscan poets on the lawn!*

Or in the all-golden afternoon
A guest, or happy sister, sung,
Or here she brought the harp and flung
A ballad to the brightening moon.

Arthur Hallam's death just when the prospects of marriage were, after two years of parental discouragement, beginning to seem more favourable, no doubt had a serious effect on Emily's extreme and rather melancholic sensibility. Three years later Mary had a similar, though less grievous, disappointment, when John Heath, a Cambridge friend of her elder brothers, to whom she had become engaged, broke off the engagement.

The move to High Beech, Epping, in 1837 must have been a good thing for both girls, for whom Somersby now held too many disturbing memories. The whole family were intermittently together at High Beech, or at 12 Mornington Place, in Camden Town, where they seem to have had a sort of communal lodging. The four sisters were all living at home, and so, for the most part, were Alfred, Septimus and Horatio. Frederick joined them when not on the Continent, Arthur seems to have been mostly at Caistor, where Charles was living in the big house on the market place until he moved to Grasby, and two or three of the brothers and sisters were generally visiting him. The family had another connexion with Caistor through the Haddelseys. Mr Haddelsey was a solicitor, who collected for Alfred the rents from a small property at Grasby which his grandfather had left him, and whose daughter Susan was a close friend and correspondent of Cecilia's. The friendship between the two families was long maintained. Indeed there is a tradition in the Haddelsey family that Alfred and Susan exchanged letters within a few days of his death in 1892.

During these years (even before leaving Somersby) Mary, Emily and Cecilia seem to have become the centre of a small group of young blue-stockings called the 'Husks' and devoted to the study of the Romantic poets – Keats, Shelley, Wordsworth, Coleridge, and, of course, Alfred

Tennyson. The Husks had their own private language; they met in the houses of the various members to 'shuckle' (Husk word for a confidential highbrow chatter), to 'sloth' in the garden and to read and discuss the 'deadly' (thrilling) poems of their favourites.

Although there is very little detailed information about these early years, the characters of the four sisters can already be clearly differentiated. Mary we find summed up by one of her Bayons cousins about 1835, as 'very handsome, very quiet, very amiable, not very gay.' Alfred, however, writes of her as 'a girl of great feeling, very warm in attachment to her female friends.' And her quiet selflessness made a strong effect wherever she settled for any length of time. This was soon apparent at High Beech, for when in the spring of 1838 she set off for the Channel Islands with Anne Sellwood in quest of health, it was said that she had already done more good than any one in the neighbourhood and that the children had got to be particularly fond of her. Emily was more egocentric and more assertive, a courageous horsewoman with something of the tragedy queen both in manner and temperament. However, she was capable of deep feeling and Arthur Hallam's death no doubt dealt her a blow which time could never efface. Its severity is shown by a letter which she wrote to her Uncle Charles d'Eyncourt on the death of his youngest son, Eustace, in 1842, nine years after her own loss:

I can well understand, my dear Uncle, that your feelings of bereavement are even more distressing than they were at first. In these overwhelming griefs the effect is frequently too stunning in the first instance for the full truth to bear with all its ghastliness of power upon the mind, but when day after day passes away and nothing breaks the mysterious silence, no letter from the beloved one whose heart was full of warmest home affections, then by degrees the full weight of the direful blow is felt crushing one's very soul.

Of Matilda's early years, there is little to say. There is a tradition in the family that she had at the age of about six months been dropped on a coal scuttle which injured her head and caused some mental derangement in after years. She had a strong sense of humour (much less marked in her two elder sisters) and a naïvety which was remarkable even in the Tennyson family. There was a vein of mysticism also, perhaps even a more psychic quality, if one is to believe the story told in Hallam Tennyson's *Memoir* of her strange experience at Somersby in the autumn of 1833. One evening, just before the day on which Arthur Hallam died in Vienna, she and Mary saw a tall figure, clothed in white from head to foot, pass down the lane by the rectory. They followed and saw it disappear through the hedge at a place where there was no gap. Matilda, it is told, was so awed by this experience that on reaching home she collapsed and burst into tears. It was, by a strange coincidence, she who a few days later picked up at Spilsby the letter telling of Arthur's death, and brought it home, ignorant of its contents, to Alfred.

Cecilia was an enthusiastic 'Husk', and had a much keener sense of humour and a lighter heart than Mary or Emily, neither of whom could have written this description of a would-be suitor – a vignette which surely would have pleased Jane Austen. It is from a letter to her cousin Lewis Fytche, dated 24th April 1840:

Now *Mon cher cousin* for a little more of the Revd. gentleman. On the evening of the day of your departure, as I fairly saw that there was to be nothing going forward but the gravest of conversations, I moved from off my seat for my work that I might continue the Scent Bag for you. Now this same work happened to be on the piano. My movement attracted the Revd. gentleman and he said 'My Cecilia are you going to give us some music?' I murmured out 'if you like.' Aunt Maryanne said 'I'm sure she will if you would like any, Mr Willson.' The Revd. gentleman answered 'I wish you would, I should be extremely happy to hear some.' So I sang a song, played some Quadrilles and then the Rev gentleman expressed a wish for a Gallo*peade* (It sounded so funny – he pronounced the last syllable in the word Gallo*peade* with A short) Having done all he wished he gravely thanked me and I began to work – The next morning before I came down to breakfast he asked Aunt Maryanne if I could make a Pudding or a Pye – I believe Aunt Maryanne said I could make both, upon which he said 'It is a very good thing to know how to make them for though you may not be required to make them yet it is as well to know.' Don't you think it looks suspicious? I declare I am quite in Spirits about it. When O when will the excellent and Revd. gentleman come again! I fear I shall quite pine away and get more and more Weasel-like until his return which will not be till the fruit is ripe – but that is nothing. You know by the Fruit he means me. To return his civilities I offered him my pony when he went away, to take him to Waltham Cross, but he said 'Thank you no. It might perhaps be throwing me.' I could not do less you know when I recollected the many civil things he had said to me, offering to go all over Lincolnshire Asylum with me, inviting me to his Lodgings and then to crown all asking me to Play. No, no I certainly could not do less.

Sometimes her humour was more robust as in the description of a boozy London coachman who peered in at the coach window 'with that drunken placidity of countenance which is the result of a certain quantity of liquor', and this of a fat man who declined to give up to her his inside seat on the coach from Boston to Peterborough. 'He was a mountain of a man and took up the whole of one side of the coach. I had an inside place at Peterborough and had the pleasure of his company to Waltham Cross. How hideous he looked when we passed through towns with the lamplight shining on his bloated countenance. Most likely had he given up his place to a lady as he ought I should have seen something benevolent in his face'. Like Mary Cecilia was 'a girl of great feeling and very warm in her attachment to her female friends'. Throughout their stay at High Beech she maintained an affectionate correspondence with Susan Haddelsey of Caistor and her letters give a strong impression of the very close relations of the whole Somersby family and her own deep sensibility. When in April 1838 Mary and Anne Sellwood, who was stopping at High Beech, set off for Guernsey in search of health and sea-bathing, Cecilia comments characteristically 'It was melancholy parting with Mary and Anne in the early morning but yet I think it is better than parting at night and knowing that those you have parted with are still under your roof and that you will not see them again.' And when, next summer, Mary went with the sisters' favourite 'Husk', 'Mimosa' Neville, to Italy, Cecilia delights to picture them sailing on the lake at Como 'in a boat lined with crimson velvet and a canopy of purple and gold' while Mimosa's favourite brother played to them on the flute.*

Cecilia's letters give many glimpses of life at High Beech shewing

---

* For the strange story of 'Mimosa' Neville see *Alfred Tennyson* by Charles Tennyson. London, 1949, pp. 169. 173,

clearly that Alfred was the mainstay of the family. His opinion on the merits of a new pony is quoted with respect, he is seen striding along with Cecilia as she rides through the forest, and there is a delightful picture of the night preceding the departure of Mary and Anne Sellwood for Guernsey, when there was much wild fun and the whole family sat up listening to Alfred who kept them laughing until one o'clock in the morning with his impersonation of different imaginary characters – perhaps some of those which were to appear later in his famous poems in the Lincolnshire dialect.

In 1840 the family moved from High Beech to Tunbridge Wells and thence in the autumn of 1841 to Boxley near Park House, Maidstone, the home of Alfred's Cambridge friend, Edmund Lushington. The house in which they lived has now been demolished. It was called Park House, Boxley, belonging to the Best family. The name of the house was later changed to Park Place to avoid confusion with the Lushington property.

Contact was still maintained with the more friendly of the cousins at Bayons and with the Rawnsleys at Halton Holgate, and Somersby continued to exercise a powerful charm. On 20th February 1841 Emily writes to her cousin George at Bayons after a visit to Halton:

I can scarcely tell you how the brief glimpse I caught of the house at Somersby, in going to Halton by Hag overpowered me, nearly every circumstance pleasant and otherwise which had happened there from my youth up came peacefully and vividly to me. The past, however painful when present, knows on retrospection a sunset glow which rest mournfully yet very pleasantly.

High Beech involved Alfred (possibly also his mother and sisters) in a serious financial disaster. A mile or so from High Beech lived a certain Dr Allen whose principal occupation was the management of three houses in which he carried on the treatment of mental patients. Allen had very progressive views about mental disease and during the years that the Tennysons were at High Beech was actually giving free treatment to the unfortunate poet John Clare and endeavouring to raise a fund to relieve him from the financial anxiety which Allen believed to have been one of the main causes of his breakdown. Though there is no evidence that Tennyson ever met Clare at this time it is known that he often visited Allen's hospital and took a great interest in the patients. No doubt the mad sections in Part II of *Maud* were largely the result of these visits.

Matthew Allen had been born in 1783, youngest of the ten children of a dissenting minister of the Sandemanian Sect at Gayle in Wensleydale on the Yorkshire moors. At sixteen he became apprenticed to his eldest brother Oswald, who had been appointed apothecary to the Dispensary at York. Three years later he married a cousin, Mary Wilson, and on her death in 1806 left York to become an itinerant preacher. The fact that Oswald's brother-in-law, Thomas Withers, who was the senior physician in York and died in 1809, left Matthew a legacy of £500 and all his medical textbooks, suggests that the young man had shewn exceptional qualities during his apprenticeship. According to his own statement young Matthew, during the years following his wife's death, began the practice of visiting asylums to study mental disease and even commenced lecturing on the subject. In 1811 he married again and settled in Edinburgh, setting up a shop in Princes Street and attending lectures at the University. Here he made the acquaintance of Thomas Carlyle who tramped from Annan to Edinburgh to become a student in 1809. Unfortunately the Princes Street venture proved a failure and in 1814 Matthew was imprisoned for debt, the faithful Oswald having to find £2,000 to secure his release and discharge from bankruptcy. Not content with this Oswald gave his brother £500 to purchase a small chemical factory at Leith, the principal product of which seems to have been soda water. But Matthew was again unfortunate, being once more sent to prison, this time for selling soda water without paying the necessary stamp duty. Soon after this, in 1818, his second wife died, and the indefatigable Oswald succeeded in getting him appointed apothecary to York Asylum, which had just been reorganised after a period of scandalous mismanagement. York was at this time remarkable for the amount of progressive thought being given to the study and treatment of mental disease. Thomas Withers had been much interested in this and fine pioneering work was being done at the Quaker hospital, The Retreat. Matthew, who had already developed a keen interest in the subject, now found himself practically involved in asylum work. In 1820 he was appointed curator of the important library of the York Medical Society, and in after years he claimed to have been medical resident and superintendent at the Asylum, though the accuracy of this claim is doubtful; some support for it may be found in the fact that in 1820 he offered Thomas Carlyle the post of tutor to one of the young patients at the Asylum. Carlyle actually visited York to see the young man and his parents but did not accept the position. In 1821 Matthew was granted the degree of Doctor of Medicine by the Marischal College of Aberdeen. This did not necessarily imply a high degree of knowledge or experience, as the candidate had only to produce two sponsors and a certificate of competence. Three years later Matthew Allen was dismissed from his post at the Asylum for reasons said to have included his habit of dashing off to London and Paris without leave. Within a year he had set up a licensed asylum at High Beech. How he raised the necessary capital and secured a licence is not known.

There is no doubt that Allen was a man of unusual intelligence and humanity. He saw that many of the symptoms which had been held to indicate mental disease, were in fact the result of situation, circumstance or unsuitable treatment, or even of the fears and prejudices of those in charge of or in contact with the patient. His conclusion was that the physician must be the servant of nature, endeavouring to discover and co-operate with her indications of cure. He particularly deprecated the altered tone of voice and manner of those in charge of mental patients, implying in every word and action that the patient was considered as a child or wholly irrational being. For these reasons he preferred not to hire his staff for long periods, fearing that they would 'decline into the mere mechanism of attention.'

Allen had embodied these views in volumes on *Cases of Insanity* and *The Classification of the Insane*. In these he described himself with a characteristic flourish as 'member of the Royal Medical Society of Edinburgh and of the Medico-Chirurgical Society of London, corresponding member of the Meteorological Society of London and of the Phrenological Societies of London and Edinburgh, and Honorary member of the Literary and Philosophical Societies of Leeds, Hull, Wakefield etc.' He had also published two volumes of sermons addressed to the staff and inmates of York Asylum and claimed to be the first man ever to have preached to the insane.

It is easy to see why Allen made so profound an impression on Tennyson, whom in the autumn of 1840 he took to Chelsea to visit the Carlyles. Alfred and Carlyle had already met at the Sterling Club, but this was Alfred's first meeting with Jane who had visited Allen's asylum with Mrs Basil Montagu in 1831 and declared it to be an establishment 'to which any sane person might be delighted to get admission.' Unfortunately Allen, whom Thomas Carlyle described as a 'hopeful earnest-frothy' kind of man, was speculator as well as alienist. Some time in 1840 he persuaded Tennyson to risk the whole of his small capital in a scheme which he was promoting for the development of a process for carving wood by machinery. Probably Allen at this time believed in the value of the process and Alfred was desperately anxious to improve his financial position in order to break down the Sellwoods' resistance to his marriage with Emily. The whole of the family had complete confidence in Allen, who was widely respected in the neighbourhood, so much so that when they left High Beech for Tunbridge Wells early in 1840 they left Septimus in his care. It will probably never be possible to say exactly what happened over the woodworking scheme. It seems that in 1840 and 1841 Allen found himself faced with demands for capital greater than he had anticipated, either by the unexpected need to purchase a French patent covering the process, or because of the defalcations of an agent. He now turned to the Tennyson family for help. It is difficult not to hold this against Allen, for he must have known their financial position and complete lack of business experience. He seems to have approached them through Alfred at or soon after the time they were leaving High Beech for Tunbridge Wells, just when Alfred, owing to the smallness of the Tunbridge Wells house and to work in connexion with his forthcoming volumes of 1842 which required his presence in London, was to be less in touch with the family than before. The first scheme adopted by Allen was to get unsecured loans at five per cent interest from members of the family – a very amateurish document covering a loan of £3,000 from Alfred was completed on 25th November 1840. Under this Allen was to pay Alfred £100 a year, in addition to five per cent on his loan, in consideration of the trouble which he had taken in raising the money. There was also mention of the transfer as security of an insurance policy on the doctor's life for £2,000 and of a mortgage on his house, but there is no record of these undertakings ever being carried out. Later Dr Allen seems to have been driven to selling shares in the project and to have made some arrangement for Elizabeth Tennyson, whose total incapacity for business he must have known perfectly well, becoming a partner or director in the concern, in consideration of substantial advances of capital by her and her daughters. Allen also pressed Frederick, who was over in England on a visit from Italy, to become a shareholder. He even tried to get £1,000 out of Septimus, who at about this time described himself in a letter to his Uncle Charles as a 'poor bill-bound biped' sorely in need of the 'petty dwindled and consumptive . . . interest' still coming to him from his much reduced capital. Rumours as to Allen's attempt to involve the young Tennysons in the scheme seem to have reached Lincolnshire and Mr Haddelsey of Caistor, who knew the young men well, wrote many letters to his agent in London urging him to prevent them from yielding to Allen's blandishments.

Early in September 1841 the four girls wrote urgently to their Uncle Charles asking him to pay over to them £2,000 out of the money bequeathed to them by their grandfather and still by a voluntary arrangement left in his hands. Uncle Charles who had heard, quite accidentally, some unfavourable criticism of Allen's scheme in the summer, when he knew nothing of the Somersby family's possible interest in it, seems to have taken no definite action on his nieces' request and they then turned to Henry Sellwood, a solicitor, father-in-law of Charles Turner and father of Emily who was later to become Alfred's wife, asking him to raise the money for them. On 3rd November they asked their Uncle to hand over to Mr Sellwood the documents needed to provide security for the lender. Two days later the four girls sent the following amazing letter to Charles d'Eyncourt, apparently precipitated by pressure from Dr Allen:

> Boxley Hall,
> Maidstone.
> Nov. 5th

My dear Uncle,
    We enclose a letter from Dr Allen – if you have had scruples before

this must remove them. We have been very mild and patient with you hitherto although we have been told by those who understand the matter that we are *shamefully treated*. We are sadly afraid the delay is on purpose, you do not deal openly with us. Is the thing not simple enough? We merely want you to give up the deed – now nearly three months since we first mentioned the matter to you, ever since 14th August. Will you be sorry that we should be a little richer than we have been, and what is it that you object to? Surely if you wish to prove yourself what you profess to be, a *kind Uncle*, there can now be no further obstacle.

Your distressed nieces

MARY, EMILY, MATILDA, CECILIA TENNYSON

This letter understandably outraged and infuriated Charles d'Eyncourt, whose distrust of Allen's scheme was fully justified by subsequent developments.

A letter which Dr Allen wrote to Frederick on 6th November 1841 shews the desperate efforts that he was making at this time to raise capital – there is no evidence that Frederick responded favourably.

High Beech,
November 6th, 1841

My dear Sir,

I really feel mine to be a cruel case, for it is now quite evident from your letter, and it has been my secret conviction all along, that the object of your uncles was to disappoint you, falsely thinking they were doing you a kindness, for their difficulties and obstacles were obviously purposely made. – What difference can it possibly make to your trustees or you whether the Deeds are in Mr Rhodes' or Mr Sellwood's custody. – I suppose the latter is just as trustworthy as the former.

That I have been most anxious and miserable in the business is most certain and this is very soon explained.

In the first place when I was driven to the necessity of purchasing the Patent, I had between three and four thousand to pay more than I had before contemplated, and this when I saw you on the 14th of August within three months, and this made me intend to offer the sale of a portion, and before I saw you I had several offers besides the promises of Mr Haslam and Mr Mayer that there would be no difficulty at all in selling a $\frac{1}{6}$ for that sum, and when I came down to you I had not the most remote idea that you would offer to purchase a share, but when you did so I rejoiced, for I believed it would give me the means of proving that I had all along intended doing your family good, when I arranged £1000 within one month, £2000 within three months, and £3000 within six months. I had not the slightest idea of the success of the Patent being so immediate and so enormous; but it was also stated and agreed at the same time that the sooner you could raise it the better, the more peace of mind you would give me, the more you would expedite the success of the concern.

Since the success, and the prospect of success has been so over-powering, the reasons for your fulfilling this impressed upon you, and if your uncles have any regard to the success of the concern and your position, it would have been here long before this time.

Those who have always been ready with £500 – or even £1000 – on simply my own acceptances I would not now ask, for I know they want to drive me into a corner to get a share. Another, however, who is intimately acquainted with all my private affairs has generously come forward to assist me without any reward, so that I shall get through without making any sacrifice of a further share or even that of selling a share in this establishment, or even my coal mines, all of which you know I contemplated, so that if you do not choose, or you choose to allow your uncles to prevent you from having this share, *tell me so at once*. The concern will soon realize enough of money and credit for all I shall want.

Yesterday it was the decided opinion of my Bankers and Solicitors that in twelve months your share would be worth Ten thousand Pounds, and that in five years it ought to give you that yearly, and really I feel that if you cannot put an end to this painful state of things *I must*.

It is not now so much the want of the money, as the feeling that with all these facts and truths I am still to bear the reflections which you all say your friends all make, that I am deceiving and duping you – all the rest of the World say to the contrary.

Mr Sellwood writes to me just in the same style as Mr Haddelsey, and I neither can, nor will bear it, but still I have refused a person every way eligible yesterday and whose services would be worth ten times the sum, from the hope that the present letters of this week have revived that the money will soon come, let not that hope again be disappointed, others have the money to lay down. – The moment the money comes I will pay you (to show my confidence) a year's interest in advance. . . .

[The conclusion of this letter is unfortunately missing].

Optimism about the scheme lasted for a few more months. Early in

1842 Alfred wrote to Drummond Rawnsley from Torquay (*Memoir* I, 215) that it was going on very well, but on 8th September of the same year he ended a letter to Edmund Lushington 'what with ruin in the distance and hypochondriacs in the foreground God help all' (*Memoir* I, 213).

The drafts (now at the Lincoln Research Centre) of letters which Alfred wrote to Dr and Mrs Allen probably early in October 1842 set out the story fully from the Tennyson point of view and shew the efforts which Alfred made to save his mother and Septimus from the wreck:

Dear Dr Allen,

My spirits have been dejected, my nerves shattered, my health affected by what I have heard. You must have seen how annoyed and worried I was the other morning at meeting you. I could not then say what was upon my mind, nor can I now fully; for you seem for a long time to have made yourself as strange to me as possible; I cannot help feeling and feeling deeply that it was not so before I lent you all I had in the world.

I think also that you must have seen that my last note to you was written in a state of great excitement and you might have answered it. My chief reason for writing that note was that I had been informed by two persons, whose veracity I had no reason to question, that you had in their presence made use of expressions to this effect 'That I had driven a hard bargain with you and that if this speculation succeeded, I could have no claims upon you.'

In the earlier days of our acquaintance if anything of this nature had been reported to me I should have rejected it at once as some monstrous perversion. At present I still hope that it is a misrepresentation and that you will be able to explain it away. The first part of the sentence is sheer absurdity; the last involves dishonour: and I am very unwilling to think ill of a man whom I have regarded with affection and admiration for the valuable qualities of his head and his heart and what seems to me his clear religious feeling. My faith in you has been strong, most strong. The stronger it has been the deeper and more poignant must be my distaste and loathing if I find you are of the herd, a mere commonplace man, ready, like all wordlings, after a 1,000 promises, at the first glimpse of prosperity, to kick down the ladder by which he mounted: for a man of your years and experience can scarcely be so childish as to dream that the selling me a 36th for £300 while all my money was risked, is a cancelling of your obligation to me. The mere man of business would laugh such a notion to scorn: but I vow to God that if you have said and meant these words seriously, your un-kindness will afflict and oppress me more than any apprehension of worldly risk or loss.

These feelings were working in my mind even when I wrote my last note: but I felt too deeply to reproach you, by stating my true reason for so writing. Your expression in your letter to me was 'As you and your sisters wish to be free of the risk', I had never said a word of *my* being willing to give up my share: but I had always *from the first* objected to *women* being involved in this sort of speculation. I know that my share is involved in my mother's 6th, but it was perfectly easy for you, who have everything in your own hands, to arrange matters so that she might have been out of the concern while I retained my 36th as indeed what risk do I run more than I have run? for I hardly suppose you would stop short in the downhill road to ruin to save *me*. It is merely giving up a chance of profit; if nothing was to be done for me in the case of success, what else was left but sheer risk? It was making me this monstrous proposition. If this concern fails, you fail: if it succeeds, you shall be none the better for it. I felt therefor that if you had said these words and meant them, it was better for me, if I parted with my share to be out of the concern altogether, to return, if possible, to my honourable poverty among gentlemen, after having drunk of one of those most bitter draughts out of the cup of Life, which go near to make men hate the world they move in, and to look on their brothers as a kind of vermin. My percentage or something like it, I could have always got by buying an annuity, which I was proposing to do, when I first met you.

Alfred Tennyson to Mrs Allen:

Monday, Oct. 15th

Dear Mrs Allen,

I believe you to be a straight-forward well-principled woman and that I do so my writing to you at this time will sufficiently prove. I had indeed wished [you] for your own sake not to meddle in any of these matters between ourselves and Dr Allen – I had wished to spare you pain, for you are not in anyway to blame, you have always been kindly and hospitable to myself – but since you will persist in a correspondence with Mary and will not avoid what I want you to avoid – hear this one thing which I have to say to you. I have learned this morning that Septimus is about to lend Dr Allen £1,000 and seeing that Dr Allen

has already at different times received from our family about £8,000 –
the result of which loan has been to my mother and sisters that they
are at this time living upon my brother Charles – and to myself that I
am a penniless beggar and deeply in debt besides – which two things
have never happened to me before – it does strike me as most remarkable that Dr Allen should again have recourse for another £1,000 to
another member of the same family – poor fellow, I don't think he
has another £1,000 in the world! . . .

It seems difficult to imagine anything altogether more indelicate
and indecorous. What I have felt and suffered may rest unmentioned,
but I entreat you, if you have any regard for your husband's honour
to do all in your power to prevent him making another victim of my
family. Security Dr Allen cannot give and he has no right to borrow
Septimus' money without.

Let me hear from you at your earliest convenience and believe me

Yours v. truly,

A. TENNYSON

On 10th November Alfred wrote again to Mrs Allen from Boxley:

I wrote to you a serious earnest letter containing a specific request
viz. that you would use your influence with your husband to prevent
his borrowing this £1,000 from Septimus; you answer *generally*,
that with regard to Septimus' money I may be sure 'all is right'. This
tells me nothing: you will much oblige me by giving a specific answer
to my petition. Will you, knowing the wishes of his family on this
subject, prevent this loan, if you can?

Early in 1843 it became evident that the wood carving scheme had
collapsed altogether, as this letter which Allen wrote to Frederick on
4th March tragically shews:

March 4th, 1843

My dear Sir,

I have done all that is possible for man to do to save your family, and
I have *utterly ruined myself* in the attempt; but I believe if you will
come here, you may get hold of the whole for Wyat's Mortgage – I
will make you a *present* of my share of Stock and Block and my
interest, which I valued at an enormous sum. – I will never consent to
their touching it if I can help it – all my suspicions of them are confirmed.

I will give you no advice, save that my ideas are the same as when you were here – I have now no private views at stake.

Yours truly,

M. ALLEN

Every stick and stave is to be sold to pay A.T. *this* day – and yet people boast! I ail! and I suffer! and I die! –

Come up ! – you must save something.

The effect of his disastrous loss on Alfred was such that his friends feared for his mental health, even for his life. The position was saved by the generosity of Cecilia's husband, Edmund Lushington, who insured Dr Allen's life at an annual expense of eighty pounds. In January 1845 Allen died and Alfred recovered a considerable part of his loss. Whether the insurance policy covered the losses of the rest of the family – and it seems certain that there must have been such losses – is not clear. Later in the year Alfred's friends were able to secure for him the grant of a pension of £200 a year from the Civil List. From this point began the slow improvement of his fortunes which was to culminate in the triumphant year 1850.

CHAPTER TEN

MARY AND EMILY

MEANWHILE the size of the family was gradually shrinking. Early in 1842 Emily married Captain Richard Jesse, R.N., a remarkably handsome man, who showed his courage not only by taking Emily to wife, but also by the two medals, one French and one English, which he received for saving life at sea. It is perhaps not surprising to find him described at his wedding as having a pale good-humoured face, talking fast and perhaps a little flurried, while Emily, oddly dressed and with hair in long ringlets down her back, looked 'singular and elf-like'. A few months later Cecilia married Edmund Lushington. In 1843 the family was further reduced when Frederick, Arthur and Septimus left England for Italy. Mrs Tennyson, with Mary, Matilda and Horatio, then moved to Cheltenham, where Mary on 7th July 1851 married Alan Ker, a barrister, whose brother was a prominent doctor in the town.

Soon after this marriage, Alan Ker, who had not practised at the Bar since 1848 and had no settled employment, emigrated to Jamaica with Mary. In 1857 Horatio married; in 1860, Arthur. Only Matilda now remained regularly at home with her mother. In 1865, Elizabeth Tennyson died. Matilda from now onward divided her time chiefly between Alfred and the Lushingtons, who, with Charles at Grasby, provided the focal points for the family during the next thirty years or so.

Information about the sisters during these years is unfortunately scarce. They seem all to have continued on terms of intimate affection, but Mary and Cecilia appear to have written very few letters and Matilda wrote with difficulty and very illegibly, owing, it is said, to an attack of scarlet fever in childhood; whether this affected her sight or muscular control is not known. Or, of course, there was the earlier accident with the coal-scuttle.

Mary led a wandering life after her marriage. Alan Ker remained for over thirty years in the Judicial Service of the West Indies. In 1853 he was acting Attorney General of Antigua, from 1854 to 1856 Chief Justice of Nevis; after that he was appointed Chief Justice of Dominica, and later he became a puisne judge of the Supreme Court of Jamaica. This office he continued to hold until the end of December 1884 when he retired because of ill-health. He died at Kingston, Jamaica on 20th March 1885, just under a year after his wife.

Alan Ker was an unusual man. His son described him as being of the utmost moral courage and of an inflexible independence of mind, so conscientious in the discharge of his office that during a colonial service of thirty-one years he allowed himself only two holidays of six months apiece with an interval of fourteen years between, and, during thirteen years of his service, saw neither his wife nor his son. He did much public work in Jamaica in addition to his judicial service, devoting several years to a consolidation of the laws of the island from the earliest times, largely at his own expense. For all this work he received no official recognition, and when, in 1882, the Chief Justice-ship fell vacant he was passed over for a man young enough to be his son. The new Chief Justice admitted that, when he came to Jamaica to take over the post, he approached Ker with some trepidation, realising the strength of his claims to the office. Ker was, however, too generous to bear malice and served loyally under the newcomer during the two years of active life that remained to him.

In spite of their long separations, Mary was a devoted wife and a devoted mother to her only child, Walter, who grew up to be a learned scholar and barrister, tall, dark, shaggy, and aquiline, and with a truly Tennysonian reserve. Like his father he never practised seriously at the Bar, but he edited law books, including the classic *Benjamin on Sales;* he translated a volume each of Cicero and Martial for the Loeb Library and wrote a considerable amount of verse with fluency and taste. Though Mary spent so much time abroad, she remained to her sisters 'the spiritual sun of the family,' as Emily called her. It was she who led Frederick and Emily into the Church of the New Jerusalem.

F

She had strange psychic dreams and was, like Frederick and Emily, deeply interested in mesmerism and spiritualism. In Jamaica she was loved by all classes of the population for her kindness and simple courtesy. Poor women would stop her in the street for the pleasure and solace of speaking to her, and when she sailed on her last voyage to England, the whole neighbourhood was, according to her husband, 'almost in tears'. It is probable that she wrote verse as a girl and a young woman, but none of this survives, and she did not resume the practice until about her fiftieth year when her son asked her to dramatise in verse a story from *Evenings at Home*, to provide a play which he could act with the two young sons of Governor Eyre. (Incidentally, the connexion with Alan Ker may in some way account for Alfred Tennyson's refusal to join in the agitation against Eyre over his handling of the Jamaican riots in 1884.)

Having once begun to write again, Mary seems to have continued regularly, and the manuscript book at the Usher Gallery, Lincoln, contains more than sixty of her compositions, chiefly sonnets. Her verse is fluent, correct, and deeply felt, but, like that of Frederick, to whom the volume is dedicated, tends to be unemphatic. There are sonnets of consolation addressed to Horatio on the death of Charlotte, and to Edmund and Cecilia Lushington on the loss of their only son at the age of thirteen, but too many of the poems deal with such refractory subjects as Swedenborgian theology. Sometimes, however, Mary writes of her long exile in the tropics, toiling through the hot days 'Mid apish chatter of the black and brown' and lying awake at night while 'The whizz, the whir and the metallic ring' of the mosquito, 'weary the breathless hours until the morn'. In these poems the bitterness of personal experience gives an edge to her words and rhythms; a sonnet to 'The White Maiden of the Tropics', with its closing couplet:

> Pale scion of the north, O not for thee
> This land of seething sun and blinding sea.

makes one feel that it is of no hypothetical white maiden that she is thinking. Most touching of all are some lines which must have been written at the time of her last parting from her husband.

A FAREWELL

Good and noble thou and I are parted –
Ever patient of life's wear and fret,
Thou the tender, true and single hearted,
Take this tribute to my deep regret.

By no fault of mine or thine this sorrow
Like a dark November wraps me round,
Whence shall I the words of comfort borrow,
Where no comfort in myself is found?

Thrice across the broad Atlantic sailing,
Far away upon the billow borne,
I, thy lonely lot and mine bewailing,
Have the cypress or the willow worn.

Cease my rebel heart thy sad complaining,
Tho' the way to thee be dark and dim,
It may be that thro' this rugged training
Was the way to make thee lean on Him.

That was Mary's final parting from her husband, for she died in England at the end of April 1884 while he was still in Jamaica. A final summary of her character may be given in the words which he wrote to his son a few days after her death.

Dear woman, never to see her again in this world! It is a sad, sad thought, and quite overwhelms me. She was a good, pious, amiable, and gentle woman, every way worthy to be her mother's daughter. A sweeter and more generous nature never shed a benign influence wherever she went. It was an education to know her, so free was she from everything unkindly, everything uncharitable, harsh, severe, and unforgiving. How placable she was! how ready to let bygones be bygones! Malice or ill-will my firm belief is she knew not the very meaning of. . . . That sweet, generous face and bearing of hers, never to behold them any more in this world! . . . At every turn I see something that reminds me of her, recalling her warm interest in myself, and the pleasure she took in any little success that befell me. Oh! the pity of it. She used to sit in the garden chair so meekly, so quietly out on the terrace there, and listen with such sympathy to my narration of my days' visits to town, and what had occurred to me in the course of business or duty. She will never do so again in this life of ours. . . .

Did ever woman keep her looks as she did? When I left England in 1873 she might have passed for forty. I never knew a woman with a finer physique. Did you ever observe what beautiful ears she had? A plaster should have been taken of them.

And so farewell to beautiful, pious, placable Mary, with her Sweden-borgian sonnets about which Alfred liked to chaff her, her sufferings, of which one may be sure she never complained, and the beautiful ears which one hopes she did not hide under the back-drawn Madonna waves of her fine black hair.

Emily's marriage to Richard Jesse seems to have been a happy one. They had two children, the younger of whom, Eustace, became the father of the late Fryn Tennyson Jesse, poetess, traveller, novelist, and criminologist. Emily's maternal instinct was slight and it seems that she never took much interest in her children, but she was sincerely devoted to her husband, who, though no doubt accustomed to command at sea, seems to have been content to play second fiddle at home and to fall in with all her whims and extravagances. Reading her letters and the descriptions of her by others, one feels that he must have had a good deal to put up with. One wonders, for example, how he liked having his eldest son christened 'Arthur Henry Hallam' and how he reacted to his Emily's conviction that a photograph taken of her at Clifton showed behind her the shadowy figure of a man strangely resembling Arthur. She and Richard lived mostly at Margate, though she was in Italy in 1851 and wrote Frederick some fine descriptions of her experiences: as, for example, of a torrent at Bagni di Lucca where 'the waters rushing over pieces of rock in the stream fell with a noise like thunder, which was taken up and echoed among the mountains, till the whole of them, placed irregularly as they are, gave out one con-tinual sound, surly and grand.'

Twenty years later she was in Paris during the *commune*. There she banged her umbrella on the pavement and shouted, 'Vive la commune,' in order to be on the safe side, although she was an extreme conservative who a few years later was fulminating against Mr Gladstone: 'How that man can exist is a marvel to me, with the murder of "that best man in all the world" [General Gordon] on his conscience – but I forgot. He cannot have one or ere this he would have died from pangs of remorse.' She was no better pleased with the state of the contemporary world as a whole: 'The longer I live, the less this rolling ball appears my home,' she writes to Frederick in 1885. 'Other people seem to be happy, they don't seem to be troubled as you Richard and myself are by the sadness . . . the world will presently be all ablaze. Nation will rise against nation and kingdom against kingdom'.

At about the same time she found herself 'thoroughly horrified and almost palsy-stricken' by the report of the Royal Commission on vivisection and immediately began a campaign to rouse to action the people of Margate, whom she found 'dark as Erebus on the subject'. Private misfortunes provoked an equal intensity of declamation – for example a cook 'a real *demon* in human form.' 'I found out too late she had false keys and had robbed me of everything pretty well worth taking in the way of apparel. Her life was a lie. People told us afterwards that she was thoroughly bad – why did they not enlighten me at the time? – and was a common prostitute . . . even the thought of her makes me shudder.'

However, as she herself wrote in one of her later letters, 'the feathered feet of time are noiseless and swift,' and the years brought relief. When Mary returned from Jamaica, Emily found in her a true affinity and through her became a convert to Swedenborg's Church of the New Jerusalem, which afforded her consolation in her later years.

Yet Emily was by no means all gloom and thunder. Her name was long remembered with affection by the villagers at Somersby. She loved her Richard and she loved animals, travelling everywhere with a stout lap dog and a raven, always fed on raw meat which had to be cut up in her presence. She had some sense of humour too, for, when she came to Farringford or Aldworth, she loved to exchange outrageous jokes and puns with her nephews.

Here is a description by Blanche Warre Cornish of a meeting with her at the Alfred Tennysons in the early 1870s:

It was one Easter holidays. The Tennysons' carriage met me at the
Yarmouth pier; in it I found Miss Thackeray and a lady with her dog
in her lap who was staying at Farringford. As we drove off through
the lanes a personal conversation, which had been interrupted by my
arrival, was resumed. The elder lady had a deep, serious voice, and she
attracted me at once by her fine blue expressive eyes, which still gave
forth light, though set in a deep-lined face. She had a well-cut profile;
dark bandeaux of hair fell with delicate curves on each side of her
brown face; they were streaked with grey. She had once been Arthur
Hallam's fiancée, Emily Tennyson. To everything Annie Thackeray
was saying in her gentle reflective way about life and its contradictions
she replied with a strong Lincolnshire accent, 'I know that; I have felt
that.' She added in a deep melodious tone, just like Horatio Tennyson's,
'I have felt everything; I know everything. I don't want any new
emotion. I know what it is to feel like a stoän' (*London Mercury*,
December 1921).

Very characteristic was Emily's reaction when the ever delightful Annie
Thackeray left Farringford at the end of her visit. Looking slowly
round the reduced party she exclaimed in her rich, deep tones, 'Now
we are flat as flounders.' Emily lived to be seventy-five, much beloved
and respected by her brothers and sisters as these farewell lines of
Frederick's eloquently shew:

ON THE DEATH OF HIS SISTER EMILY

> *Farewell, dear Sister, thou and I*
> *Will meet no more beneath the sky:*
> *But in the high world where thou art*
> *Mind speaks to mind and heart to heart –*
> *Not in faint wavering tones, but heard*
> *As twin sweet notes that sound accord.*
> *Thy dwelling in the Angel sphere*
> *Looks forth on a sublimer whole;*
> *There all that thou dost see and hear*
> *Is in true concord with thy soul –*
> *A great harp of unnumbered strings*
> *Answering to one voice that sings –*
> *Where thousand blisses spring and fade*

Swiftly, as in diviner dream,
And inward motions are portrayed
In outward shows that move with them.
After the midnight and dark river
No more to be o'erpast for ever,
Behold the lover of thy youth,
That spirit strong as love and truth,
Many a long year gone before,
Awaits thee on the sunny shore.
In that high world of endless wonder
Nor space nor time can hold asunder
Twin souls (as space and time have done)
Whom kindest instincts orb in one.

CHAPTER ELEVEN

MATILDA AND CECILIA

CECILIA, after a 'husky' youth, settled down into a quiet affectionate, and intellectual domesticity, as the wife of Edmund Lushington, Fellow of Trinity and Professor of Latin at the University of Glasgow. She suffered a good deal from genuinely poor health, partly brought on by the necessity of wintering in Glasgow, where she looked out every day – to quote her own words – on 'black and thick fog . . . made more hellish often by a red glow through it all – proceeding from the numerous fires in this city of dirt and dumps.' She loved her husband and four children, the laughing references to whom in her letters are always marked by a charmingly affectionate pride: 'This ugly boy of mine,' or 'Thy little niece is now two months old and has already three chins.' But her children were all taken from her by early death, except one daughter who never married.

Park House, under Cecilia's sway, always remained a haven of refuge for the rootless sisters and brothers. According to the sprightly and rather malicious Mrs Brookfield, 'The Tennyson habit of coming unbidden and staying unwashed was, is and will be, the great burden and calamity of the Lushington existence.' 'They actually groan,' she wrote in 1847, 'under Mary who they expect will stay and keep up the establishment when the original family retire to Malta' (where Cecilia's brother-in-law Harry Lushington had just received an appointment, Edmund being absent most of the year at Glasgow). 'I did not venture to touch upon the delicate ground of E [mily], but I expect they labour under the undefined but not ungrounded alarm that Mr J [esse] will be a permanent fixture.'

Perhaps one should not take this flight of fancy too seriously, for the bond between the Lushingtons and the Tennysons was very close, and at Park House Cecilia's eccentric and endearing personality held unquestioned sway. Tall, dark, handsome, rather ungainly and totally unselfconscious, she would sing strange ballads with passion, though she insisted on beginning her song behind the drawing room door and gradually emerging into the room. Like the rest of the family, she read verse beautifully, in a rich deep voice, liking particularly to declaim Alfred's 'Northern Farmers' from the passage outside her drawing room with the door open. Her good nature, deep voice, and talent for acting made her much sought after for charades, when, dressed in a rough jacket and flashy neckerchief and waistcoat and well primed with slang phrases which her sensitive soul abhorred, she would play the most unsuitable parts with gusto. She attained the great age of ninety-two, outliving her Edmund by sixteen years and dying in 1909.

Matilda, lived on well into the twentieth century – a tall, swarthy woman, with a strong, rugged, rather equine face – 'A creature without gall or guile' (so one of her friends described her). To her nephew Lionel she seemed a female 'my uncle Toby': 'infinite pity, infinite innocence and great cleverness in hitting the nail on the head, yet seeming, to a superficial observer, almost what country people call a "natural".' With her brothers she was always a prime favourite. Many were the jokes which passed between Farringford and Park House about the doings, sayings, and alleged flirtations of 'The Empress Maud'. If it was draughty in church she would put up her umbrella and sit under it without embarrassment for the duration of the service. It is recorded also that, once finding herself in disagreement with the salesman in a crowded London shop about the capacity of a hip-bath which he was trying to sell her, she gathered up her ample skirts, stepped into the bath and lay down in her black bonnet and veil, button boots, flowing cloak, umbrella, and jingling jet beads, to the consternation of the salesman and the delight of the other customers. Yet poor Tillie did not entirely escape the black-bloodedness of the Tennysons. She had, like the rest of the family, a deep underlying sensibility which led at times to religious obsessions. At such times she succumbed to a peculiarly austere form of Calvinism and would spend whole days weeping over the fate of her brothers and sisters, whom she passionately loved and whom she believed to be all eternally damned. At one period of her life, her intense love of music found issue in a passionate admiration for the great opera singer Therese Tietjens, who died in 1877. Amongst Matilda's papers were found several scraps of wild irregular verse about Tietjens' death and a sheet of deep-edged mourning paper, enfolding a lock of hair and inscribed in Matilda's hand: 'This paper holds my beloved Therese's hair – I have kissed it many times. It is a great comfort to have it – oh, when shall I see her again? I shall never have another friend upon earth like her – I hope God will permit me to meet her again. This thought bears me up.'

When she first came to live at Farringford after her mother's death, Matilda was uneasy, and distressed her sister-in-law, Emily, by complaints about the beloved house, its climate and surroundings. But Hallam and Lionel, then boys of fourteen and twelve, took her to their hearts, making her join in all their games and adventures. Gradually she became acclimatised and indeed grew so passionately devoted to Alfred that after his death in 1892, she never felt able to visit the place again, though both Emily and Hallam were deeply attached to her. Thenceforward she lived entirely at Park House with Cecilia. After Edmund Lushington's death in 1893, the two old ladies, with 'Zilly', Cecilia's only surviving child, had the place to themselves. It must have been a singular household. Fate had dealt harshly with Cecilia. Of her four children, the only son, Edmund, born in 1843, had died in 1856. Emily, the eldest girl, died in 1868 at the age of nineteen, and Lucia Maria, five years later at twenty-one. Only the second daughter, Zilly, lived to grow up. All the children seem to have had considerable ability and charm, and a little volume of Lucy's verse, which was privately published in 1880 by Frederick Bunyard, Maidstone, shews at least some poetic talent. Though tradition speaks of her as having been cheerful and high-spirited as a young girl, her poems suggest that the death of her sister Emily had been a severe blow from which she never wholly recovered. They shew also that she had a good ear and a highly sensitive temperament. Was there more? Had she a gift which time might have matured into solid achievement? The following fragment – not better than a fair sample of the whole – suggests this possibility:

> *O sweeter far the dying day*
> *Than golden sunrise on the hills,*
> *To watch the faint light fade away*
> *Altho' the evening shadow chills.*

O sweeter far the falling leaves
  Than verdant groves in summer's prime,
Altho' the heart grows faint and grieves
  To watch the fair decay of time.

O sweeter far the close of life
  Than youth in all its vain unrest,
The peace of death than earthly strife;
  To love and grieve and die is best.

Cecilia herself published three books. The first, *Fifty Years in Sand-bourne*, was issued by Griffith and Farran of St. Paul's Church Yard (in New York by E. P. Dutton and Co.) in 1880. This story, of only 105 octavo pages, was in many ways her best work. Its scene is laid in an old south-coast fishing village, fast growing into a fashionable watering place, and the story centres on an old fisherman of ninety, his daughter-in-law, Jane Knight, and her three-year-old granddaughter. It is a tale of tragedy. Jane has lost her husband six months after marriage; her only children, twin boys, have both been drowned as young men within sight of the cliffs, the little boat in which Jack Knight had taken his paralysed brother Dick out for a row having been overturned by a sudden storm. The shock had been too much for Jack's sickly young wife Mary, who had died, leaving Jack's three-day-old baby girl an orphan.

The little fishing village and the rapidly growing watering place are vividly described. The story is told simply and forcibly and one guesses that in it Cecilia sublimated the piercing sorrows which she had known through the early deaths of her own children. The description of the accident, which makes Dick Knight a hopeless cripple at the age of fourteen, is very poignant. Cecilia herself had surely felt the resentment, 'impatient, bitter and even fierce,' which shakes poor Dick when kindly neighbours come to console him, urging resignation to the will of God. In the end he is saved by the old parson. 'How should I make that poor boy resigned? . . . If I were to go and tell him he ought to be "resigned" to a shock and a blight on his life such as this, wouldn't he feel, if he didn't say, "You talk of what you know nothing about," and wouldn't this be the truth?' In the end he gives the poor boy strength in a touching scene which has the force of true feeling in every line. The same feeling animates a short essay at the end of the little volume, *Two Pictures of Old Womanhood*, reprinted from *Good Words*. Here is a brief but characteristic extract:

I have read of one old woman who for years was paralysed from head to foot, yet never saw a friend without expressing her gratitude because she was able to move *one* joint of *one* thumb, so that with a fork tied to it she could turn over the leaves of her Bible.

Fifty Years in Sandbourne was followed in the succeeding year by *Margaret the Moonbeam, A Story for the Young* (London: T. Fisher Unwin, 1881). This is a small volume of 180 pages, which Cecilia evidently wrote largely for her own enjoyment. It is sunnily sentimental, although, like its predecessor, founded on a tale of bereavement, for little Margaret is left an orphan and taken by her bachelor uncle to live with him in his house near 'Adimstone' in the Kentish hoplands – an obviously disguised spelling of Maidstone, near which the Lushingtons lived at Park House. The book patently aims at instruction and guidance, but this is so naïvely and appealingly imparted that one accepts it readily, and the little book charmingly illustrates Cecilia's love of poetry. Uncle Edward and his friends unashamedly describe themselves as 'poetry people' and poetical quotations introduce every chapter and adorn quite half the pages. Wordsworth is the favourite poet with fifteen separate extracts, Alfred Tennyson comes next with twelve, Longfellow has five, Charles Turner, Milton, Shakespeare and William Barnes four each, and odd lines are taken from James Montgomery, Keats, Shelley, Bryant, Southey, Scott, Browning, Charles Mackay, Coleridge, Kirk White, and the Border Ballads. Especially characteristic is one by George Macdonald, 'Where did you come from, baby dear' (*At the Back of the North Wind*, 1871, ch. xxxiii). Now and then a stanza is evidently Cecilia's own – certainly she must have been the author of these verses put into the mouth of a dog, reproaching his master for stopping too long to look at a waterfall on their afternoon walk.

Why Master, good Master, why do you stop?
   What can you be looking at there?
Did you never see water spin round like a top
   That at it you stupidly stare?

It's that new little girl who has made you so queer,
   Why can't she come on and make haste?
I would not for worlds disrespectful appear
   But I'm really surprised at your taste.

I'm ready to swim or to race at your call,
   Or to leap to and fro like a frog,
But to stand idly staring at nothing at all
   Is too much for a sensible dog.

Cecilia certainly wrote a good deal of verse during her lifetime, though it is not known whether any of it was ever published. Unfortunately the poetic manuscripts found among her papers at her death, which were very melancholy in tone, were all destroyed.

Margaret the Moonbeam evidently had some success, for a second edition came out in 1883. Meanwhile the favourable reviews of *Fifty Years in Sandbourne* in *The Queen,* *The Non-Conformist, The Rock* and *John Bull* encouraged Griffith and Farran to bring out Cecilia's third book, *Over the Seas and Far Away* (1882).*

This is a romance in the Victorian manner. It has not the individuality of either of the earlier books and it is intensely, but sincerely, pietistic. There are nearly as many quotations as in *Margaret the Moonbeam* and all are from the hymnals. Now and then one recognises the sister of poets, as for example in the description of a first sight of the sea: 'In front nothing but this boundless open plain of water; all silent, except for a soft, hushing hiss pressed on the sand by the tiniest ripple; all motionless except for the wavy tremor which told that in the midst of its calm the heart of the mighty sea was living' (p. 122). The following passage transmits a flash of mystical insight: 'The hours when we most

---

* There are copies of all three books in the British Museum. The Tennyson Research Centre at the City Library, Lincoln, has a copy of *Fifty Years in Sandbourne*.

truly seem to live are not those whose details we can always repeat most accurately. The spirit's life seems too vast at such moments for the faculties of our brain and body' (p. 214).

Occasionally, too, a very unexpected opinion bursts from the conventional page, as for example this sudden explosion against the Victorian prison system: 'I have seen bright, affectionate lads, who had been led into bad ways half blindly, or who had broken the law more from folly than from meaning harm. They looked like innocent boys when they went into prison, but when they came out they were hardened criminals. It has made my heart ache more than anything in the world' (p. 186).

Park House is curiously designed in depth. It stands high up on a wooded ridge looking south across the valley through which the main railway line runs from London to Maidstone. The front is narrow, containing only the large entrance hall and to east and west of this the drawing room and dining room. Behind the entrance hall is another large hall into which a fine circular staircase descends from the first floor, with what was once Edmund's library on the east; behind this lie the spacious kitchen and offices. This long recession of rooms is enclosed east and west by fine Georgian façades. Each of the two old ladies occupied large rooms on the first floor with glorious views southward over the valley, Cecilia on the east side of the house above the drawing room and Matilda on the west over the dining room. Each was looked after by a personal maid and neither was ever seen out of her room before luncheon. To the small nephews and nieces, who visited Park House from time to time, the old ladies were rather terrifying and their respective corners of the house were strictly forbidden territory. One, the late Mr Godrey L. Lushington of Woodlawn Park, Loose, near Maidstone, remembered Cecilia as a very old woman always wearing a white knitted woollen cap, carrying a large black bag, and walking with a stick. She went out very little either in summer or winter, but sometimes after tea (never before) she would wander out through the hall, stopping on the way to stroke the bust of her long lost little son and talk to it affectionately for a few moments. After roaming about the lawn for twenty minutes or so, she would wander back into the drawing room, invariably saying to her daughter (if it was winter time) in a deep, complaining, rather mournful voice, 'Very dark tonight, Zilly,' to which Zilly would invariably reply, 'Of course it is, dear. The sun has gone down.' She used her stick almost like an extra limb, and if she passed one of the children she would prod him with it, not with intent to give pain, but as some creatures use their antennae. She would embarrass Zilly by pointing with her stick at any visitor whom she might find at tea or lunch, and asking in her deep voice, 'Zilly, who's that?' Equally important was the black bag. Into it she would cram a generous selection of any delicacies which might take her fancy at tea, and, if guests were expected, great care had to be used to keep tempting cakes or buns out of sight until the last minute. She had even been known to slice the whole top off a large iced cake and add it to the loot in the black bag.

By comparison Matilda seemed during these years less eccentric and less frail than Cecilia, though she was the older by just over a year. She too kept closely to her room and very seldom left the house. When she expressed a wish to do so, a donkey was fetched from an adjoining paddock and harnessed to a large bath chair. In this Matilda would drive for half an hour about the garden paths, followed by an old brown and white spaniel to which she was deeply attached. Although Cecilia lived to be ninety-two, not dying until March 1909, Matilda survived her. Zilly, to whom Park House passed on her mother's death, did not wish to live there, and she and Matilda moved first to Lexham Gardens, South Kensington – Matilda still tall dark and equine, Zilly short and squarely built and priding herself on her likeness to Queen Victoria. From Lexham Gardens the two moved to Eastbourne and there Matilda died in 1913 at the age of ninety-eight, the last of a remarkable family.

Although the Somersby Tennysons had all been born within a period of just over twelve years, their lives had spanned a hundred and six – from the middle of the Napoleonic wars to the very verge of the World War of 1914. The average length of life of the eleven brothers and sisters (including poor Septimus, who died at fifty-one) was over eighty years. Very few families can have surpassed them in longevity; in

CHAPTER TWELVE

UNCLE AND AUNTS

B EFORE we take final leave of this extraordinary brood which
Dr Tennyson produced at Somersby we must say something of
his brother and sisters whose temperaments are surely relevant
to the study of the psychology of his children as deriving from the
same sources as his own. Of the three one feels that the eldest, Elizabeth
Russell, was the nearest in personality and temperament to her
Somersby nephews and nieces. Dangerously sensitive and imaginative
from childhood she contrived to develop a truly Christian and yet
humorous tolerance which enabled her to retain and return the affection
of her parents and of both her brothers and their families. Her surviving
letters shew a delightful generosity of affection, as, for example, this
which she wrote to Charles on the loss of a stillborn child in the
autumn of 1819:

I did weep, my ever dear Charles, and found my eyes repeatedly
filled with tears during the whole of yesterday and even when I laid
awake in the night. There is something in the death and burial of an
infant which touches the tenderest chord in our hearts, especially when
it has belonged to those who are inexpressibly dear to us – dear Fanny
could weep for it as yours, you would regret it as hers and I feel that it
belonged to you both – I think Tasso (?) speaks of an infant's death
beautifully. I cannot recollect the words but it sipped the cup of life
and perceiving its bitterness turned its head and refused the draught.
I can so well imagine from your own expression all you have felt and
it is so happily expressed that I shall treasure your letter as a bit of your
mind and heart embodied. Write a line and tell me how poor dear
Fanny recovers. I would tell her how much consolation there is in the
loss of an infant, but she knows this and will feel it, and that she ought
to be happy in the thought that it has (if there be truth in revelation)

gone to God; 'for I say unto you' are Christ's words 'that in Heaven their angels do always behold the face of my Father who is in Heaven . . .'

Her relations with her father may be illustrated by two letters written to him after the death of her mother, the first on 21st January 1826:

Do not try, my dear and now alas! my only parent, to encourage the idea that you can be in the way of any of your children; even a wayward one must sympathise in your deep sorrow, and more so when afflicted in your poor shaken frame, every ache and pain of which has formerly been watched and mourned over by her blessed tender mother and how do we know that she is not now a ministering spirit about your path and about your bed. I try to realise a conjecture so happy and so elevating. It is in this bringing into life those who are passed away from our senses that we cheat ourselves out of that sorrow which withers up the heart, and so indebted have I found myself to imagination when double darkness and gloom left my mind to its influence that I can never hear it denied without internal opposition.

All your feelings have been and perhaps are now mine, they belong to the desolate, to the mind which feels its loneliness and yet how can we smile and trifle, just as the sunbeams dance upon the dank cold tide . . .

The second letter was written just six months later

Do not believe my beloved Father that any apprehension of renew'd sorrow weighing against an idea that I might prove a comforter under yours should prevent my going to Tealby. Sorrow like ours can neither be increased or diminished by outward circumstances or scenes, it lives a life independent of them, and however at different times it may vary in its modification it is always *there, in the heart* pressing with the same weight upon those finer springs of hope and joy belonging to existence, before it had so tasted of adversity, in its bitterest form.

Relations with her difficult sister Mary were more precarious. When in 1850 Charles proposed to dedicate to her his Elegy on the death of his youngest son Eustace, the letter which Elizabeth wrote to him on 16th December is significant – and characteristic. 'Is it advisable to dedicate your poem to me having a sister who might claim herself offended by the preference? She is I know, considered the one of your heart and may at present, as formerly, so consider herself. Of this I ask not. There is among the mysteries of our being something like mesmeric influence and we are (I think) scarcely responsible for our taste and distaste of individuals'.

With Alfred she maintained affectionate communication until the end of her life. This was facilitated by her retirement to Cheltenham where Alfred's mother was living from 1842 to 1853. Alfred was often there until his marriage in 1850 and the two saw much of one another. This extract from a letter which she wrote to him about 1848 or 1849 shews the plane on which they held communication:

A sorrowful-hearted aunt watches for her dearest nephew's fresh spring. When will it sparkle under her dim eyes! Nothing to add, but a lately strengthened conviction that there are from time to time, letters from an invisible world, preparing some hearts for sorrow – You, my dear Alfred, will not mock at this belief, as some do. It is pleasant to speak to the very few rich minds who accept the truth.

Their last meeting was at Cheltenham in 1865 when Alfred and Emily found her, now close upon eighty years of age, half blind and partially paralysed, but peaceful and still beautiful and able to have long and intimate talks with them on the subjects nearest their hearts.

For her brother Charles she had a deep and lasting affection, thoroughly understanding his anxious and fretful temperament and being able to chaff and gently criticise him without offending his pride or sensibility which often made him uneasy or even resentful at the kindnesses which her lavishly open-handed Matthew showered upon him. 'Never trouble yourself about obligations to Russell which your excellent head is working out or has already worked out. What would we do in many emergencies without you, who extricate him so handsomely and spare his purse. But nobody has a head like you and nobody else has a heart to match such a head.'

A letter written to Charles fourteen years after Matthew's death shews that this demon was not yet exorcised. 'I would do anything to make you happier, you cannot imagine how *miserable* I feel under an idea that a cloud sometimes passes over your heart and mind respecting a subject which ought never to be thought of between us, any more than it was or ever would have been, had my husband who thought you his *own* brother lived to bless us today.'

All these difficult relations she managed to maintain with a humour and a sense of style which make her remaining letters still a delight to read and which approximated more to the Somersby children than to their father, whose writing though forcible and fluent was rather ponderous and conventional.

One cannot imagine the Doctor writing of his butler 'he has no more head than asparagus when it has fulfilled the end of vegetation' – or of himself, 'I thank God for possessing the prudence of the family, as it leaves me some paws to suck' or 'other people are like armadilloes while my coat of mail (if indeed I possess one) is as pervious as a cullender'.

How delightful is her sympathy with the bull which she suspected of threatening her only daughter's prospects of producing an heir to the Boyne Viscountcy:

Emma has never hinted to me any fright from a bull; do let me hear all about it – I dread alarms for her and am always talking and writing to her of the risk there is in country walks with little dogs – alas, she turns a deaf ear to the cries of wolf – there ought to be a heavy penalty on bulls at large – though poor things one cannot help pitying them.

It is not surprising that she often rebelled against social formalities. 'How easy it would be', she writes wistfully, 'to see one's fellow creatures if stomachs did not require petting', and there are months of boredom suggested in these few lines about Leamington Spa.

This is the most disagreeable damp hurrying place I know; everlasting callers, requiring me to become one! My heart gets worse, scarcely beating with the force of a fly's – it would be easily stopped till the day of Resurrection.

Mary Bourne too had a style of her own – but a much more formidable one, which well matched her formidable Calvinism. She would weep with emotion at the infinite goodness of God, 'Has he not', she

would exclaim, 'damned most of my friends? But *me*, *me* He has picked
out for eternal salvation, me who am no better than my neighbours!'
And Alfred would recall with grim amusement her saying to him in
his impressionable boyhood, 'Alfred, Alfred, when I look at you I think
of the words of Holy Scripture "Depart from me ye cursed into
everlasting FIRE".'

Yet in spite of her doubts about their ultimate fate Mary Bourne
always regarded the Somersby family as 'the dearest and most interesting of my connexions'. Now and then she openly took Dr Tennyson's
part against his father and brother and while the children were young
there were times when they looked on Dalby (not five miles from
Somersby) as almost a second home. Mary took a keen interest in poor
Emily's frustrated engagement to Arthur Hallam in 1832 and busied
herself actively in the negotiations with her father though 'under the
dreary conviction that no suggestion of *mine* could be successful at
Tealby', and she was pleased when, five years later, Alfred, Charles and
Cecilia called at Dalby at ten o'clock at night and demanded supper on
their way to the Rawnsleys at Halton Holgate to take their final leave
of Lincolnshire. That seems to have been the end of her direct contacts
with the Somersby family. When she died in 1864 after many years of
ferocious and wandering widowhood, Alfred summed up the story in
a letter to his cousin Louis d'Eyncourt:

She had been hidden from me and my family for so many years –
ever in fact since we left Lincolnshire – that the grave is only a deeper
hiding. Had she ever expressed a wish to see me or any of us, I or they
would have gone to her immediately. But I don't suppose she did.
Peace be with her! I remember her in her days of kindness when we
lived near each other, and should have been glad to have seen her
once again – and I don't know why I never volunteered to go to her
– except, perhaps, that I knew her to be one of the most wayward and
at times violent of human beings, and might possibly have been
received very harshly. Still, I ought to have gone, I think.

The few letters from her which survive are marked, even before
the loss of her home and the death of her husband, by a ferocious
pessimism which begets its own grim style:

'To all but friends I should have been a poor, despised, troublesome nuisance.'

'I have often noticed whatever I set my heart on quickly vanishes from my grasp.'

'I do not wish to wound you or your dear kind father with my many miseries arising at home and abroad, but I am indeed a wounded pilgrim.'

'My heart is . . . ever anticipating a worn out body and mind in 10,000 formidable shapes. Still the Tennyson stamina continues to rally and I sometimes feel myself only yet half old or dead.'

'I have had a savage touch of the prevailing plague in town, where I dragged five months of a wretched existence.'

Even when writing to her father after her mother's death she could find nothing more consolatory to say than this:

Could a daughter's presence or sympathy have beguiled you of woe, you would have commanded my time and tenderest attention, but alas I know too well your inconsolable case; the wound you have received neither time nor friends can heal, there is but one true comforter under affliction such as ours, and when time shall have closed on our sorrows, may we join the dear saint we deplore, in everlasting joys.

Poor Mary Bourne, one feels that there is nothing she would have resented more than being condemned to 'everlasting joys'. On earth she found some consolation in the love of animals and when, as so often happened during her stormy wanderings, she had to change her lodgings, she would never allow her dogs to travel in a cab, but always hired a carriage for their benefit.

Charles had not the marked personality or sense of style – either in the written or the spoken word – which characterised, in widely different ways, his two sisters. He was a voluminous correspondent, but his letters are diffuse and uninteresting, while his speeches, so far as one can see, though well argued, have not much distinction of language. Though he did not inherit his father's conciseness, he did

inherit his instability and fretfulness and it is probable that he felt
throughout his life – though he would not have admitted it even to
himself – some sense of guilt at the preference which his father had
extended to him. This perhaps made him exaggerate the importance of
the Hildyard pedigree and of his obligations as the leader of a county
family and led him into actions, which, as he had not a very strong
sense of humour, made him a little ridiculous. All this helped to blind
his contemporaries (and subsequent historians) to his very real achieve-
ments in the arts and sciences and in politics. In the latter field he seemed
exceptionally qualified for success. He was hard working, able and
pertinacious. He had a fine rich voice which he could use with effect
and he was romantically handsome (Elizabeth Russell used to chaff
him about his 'melancholy Charles the First Countenance') – dark like
his brother and like him in feature though of less formidable build and
more subtle and refined in expression. In thought he was progressive
and independent, perhaps too independent for ultimate success in the
House of Commons of which he was a member for 33 years through
ten successive Parliaments, for though he sat as a radical, he always
spoke as a member of the landowning class and was apt to adopt
positions which his radical colleagues found very uncongenial. Indeed
there were times when it was rumoured that he was trying to form a
third party and it was characteristic that, when in 1845 the coming
of the Sheffield and Manchester Railway at last – after more than
fifty-five years of struggle – enabled the shareholders of the Grimsby
Dock Company to recover something of their investment and the
amalgamation agreement came up for ratification, the only member
of the Dock Company to vote against the proposal was the Right
Honourable Charles d'Eyncourt, M.P., one of the directors. His
antiquarian interests were apt to make him more than a little pedantic
now and then, and, as a radical, he very often found himself in conflict
with the Whig members of the opposition. All parties found it difficult
to understand a kind of naïvely devious subtlety of which examples
recur throughout his political career. As a result, with all his abilities
and advantages the last twenty years of his political career were
completely ineffective.

Unfortunately for Charles and his family, disappointment in politics tended to produce discontent at home. In such moods he would shew all his father's fretfulness and irritability. Thus we find him on 29th June 1840 writing to his son George: 'I sometimes feel so disheartened and so hopeless that I think I must give up altogether. . . . I should like when I am at home to have peace and feel all to be happy about me – if not I had rather do anything than be plagued as I do plague myself when there – I have not the heart to take hard steps, tho' my words often imply the contrary'. It was probably in such moods of depression that he coined for his children the opprobrious monosyllabic nicknames preserved by family tradition. George Hildyard, the eldest, a man generally beloved – even by the Somersby family – who is said to have been deeply in love with Bulwer Lytton's daughter Emily and driven by her tragic death at 20 years old to seek solace in drink, he nicknamed 'The Sot'; Edwin, who married a sister of the Duke of Northumberland and became an admiral was 'The Snob'; Louis, whom Charles thought deficient in filial affection, he called 'the Stone'; Julia, whom everyone loved, was 'the Saint', and Ellen who had a violent temper 'the Shrew'. There is no tradition of any nickname for Clara, whose good nature was always a pacifying influence and who was responsible for bringing the Bayons and Somersby branches of the family together after her father's death; Eustace, whose early death was the great sorrow of his father's life, would, had he lived, no doubt have been canonized with Julia. Probably Charles was not altogether sorry when at the General Election of 1852 he was defeated at Lambeth by a majority of 193 out of a total electorate of over 18,000, especially as his admirers entertained him at a great dinner and presented him with an elaborate piece of plate worth more than £400. And retirement from the political scene had its compensations. Charles had always been meticulous in the discharge of his obligations to the Borough of Lambeth and his constituents there. This became a weariness of the flesh and he was never able to accept the advice of a leading member of his committee – 'Why, Sir, in the name of the Father, the Son and the Holy Ghost, don't you tell them to go to the Devil?'

Charles's real creation was the rebuilding of Bayons Manor. Sir Nikolaus Pevsner in his Penguin volume (1964) on the buildings of Lincolnshire describes the later stages of this work as becoming 'positively operatic'. 'Inner and outer defensive works were erected,' says Sir Nikolaus, 'a moat dug and an embattled barbican with a drawbridge provided – in 1842 the huge keep was built by the East inner wall. The character of these works,' he continues, 'is remarkable. Debouching from the barbican to the inner bailey is one of the most convincing of post-mediaeval experiences.'

However even the rebuilding of Bayons on so grand a scale did not satisfy Charles.

In 1848 he purchased a house at Aincourt (Seine-et-Oise) where the Barons d'Eyncourt had possessed their original castle. The idea of a secondary residence at the little French town from which his mighty ancestors had come to England had long been in his mind, and during the fifteen years which remained to him he spent more and more time at Aincourt with ever greater enjoyment. The town council gave him leave to enclose part of the 'Place des Ormes' between the house and the street, the town people were 'very obliging and attentive', he made friends with the *curé* 'a very well informed, intelligent and agreeable young man', and one may be sure that neither the *curé* nor the citizens of Aincourt were allowed to forget his pedigree, and that his visits to the little town did not diminish Charles's belief in its importance.

One other highly romantic activity, which seems to have occupied Charles for at least twenty-five years, was the attempt to revive the order of Knights Templar. The order had begun during the Crusades as a charitable organisation founded to succour and assist pilgrims to the Holy Places. By the later thirteenth century it had become, through the gifts and bequests of the faithful and the ruthless ability of its leaders, one of the wealthiest and most influential factors in European politics, with the Paris 'Temple' as the centre of the world's money market. Early in the fourteenth century the king of France determined to destroy the order. He secured the support of the Pope and other European monarchs, and by 1314 the final act of what has been called 'this stupendous tragedy' was completed, many of the order's leaders being burned at the stake. The movement for its revival had apparently started amongst the 'ancient' division of the Freemasons, located mainly in France, and it was probably owing to his French association (perhaps longer and closer than we can realise today) that Charles

became interested. When elected a Member of Parliament he soon
found himself working in the liberal interest with the eccentric and
wayward Augustus Frederick, Duke of Sussex, sixth son of George III.
Augustus Frederick had, at the age of seven, been sent supperless to
bed by his Royal father for wearing election colours of which he
disapproved, and he had continued ever since to profess opinions
most unusual for a Royal Duke.

Probably both he and Charles were attracted not only by the
romantic history of the order, but by the loftiness of its aims, which one
of its supporters set out as follows:

True Knights as armed mediators and pacificators, supporters of
lawful authority, of charitable institutions, protectors of the weak,
helpless and oppressed, particularly females, orphans and the aged.
. . . practising courage with circumspection, prudence, humanity in
combat, generosity in Victory, humanity to vanquished prisoners, the
wounded foe as well as friend, good faith in truces and treaties towards
pacification and ultimate good understanding and harmony – the
extension of civilisation beyond its present known limits, the liberation
of slaves and the gradual abolition of slavery . . . in short, manifesting
on all occasions self devotion, offering in themselves an actual, not
merely passive virtue, and acting as true Knights, whose device
ought to be 'Homo Sum et Nihil humanum a me alienum puto' –
thus forming a select and prominant Aristocracy amongst mankind,
no longer allowing the justice of the remark to subsist that chivalry is
become merely *une affaire de toilette*.

The 'ancient' freemasons of France and the 'moderns' of the United
Kingdom had become reconciled in 1811 and the Duke of Sussex had
become Grand Master of the combined body in 1813. By the beginning
of the 1820s the Duke was working closely with the Radical Reformers
and Charles actually became his equerry. It seems that Charles quickly
got into correspondence with representatives of the 'ancient' freemasons in Paris – particularly Sir John Byerley and Sir William Sydney,
who were enthusiastic supporters of the scheme to revive the order of
the Templars. From the first they seem to have regarded Charles as
their main hope of English leadership. Though the Duke of Sussex was
Grand Prior, Charles soon appears as provincial Grand Master for
England, and there is talk of making him Baillie of Cyprus or Com-
mandant of Acre and later County Palatine of the order. There is

mention also of an order of St Sepulchre but Charles reluctantly turned down the idea of becoming a Knight of Malta on the ground of expense. Charles is consulted on the design and specifications for rings, swords and crosses in gold and silver and there is talk of a Grand Diploma of Grand Croix for him, with his arms and supporters emblazoned on a magnificent skin from a specially engraved plate and all his 'Titles' fully set out.

There was considerable correspondence about the need to extend the membership of the order and it was suggested that Charles should not only 'make a suitable selection from among the distinguished characters with which our country abounds' but should also canvass for support amongst 'the intermediate class between the gentry and aristocracy, including the Baronets of England and Nova Scotia, the Scottish nobility, the gentry and learned Professions'.

Unfortunately the Duke of Sussex, though he continued his membership of the order, did not approve of the Freemasons wasting energy on subsidiary activities, and, in spite of the enthusiasm of Charles and his friends, the order made very languid progress. Indeed James Burnes in his *History of the Knights Templars* (Edinburgh: William Blackwood & Sons, 1837) lamented that 'scattered over the mighty Empire of Great Britain there are not forty subjects of His Majesty who are Knights Templars and the whole members of the order do not probably at this moment exceed 300'.

In 1843 the Duke of Sussex died, and Charles's enthusiasm in matters chivalric was probably stimulated, for in the following year his long-suffering wife Fanny was appointed Dama Cavaliere and Viscontessa of the Order of the Redeemer and the appointment is evidenced by a superb certificate (now in the archives at Lincoln) signed by Alexander the First, Prince of Gonzaga and Duke of Mantua, a direct descendant of the Emperor Charlemagne and Lothario King of Lombardy and Successor (?) to the Kingdom of Jerusalem. The appointment seems to have conferred on Fanny little tangible benefit beyond the right to carry the cross of the order on the left side, suspended by a ribbon, and to wear its costume.

However Charles's interest was not long maintained and in 1849, now sixty-five years old, he resigned from the order.

In literature Charles's tendencies were, it need hardly be said, both

romantic and antiquarian though he shared the prejudices of Lockhart
and Croker against the 'Cockney School' of poetry and was contemptuous of his nephew Alfred's 'lame and affected' style. His one
public venture into the poetic field was significant. In 1851, the year
after the publication of *In Memoriam*, he published *Eustace* a very
sincere and efficient elegy on his beloved youngest son who had died
nine years before, shortly after joining his regiment in the West Indies.
Eustace contains 750 lines in rhyming couplets divided into three cantos
and an invocation. The middle canto describes a great banquet of
four hundred covers given at Bayons to celebrate the baptism of the
Prince of Wales on 25th January 1842, and to bid farewell to Eustace
before his departure to join his regiment. The lights stream gaily
through arch and oriel, mingling the blazonries of painted glass with
the richly coloured trophies that adorn the long tables. Among these
stands conspicuous the Prince's emblem of ostrich feathers, the origin
of which is explained in a learned footnote. The shouts of the guests fill
the lofty hall and shake the armour beaming on the walls; banners
wave from the rafters and the roof rings again as the loyal anthem is
sung. At last, as the festivities draw to a close, Charles hands his son a
golden chalice as a memorial of the evening. This Eustace receives,
declaring in an impassioned speech that he accepts it not as a gift, but
as a pledge of paternal affection:

> *Thus let me keep it till I cease to be*
> *What now I am and feel – a son to thee.*

Within a month Eustace lies dead at Barbados and the cup, sent home
by his dying wish,

> *To Bayons Hall restored*
> *Now stands apart – and sacred – on the Board –*
> *Fulfils the soldier's wish when it renews*
> *A sweet remembrance of his last Adieus –*
> *Recalls his fond and dying thought of Home*
> *And Forms a link with EUSTACE – in the Tomb.*

The book, which was published in 1851, was illustrated with fine engravings of Bayons Manor; of the park with Eustace in the foreground, reclining on an eminence and surveying the deer and the antique towers recently added to the home of his boyhood; of the banquet proceeding in the great hall, with Charles and Fanny seated at the head of the table, the chalice before them and a long vista of guests stretching on either side into the distance. Turning over its handsome pages, one cannot avoid the feeling that one, at least, of its distinguished author's aims in publishing the work was to show the world that Alfred's 'lame and affected style' was not typical of the family, the head of which knew very well how this kind of thing should be done.

Meanwhile, in 1848, Charles had presented to the annual meeting at Lincoln of the Archaeological Institute a paper on an ancient inscription on lead to the memory of William d'Eyncourt who had died in the reign of William Rufus.* This William was a son of the first Baron, Walter d'Eyncourt who had come over with the Conqueror. He had apparently died as little more than a boy at William Rufus' Court in London and his body had been sent north to Lincoln, sewn up in a protective leather bag, to be buried by his cousin Remigius, first bishop of Lincoln and founder of Lincoln Cathedral, near the west door of the great new building. The leaden fragment had been discovered in 1670 and Charles's paper, besides containing a learned disquisition on the use of lead in funerary inscriptions, pointed out that as this fragment described William d'Eyncourt as *a regio stirpe progenitus*, his mother had probably been a Saxon Princess whom the Conqueror had, for political reasons, arranged for Walter d'Eyncourt to marry. Charles thus, without making any specific claim, traced his own ancestry to the Saxon Royal house as well as to the Norman nobility and the Royal Edwards of later times.

In 1852 Charles gathered together in a privately printed and distributed volume, *Memorial of Bayons Manor*, this address to the Archaeological Institute, his own poem *Eustace* and two papers recently published by John Bernard Burke (afterwards Sir John and Ulster

* *Memoirs Illustrative of the History of Lincoln*, Archaeological Institute printed by W. Davy and Son, Gilbert St. 1850.

Herald), the first in *A Genealogical and Heraldic Dictionary of the Landed Gentry of Great Britain and Ireland* (London: Henry Colburn, Great Marlborough St.), the second volume of which contained on pp. 1,377–1,382 a genealogical history of the family of Tennyson d'Eyncourt in the County of Lincoln. This account explains that the names and arms of d'Eyncourt had been superadded to those of Tennyson by Charles in compliance with a codicil to the will of his father, to commemorate his descent from the ancient and noble family, and traces that descent continuously from the barons of the Court of William the Conqueror through Dorothy Hildyard of Kelstern and poor Elizabeth Clayton, the short-lived and not so literate wife of Michael the apothecary. The second paper, which appeared in 1852 in John Bernard Burke's *Visitation of Seats and Arms of the Noblemen and Gentlemen of Great Britain* (London: Henry Colburn, Great Marlborough St.) was an equally exuberant description of the rebuilt Bayons Manor, 'a castellated Manor House of dark-coloured stone with all the attributes of a baronial residence of the Middle Ages, its external aspect and interior arrangements . . . recalling the expansive and dignified hospitality of the olden time.' Burke lingers with relish over the library 'well stored in every department of elegant literature . . . the principal withdrawing room fifty-four feet in length by thirty-six feet in the transept with an oak ceiling thrown into Gothic arches resting on highly decorated corbels . . . the floors of oak and windows and oriels of stone . . . the whole presenting an interest and charm beyond the average of our manorial residences which the vitiated taste of the eighteenth century in too many instances degraded from their national and antique costume and thus . . . destroyed those historical and domestic associations which are calculated to inspire attachment to the soil and insure defence in the hour of danger'.

In 1859 Charles brought this burst of genealogical activity to a fitting close by presenting to the Cathedral the Cinquefoil window, which still adorns the west end and commemorates in correct thirteenth-century style Bishop Remigius the cousin of his baronial ancestors.

But the scheme which absorbed most of Charles's energy and interest during the years that remained to him was the establishment in Tealby

village of a 'D'Eyncourt School and Institute' for the boys and girls of
Tealby and the neighbourhood, without regard to religious differences
and open to government inspection. He must have devoted much time
during the years following his retirement from Parliament to working
out a constitution and curriculum for the school and institute and to
the erection of a handsome school building in correct perpendicular
Gothic with a fine open timber roof, modelled on that of Westminster
Hall (built in the reign of Richard II and reputed the finest timber roof
in Europe).

One must not allow the distinctly feudal relation which Charles
adopted towards his enterprise nor the volume of Victorian clichés
with which he often described it to obscure the imaginative, progressive
and humane spirit in which it was conceived. Over the door of the
school building were carved the words *Deo Patriae Vicinis* ('To God,
my country and my neighbours') but Charles retained the ownership
of the whole. Though the school was to be managed by trustees, the
Lord of the Manor was to be chairman with a casting vote in the event
of deadlock, and many detailed powers were reserved to him, including
the appointment of the headmaster.

The school building was criticised as being 'too stately for its
apparent object'. Charles replied that it was 'intended to bespeak a
great object', for which it could not be too stately. On the other hand
he rejected all suggestions for a ceremonial opening with VIPs on the
platform because, situated as he was in a large parish in which there
was no educational provision whatever, he felt it to be his simple and
paramount duty to do what he was doing. He had waited a whole
generation for the government to make some Parliamentary provision
for national education and waited in vain. More than half the adult
population of England and Wales still could neither read nor write and
even where schools existed parents too often withdrew their children
and sent them out to earn money before they were eleven, thus
condemning them in later life to 'the cruel discouragement under
which men labour who have to compete with others better educated
than themselves although they may in natural ability, energy and
industry be their superiors'.

Though Charles rejected the idea of a ceremonial opening he was able to give his views on education generally and outline his intentions for the school in replying to an address presented to him on behalf of local interests shortly after the school actually opened.

The curriculum was conceived on very practical and progressive lines. Besides the 'three Rs' for the young of both sexes and domestic science for the girls there was to be instruction in grammar, composition, geography, history and vocal music. The more advanced subjects mentioned in Charles's speech were perhaps to be reserved for the institute, e.g. agricultural chemistry for the farmers' sons as well as botany, geology, geometry (for mensuration) and, in order to keep pace with the already growing use of machinery on the land, mechanics. Such technical subjects would surely be beyond the scope of the headmaster and the 'two amiable ladies' appointed to assist him – one as sewing mistress. More within their scope would be natural history and astronomy, the former being justified by its power to cultivate in the farmer and labourer 'a feeling of mercy and protection towards the animals submitted to their power', and the latter 'by its ability to excite wonder, then delight and finally to call forth sublime contemplation, which would lead to the establishment in the mind of a reverential religious feeling likely to influence conduct through life'.

Charles shewed a typically Victorian attitude to the education of women, urging that no pains should be spared to strengthen that heroic self-denying element which, when duly cultivated, renders woman 'a beautiful example of forbearance and resignation – of sympathy, mercy and goodness'. At the same time he felt female education to be in many ways more important than male, for the mother was the child's first ruler and teacher – if she had not a deep sense of truth, gentleness and justice the child would resort to deceit and falsehood, the offspring of fear. A similar humanity appears in Charles's views on punishment. Corporal punishment and public disgrace, he said, were to be avoided, since they tended to harden instead of correcting and to undermine the most valuable of all moral possessions, self-respect.

Charles dealt characteristically with the controversial subject of religious education. Religion would be carefully, anxiously, and diligently cultivated in the school, by instructing the scholars in the Christian faith, so far as was consistent with every principle of religious liberty, upon which he had acted in his public life. . . . Portions of the scripture would be read daily in the school, and an explanation given by the master of any obscure passages, but it would be unsectarian in character. His decision to include 'the inculcation of moral philosophy' was objected to by some who thought that it was needless to teach morality, as it would be a consequence of religious instruction. This he admitted, if religious instruction always found its way to the heart. . . . But this was too rarely the case, and therefore he considered it right to instruct children in their moral duties by the conclusions of reason as based on the will of God. Moral philosophy afforded some means of ascertaining the Divine Will, and we must never forget that children have hearts as well as heads.

Charles ended his speech with a characteristic peroration, of which his nephew Alfred would surely have approved. 'Man may have millions of ages before him and be in a state of progress to a nobler destiny. Man appears to have walked forth hitherto scarcely conscious of the divine spirit within him. Let us endeavour to unfold it so that he may attain that more glorious station which the Creator may have designed for him on Earth or at least be prepared for eternity.

'You may think me too enterprising and sanguine', he concluded 'but my heart is in the matter and if zeal and perseverance of which I have abundance can ensure success I feel I must succeed.'

The school started with the headmaster and the 'two amiable ladies' already mentioned. There was a scale of fees, labourers paying a penny a week for each child, artisans threepence and others sixpence. Books were to be provided *gratis* but parents would have to buy slates, drawing books, pencils and books for home lessons. Parents were requested to send their children to school neatly clothed with dress, hands and faces clean, hair combed and boys' hair cut short and with pocket-handkerchiefs.

Charles's school was evidently popular from the start, for early in 1859 he issued a statement that owing to its success he had determined to realise his original conception by extending the scheme to include a rural institute for the benefit of Tealby and its neighbourhood, with a library and reading room and courses of lectures on scientific, literary and moral subjects. There was to be a scale of subscription for member-

G

ship of the Institute, four shillings for labourers, six shillings for artisans and ten shillings for others (annually). In June a general meeting was held to launch the scheme and a course of twelve lectures announced for the season 1859–60, the last of the series – on astronomy – to be given by Charles himself on 1st June of the latter year.

This lecture must have been a considerable success for it seems that in the next year Charles undertook to deliver a course of several lectures on the same subject 'with all the illustrations necessary to give the village mind a due notion of the magnitude and grandeur of celestial phenomena'.

But the full course of lectures was never to be delivered. On 21st July 1861 Charles died at the London house of his son-in-law, John Palmer Esq, QC in Gloucester Place, Portman Square. The school continued and continues today as a primary school under the national system. What happened in regard to the institute, library and reading rooms is not known. They do not exist today.

Perhaps we should regard Charles as a poet *manqué* and the rebuilding of Bayons as his *Idylls of the King*, less significant and less enduring than Alfred's, but nevertheless a real feat of the romantic imagination.

Alas, the great house with its keep, barbican, curtain walls, machico-lations, louvres, niches, turrets, oriels and finials, is now reduced to a heap of rubble waiting to be carted away for road-stone.

Charles remains an enigmatic, if fascinating, figure, whose import-ance as a sharer of those qualities in his nephews and nieces of which he so heartily disapproved can be suspected but hardly evaluated.

EPILOGUE

The Somersby Tennysons could never have arisen in any previous age and the likes of them are not likely to be seen again. They would all now presumably be classed as, in some degree, manic depressives; they all succumbed at some time or other and for varying periods to some form of religious obsession. They all always thought themselves ill, yet the average length of life of the eleven brothers and sisters was over eighty years. None of them ever did any normal work, except Charles, who devoted the years which his neurosis and drug addiction allowed to the dedicated if eccentric service of his remote country parish. All spoke exquisite English without any suggestion of priggishness; all read verse with wonderful sensibility and humour. Though only three attempted to publish, all wrote verse and one feels that, given Alfred's concentration and stamina, all might have found honourable places in the roll of British poets.

How are we to trace the spiritual origins of this extraordinary brood? We have already mentioned their grandmother, old George's wife, as a possible source. She was said to have been fond of poetry and a gifted artist and musician, and a faint fragrance of style and fancy still breathes from her remaining letters. But one cannot credit – or debit – her with all the Somersby peculiarities. The germs of some are no doubt to be found in the morbid and romantic sensibility of old George, her husband, which the prosperous lawyer and county magnate in him so successfully disguised. Certainly he and Mary had four remarkable children. The most remarkable was no doubt the eldest son (the father of the Somersby brood) whose singular and unhappy temperament we have endeavoured to describe as fully as surviving evidence permits. But how can we hope to evaluate the impact of his remarkable library and his ineffectual and indulgent wife's addiction to Beattie and Mrs Hemans; of the scandal and gossip caused by his 'disinheritance' and his own moral and mental deterioration which this gradually brought about; of the children's lack of regular education and the beauty and isolation of the countryside over which they were allowed to roam so freely?

Canon H. D. Rawnsley in 1892 asked the eighty-five-year-old Frederick Tennyson to which of their ancestors the poetic genius of the Somersby Tennysons could be attributed. Frederick replied from Jersey in a clear bold hand and in characteristically rotund, but slightly incorrect, phrases:

With respect to your query as to what fountain of inspiration the Tennysons are indebted, the Creator himself only could give a perfectly definitive answer. From many generations of ancestors posterity derives collective influences, and therefore it is difficult to assign to any single individual what may have been mingled in an accumulated form in the last inheritor.

Our survey has involved even more difficult questions and we can only hope that we have been able to contribute something to the understanding of these, if not to their solution.

TENNYSON'S CONVERSATION

MANY of Tennyson's contemporaries wrote of the extraordinary charm and force of his conversation – among them Edward FitzGerald, Benjamin Jowett, Frederick Locker, Annie Thackeray, W. E. H. Lecky and F. T. Palgrave. All these seem to have agreed that, although in uncongenial company he could be self-conscious, unresponsive, sometimes even positively rude, amongst those he loved and respected he was one of the most spontaneous and delightful talkers of his day.

It is notoriously difficult to reproduce in cold print the charm of the spoken word, but Mrs Rundle Charles' record of her talks with Tennyson in 1848 (*Memoir*, p. 230 *et seq.*), Frederick Locker's account of the Swiss tour of 1869 (*ibid.*, p. 472 *et seq.*), Dr Symond's account of the dinner party at Thomas Woolner's at which both Tennyson and Gladstone were present in 1865 (see my *Alfred Tennyson*, pp. 359 and 360), and many pages of William Allingham's diary and Hallam Tennyson's memoir, give, with due allowance for Victorian discretion, a fair idea of the wide range, terse felicity, imaginative force and pervading humour of Tennyson's familiar conversation.

There exists another important body of evidence in a notebook in which the poet's eldest son, when a schoolboy at Marlborough, jotted down rough notes of his father's talk. This is about 20,000 words long and covers, I should say, the years 1867 to 1870. The notes are devoid of literary artifice and this makes them more valuable as evidence, though less easy to use effectively, for where literary friends tend to dress up what they remember, a schoolboy's rough notes are apt to err by blunting points and by inadequate and even inaccurate reporting.

To construct a coherent and lifelike picture from Hallam Tennyson's notes is extraordinarily difficult, both because of their inevitable in-accuracy and because of their extraordinarily wide range.

Perhaps the most interesting refer to the poet's reminiscences of his own youth and of the rough old Lincolnshire in which he was brought up. We see him, as a little boy, wandering alone about the Somersby pastures with a little stick, conquering kingdoms with curious and resounding names – no doubt a sublimation of the literary world which he even then hoped to conquer. We catch a glimpse of the grim and terrifying Calvinistic aunt, Mary Bourne, glaring at him across the street at Spilsby and shouting at him, 'This reminds me of the great gulf which shall divide the wicked from the blessed.' There are queer glimpses of the grammar school at Louth where Alfred spent four years, from seven to eleven. One of the few boys who was kind to him during that unhappy time was, he tells Hallam, afterwards hanged for horse-stealing, while a boy who used to hit him in the stomach, when he stood weeping in a corner from home-sickness, with the words, 'That'll teach you to cry,' grew up to be a popular physician, generally respected for his kindness and sympathy.

Another reminiscence of those unhappy schooldays tells of little Alfred's haunting fear that one day at the catechism class he would be asked to repeat the Lord's Prayer and would find himself unable to. The day came, the question was asked and the poor boy found that the words had completely vanished from his memory.

Another personal memory describes his horror on seeing at a dance his partner's white glove come away from his shoulder completely black. The servant at the Rectory had brushed his coat with the shoe-blacking brush. There is rather a wry reminiscence of a breakfast at sardonic Samuel Rogers' when Tommy Moore was monopolising the conversation and Tennyson sitting shy and silent in his corner. 'Well, Mr Tennyson,' said Rogers drily, 'I suppose we shall hear from you when Mr Moore has gone.'

There are plenty of stories about old Lincolnshire:

'What is sin, boy?' 'Faïäth, sir.'

'What is the outward and visible sign of baptism?' 'The baäby, sir.'

'How is your wife, gardener?' 'Been four and a half days in heäll, sir.'

A swain, proposing to a milkmaid, shies a rotten stick at her, 'Taäk that if thou loves me, as I loves thee – now it's out.'

Perhaps it was the same swain who gave this eulogy of the same milkmaid: 'She has good walloping hands and a fine pair of staddles.'

A maid says to her mistress who is wearing the newly fashionable 'bustle,' 'If thy Maäker had meant thee to have a loomp there, thou'd have had one.'

A.T.'s aunt, Mrs Matthew Russell, finding her head-dress on fire, rang frantically for the footman, 'William, I am on fire.'

'Very good, madam,' replied William, unperturbably, 'I will go and tell Amy.'

A burly dissenter paying a visit of sympathy to a poor little man who was dying, 'Why, you beänt half a man, you should see me die!'

A daughter ties her poor mad father to a tree and beats him.

A neighbour, on a visit of condolence to a widow, asks her, 'Who was thy mate's carpenter?'

Aunt Bourne's coachman, trying to kill a sheep which obstinately refuses to die, bashes it on the head, shouting 'Die, will thou, thou beeäst!'

The remark of a Lincolnshire bookseller: 'Go away with your books, they are more of a reading lot at Louth,' suggests that the Tennyson brothers may have offered the MS of Poems by Two Brothers in Lincoln before taking it to the Jacksons.

One would have welcomed a fuller gallery of Lincolnshire eccentrics – here are two specimens:

A gentleman who deserted his wife for twenty years and then suddenly appeared in church with a long beard and sat down in a pew by her, neither shewing any sign of unusual emotion; and the eccentric old deaf clergyman at Louth who used to eat a leg of mutton a day and spend hours swinging from apple tree to apple tree in his garden for exercise to work off the excess. There is a pathetic picture of this old man conducting the funeral of a dear friend and sobbing aloud, 'Oh, my God, oh, poor old lass, how I loved her,' and pointing upwards with his forefinger at the words 'Eternal life.'

Finest of all the Lincolnshire stories, even in Hallam Tennyson's halting prose, is that of the Fen murder. It must have gained enormously from the poet's telling. I quote Hallam's version. 'There was an old man and his old, grey-haired maid, Bess, that could jump over the Fen-dykes better than anyone. They lived in a solitary clay cottage [in the Fen]. Mr Jones went to knock at the door; he could not get in but went round the house and discovered a hole pick-axed through the wall, and through the hole he saw the big, fierce dog licking up his master's blood which trickled through the ceiling. He found Bess with her hand on goose pies in a sentimental manner, with her skull stove in and the old man was murdered on the stairs, a knife stuck in at his mouth, which came out at the back of his head. The murderer was discovered by his going to the doctor and saying 'I have cut my hand with a hay cutter,' when it was really pierced with a hay fork with which the old man defended himself. When he went from his village, sudden remorse seized him and he cried out, 'Goodbye, my son, my life, I shall never see thee more.' Mrs Joliffe told A.T. she had seen the man grown quite a bag of bones through remorse in prison, and he died killed by remorse, having constantly told Mrs Joliffe the story, saying, 'The old man had me down six times on the stairs, and the old woman clinging round my legs cursing – I shall never forget it – it will kill me.' So it did.

What a story for Crabbe – a pendant to Peter Grimes. No doubt it appealed to Tennyson's sense of the macabre and sadistic which peeps out very occasionally in his poems, as for example in *The Vision of Sin*, *St Simeon Stylites* and a passage or two in *Queen Mary*, *Harold* and *Becket*. Here are a few examples from the notebook – strange subjects for conversation between a Victorian father and his schoolboy son.

'A walled up room found with the skeleton of a man crawling from under the bed and the woman in bed.'

'A chieftain in Dahomey, I fancy, killed young girls to warm his feet in their bowels.'

'On the accession of a king in Dahomey enough women victims are killed to float a small canoe [with their blood].'

'In Mexico the priests sacrifice hair all clotted with blood. 50,000 human victims a year, ripping them up the chest, victim pampered beforehand and worshipped as a god.'

'A barbarous king had his subjects' heads cut off. Gave a little hop each time he saw one [fall].'

'A pig ate a man's face and nose to the bone while he lay drunk in a ditch.'

'A.T. walking through Didcot churchyard found a young girl's shin bone stuck in the heel of his boot.'

'A man scalped twice and the sinews of his arms taken out to make bow strings.'

'A man came to a crowded inn. The landlord said he could give him a bed provided he did not make a noise and did not look out of his bed in the morning, as an old lady was in the room. He awoke in the morning and heard a rustling – of the lady getting up, as he supposed. He came down and remarked to the landlord, "I heard the old lady getting up, but I am sure I didn't disturb her in the night." "I didn't think you would," said the landlord. "She was in her coffin." '

'The Princess Belgoso saw in Angora jugglers who cut open their cheeks and made her feel inside the wound, then healed it. Others who cut open their bellies so that dark blood gushed forth, but stroked the place and healed it. One man, when he wanted to decide his course, regularly cut open his belly, pulled his bowels out on a tray before him, consulted them, packed them up again and healed the wound with a stroke.'

'While they were preaching Christianity to a tribe, a woman, because her child cried, broke its back across her knee.'

As an antidote to these tales of horror and disgust (and I have not quoted the most disagreeable), here are some of a finer caste:

Hallam notes that his father thought 'very fine' the Scandinavian legend of the king who was tired of life and sailed out to sea, having ordered his ships to be set on fire before launching. He liked, too, Scott's story of the Highland chieftain who, discovering one of his men asleep on a pillow of rolled snow, kicked it away exclaiming against the man's effeminacy. He liked also a story told by his friend Archie Peel's brother-in-law, who had seen a soldier at Balaclava bleeding profusely from two great gashes across his thigh. 'Well, Jack, I am afraid you're badly hurt.' 'I don't care a damn,' Jack answered. 'Those bloody Heavies can't chaff us again.' Another martial story which he used to tell with delight was of Stark, a gallant American officer, who when the British force came in sight, cried out, 'There are the Britishers, my boys, we'll lick 'em or Molly Stark will be a widow to-night.'

He would also tell with relish an ancient legend of the Lambton family. Here it is in Hallam's words:

'In Durham one of the Lambtons was fishing and a worm would not fit on his hook. He swore and cast it down a well and went off soon after to the Crusades. The worm grew and became a serpent with nine eyes and came out of the well and coiled itself round a conical hill nine times. The Crusader Lambton came back and fought with the serpent in the middle of the River Ware (sc. Wear), clothed in mail made of razor blades. The serpent was cut into a thousand bits and floated down the river.'

Hallam's account here is rather confused, but it seems that Lambton had been persuaded by the wizard who armed him for the fight to promise to sacrifice the first person whom he met on coming out of the river. This proved to be his father, and as he refused to kill his father a curse was laid on the family that no Lambton should die in his bed for nine generations.

Tennyson's keen interest in natural science is shown by the great number of scientific references in the notebook.

Many deal with the apparently rational behaviour of birds and insects, for instance:

Goose's egg placed in crane's nest. The crane hatched it. Father crane inspected it and called his comrades. They held a council, pulled mother crane out and smashed her neck.

Rooks have been seen pecking an offender to death after judging him.

Dean Stanley's parrot having escaped and seeing a large assembly of people in the street, called out 'Let us pray'; and the parrot at Somersby rectory startled the household at family prayers by suddenly exclaiming, 'Oh, God.'

Bees wall up maggots.

Ants have athletic sports and mock wrestling matches.

Earwigs hatch their eggs like hens.

One spider lays all its eggs until it is quite empty, then stretches its skin over them to keep them from the weather and dies.

Leeches in Ceylon all rise up on their hind legs when they hear a man coming. They hang like bunches of grapes on horses' thighs.

There is a story of four men sitting motionless round a card table in

India because a cobra had wound itself round the leg of one of them. At last a servant came in and they asked him in a whisper to bring bread and milk. When this appeared the cobra went off to it, but the man went mad.

There is a fearsome picture of a cobra pursuing a British officer across country 'in loops', and one of a dromedary turning round and biting off the head of a boy who was riding him, because the boy had insulted him three or four days before.

Bats are said to have fought in an empty room until the floor was stained with their blood.

A house is said to have been set on fire by a bottle of water, placed before some curtains, acting as a burning glass in strong sunlight.

When a volcano in Mexico, which is above the level of eternal snow, erupts, all the snow comes down in boiling water.

In Switzerland an avalanche coming down near a newly built church puffed it away without touching it.

The top of the atmosphere goes in waves under the sun, and there is a great November wave.

The crust of the earth is like a gooseberry tart baking.

Wonderful hills are built up by millions of animals.

Dead grasshoppers in the Andes make ridges on which people can climb above the snow.

It is surprising that, having regard to Tennyson's enthusiasm for astronomy, there are only two references to this subject in this notebook – one of them obviously incomplete.

There is a rich store of anecdotes about famous people. Amongst these Goethe's comment on a picture of the Crucifixion is recorded '. . . it is too much for a young man to look on the Divine agony. Christ crucifying Himself for a miserable little race on a miserable little planet seems unintelligible'; also the poet Cowper's description of his sensations when he attempted to hang himself, as 'pursuing a red object through a green field.' Then there is a curious reminiscence of Lord Russell (? Lord John Russell), who recalled having been told by Mrs Charles James Fox to sit by her great husband after dinner and tickle his neck with a feather, as she feared apoplexy if he should fall asleep. These two may have been previously printed, as I think perhaps has Tennyson's record of an interesting talk he had with Wordsworth about the beauty of mountains, much of which, he thought, would be lost when balloons could float above them and people land on them in shoals to see Nature's great effects. 'Ah,' said Wordsworth, 'I do not like to look into the common-placing future.'

Another interesting Wordsworth item is reported through Aubrey de Vere, to whom Wordsworth is said to have observed that his wife had been good to him in many ways – particularly in that she never objected to him loving many women.*

I do not remember to have seen elsewhere the remark attributed to Leigh Hunt: 'Talk about drink – the Devil often lies in wait for a man at the kidney end of a loin of veal,' or Ruskin's comment that the brutality of the English can be seen on any bridge over a beautiful stream – wherever there is such a bridge you will see English boys spitting over the sides into the water. Pleasanter is Jenny Lind's saying – which may well have been a personal memory of Tennyson's – that when she was being applauded for her singing she had time to thank God for having put such a voice in her vile body, but did not feel any elation. Delightful is the picture of Herbert Spencer utilising the enforced leisure of a wet day in a Highland inn by dictating some philosophical work to his secretary in the coffee room. After a time the rest of the company got so bored that they asked if the secretary could dictate and the philosopher write.

In a broader style of comedy are two Episcopal dialogues – the first between MacGee, Bishop of Peterborough, and his gardener, 'John, John, you must give up the drink. It is a sin in the eyes of that Being of whom both you and I stand in awe.' 'Yes, my lord, I know – the missus.' The second between the Bishop of Winchester and the gamekeeper with whom he had been shooting:

Bishop: 'James, you haven't been very regular at church lately.'
Gamekeeper: 'Well, my lord, you see I must look after the birds. If I go to church the poachers get them.'
Bishop: 'Nor at family prayers.'

---

* Here I may record that my uncle Hallam, Lord Tennyson, told me when the account of Wordsworth's love affair with Annette Vallon was first published in 1922, that Tennyson and his circle had always known the facts about this but had kept it to themselves.

Gamekeeper: 'That is not a rule of the Bible, my lord.'

Bishop (rather staggered): 'Many things we have to do are not in the
Bible.'

Gamekeeper: 'But your Honour and Lordship, is there a precept in the
Bible telling the Apostles to shoot?'

Bishop (still more staggered): 'No – but the truth is that there was such
bad shooting in Galilee, they all took to fishing.'

There is a curious story of J. A. Froude going down into the crypt
of Westminster Abbey after the publication of his *History of England*
and being terrified by the sudden and inexplicable waving of the
banner of Queen Mary whom he had so fiercely criticised in his book.

Very picturesque is the reminiscence of Sir John Swinburne,
Algernon's grandfather, being appealed to for help by an ugly little old
gentleman in a flowered waistcoat, whose carriage had broken down.
This was Mirabeau. After a short time Sir John's carriage overturned
and one of the irons gashed Mirabeau's face and drew blood. The Irish
footman looked in quivering with fear, and exclaimed, 'Damn it,
we've killed the Frenchman!' Sir John used afterwards to say that
Mirabeau was as much superior to Wilkes as Wilkes was to the rest of
the world.

There is a characteristic, though perhaps exaggerated, tale of the
eccentric and violent J. M. Kemble, Anglo-Saxon scholar and lifelong
friend of Tennyson, who is said to have turned his wife out of doors,
hurling his slippers after her, and then reviled the policeman, who ran
and picked up the slippers off the doorstep, for violating the time-
honoured principle that an Englishman's home is his castle. A kindlier
view than that usually taken of the sardonic W. H. Thompson (Master
of Trinity, Cambridge), and another lifelong friend of Tennyson's,
is given by the story of an undergraduate who was persuaded by a
practical joker to go to a party at the Master's lodge in a surplice, and
was courteously relieved of it by the Master with the explanation that
'It is not surplice night to-night.' An excellent 'period piece,' attributed
to Lord Houghton, describes Lady Cork driving along a road where
there were two stonebreakers at work. 'Get up behind my carriage,'
says she imperiously. 'Why?' asked the stonebreakers. 'Look at your
calves.'

There are several references to Carlyle – most of which occur also in Hallam Tennyson's *Memoir:* one is a description of Lord Houghton, who had just included Spurgeon, Father H— and a notorious atheist at one of his parties, 'Houghton would have Christ and the Devil to meet at dinner if he could manage it.' I am not sure whether this has appeared elsewhere, or the old man's alleged outburst to a doctor who came to visit him: 'You most unprofitable among the sons of Adam, one might as well breathe one's laments into the long hairy ears of a jackass as into your ear.'

To finish this group I will add a delightful story of Queen Alexandra, who came to Aldworth with Mrs Greville, one of her ladies-in-waiting, to hear the poet read, and as she was leaving took one of his great hats off the peg in the hall and clapped it on Mrs Greville's head before the footman.

But the form of anecdote in which Tennyson most delighted was what one may call the classical anecdote of humour and character, concise and epigrammatic in form, like, for example, Tallyrand's 'Déja?' or Beau Brummell's 'Who's your fat friend?' He used often to announce his intention of making a selection of the hundred best anecdotes of this kind, asserting that it would be the most valuable of all his works. The notebook contains several examples. Many of these are, no doubt, well known, such as the dying Swift's complaint that he had no longer strength even to stick a knife into a dissenter, and Sidney Smith's reply to a bore who badgered him about his ancestry, 'All I can say is that my father disappeared about the time of the Assizes.'

A story which seems to have particularly pleased Tennyson was of the seaman who saved the life of his Admiral and was rewarded with sixpence – 'You see,' said the seaman to his friend, 'he knows the value of it better than we can.'

Then there is a delightful vignette of a Parisian, seeing a crowd round the entrance of the Madeleine, poking his head in and hurriedly withdrawing it, 'Mon Dieu, on prêche.'

Here is a pleasant dialogue, quoted by Hallam Tennyson, 'How beautifully alabaster white are your shoulders, my dear,' said a patronising old man to a young lady. 'I am the same all the way down,' the ingenuous maid replied. And I like the undergraduate quip about Dr

Perry, Bishop of Melbourne, 'If all flesh is grass, Perry must be hay.'

There are several stories with a marked Regency flavour – perhaps favourites of Dr Tennyson at Somersby. Here are three examples:

'Huddlestone, lying drunk under the table, to the Duke: "Pick me up, Duke." "Can't," says the Duke, "but I'll come and lie beside you".'

'When we both get drunk, I can walk but can't talk, and Jack can talk but cannot walk, so I get up and ring the bell and Jack asks for another bottle.'

'Judge Plunket and his brother, a clergyman, were playing whist, when the clergyman revoked. They began to quarrel, until the Judge got up saying, "As to blackguarding, I am any man's equal, but when you come to blasphemy, your knowledge of theology beats me".'

Charmingly characteristic is Lord Melbourne's comment when Lord Lansdowne was urging on Queen Victoria the importance of national education, 'Education isn't everything. Look at the Pagets.' As a pendant there is this dialogue between two Victorian (?) senators:

First Senator: 'You a Senator! You ain't 'ad twopennorth of education in your life.'

Second Senator: 'I've 'ad more than you.'

First Senator: 'I'll lay you five pounds you can't say the Lord's Prayer.'

Second Senator: 'Done! I believe in God, The Father . . .'

First Senator: 'That'll do. I never thought you'd have known it.'

The poet seems to have been pleased with this story of the evangelist, Moody, arranging to insure his life before crossing the Atlantic. 'Oh, my friend, I wish we could insure our immortal souls as easily.' 'We don't do that kind of business here,' replies the clerk. 'All the fire business is done over the way.'

Lastly, as illustrating Tennyson's attitude towards revolution, I will quote his description of the visitor to an Italian town finding the streets in a turmoil and asking a passer-by the reason – 'Nientissimo, nientissimo, rivoluzione,' replies the Italian with a shrug of his shoulders.

Of course, this schoolboy record of Tennyson's talks with a schoolboy only reveals a limited range of his personality. But, if it gives no rounded picture of the man it certainly adds a few more facets to his incredibly complex figure. One can print and put between covers

Claribel, The Lady of Shalott, St Simeon Stylites, In Memoriam, Maud, The Idylls of the King, The Grandmother, The Wellington Ode, Rizpah, The Lincolnshire Poems, and *Crossing the Bar,* and make a book. I have been trying for thirty years to assemble as many equally diverse elements to make a portrait, and I do not feel that I have yet succeeded.

CHARLES TENNYSON

SELECT BIBLIOGRAPHY

Many of the early Tennyson family letters and records are deposited in the Lincolnshire County Archives, The Castle, Lincoln (The Tennyson d'Eyncourt Collection). Some originals and a number of photocopies of items in the Lincolnshire archives can be found at the Tennyson Research Centre, Lincoln, together with much other material. This is being catalogued and is appearing in a three-volume catalogue entitled *Tennyson in Lincoln: a catalogue of the collections in the Research Centre*, compiled by Nancie Campbell, F.L.A.

Volume I, published in 1971, covers the libraries of the Tennyson family including the poet; his father, Dr George Clayton Tennyson; Hallam, Lord Tennyson; Charles Turner; Emily Sellwood, etc.

Volume II, published in June 1974, covers books, pamphlets and other material by and about Alfred, Lord Tennyson, his family and friends. Included also are proofs, trial books, illustrative material, parodies and music.

Volume III, to be published possibly in 1976 or 1977, will contain in Part I manuscript material and family letters, and in Part II letters from friends (many famous Victorians).

A. *Published and Unpublished Works by Individual Members of the Family*

1. FREDERICK (1807–98)
1827 (with Alfred and Charles) *Poems by Two Brothers* (Louth: Jackson).
1853 *Poems* (privately printed).
1854 *Days and Hours* (London: John Parker, West Strand). Poems.

1874   editor, with A. Tudor, of Henry Melville's *Veritas: the Median and Persian Laws* (London: Arthur Hall & Co., 25 Paternoster Row).

1890   *The Isles of Greece* (London: Macmillan). Poems.

1891   *Daphne and Other Poems* (London: Macmillan).

1895   *Poems of the Day and Year* (London: Lane). Selected from the volumes of 1853 and 1854.

One poem in Mary Tennyson's notebook in the Tennyson Collection, Usher Gallery, Lincoln.

Posthumous: *Shorter Poems of Frederick Tennyson* (London: Macmillan, 1911).

There is a large collection of Frederick Tennyson's papers and correspondence in the Lilly Library of Indiana University, Bloomington, Indiana. Some letters in the Lincolnshire County Archives.

2. CHARLES (1808-79) (changed his name to Turner *c.* 1836 on inheriting a small property in north Lincolnshire from a great-uncle)

1827   (with Alfred and Frederick) *Poems by Two Brothers* (Louth: Jackson).

1830   *Sonnets* (Cambridge: Bridges).

1864   *Sonnets* (London: Macmillan).

1868   *Small Tableaux* (London: Macmillan).

1873   *Sonnets, Lyrics and Translations* (London: King).

Posthumous: *Old and New* (London: Kegan Paul, 1880). Collected sonnets.

  A Hundred Sonnets by Charles Tennyson Turner (London: Hart-Davis, 1960).

Letters in the Lincolnshire County Archives and one to Frederick in *Letters to Frederick Tennyson*, ed. Hugh Schonfield.

3. ALFRED (1809-92)
See:

Madden, Lionel, 'Tennyson: select bibliography', in *Tennyson*, ed. D. J. Palmer (Bell, 1973).

Tennyson, Charles, and Fall, Christine, *Alfred Tennyson: an annotated bibliography* (Athens, Georgia: University of Georgia Press, 1967).

4. MARY (1810-84)

'Journal in Antigua'. Manuscript notebook at the Tennyson Research Centre with note dated 'Freshwater, 25th July-27th October, 1852'.

Manuscript notebook of poems in the Tennyson Collection, the Usher Gallery, Lincoln, with dedication to Frederick Tennyson dated 19th July 1879. There are 132 'Sonnets and Fugitive Pieces' indexed and written by Mary, one poem by Frederick, six by Edward and eleven by Septimus.

One poem by Mary is published in *The Other Tennysons*, ed. Peter Hall.

Letters at the Tennyson Research Centre and in the Lincolnshire County Archives.

5. EMILIA (1811-87)

Unpublished letters in the Lincolnshire County Archives.

6. EDWARD (1813-90)

'Thoughts on Pre-existence'. Manuscript poem copied in unknown hand with note 'Freshwater, August 24th' (no year given) at the Tennyson Research Centre.

1831   Two sonnets published by Charles Tennyson in 'Tennyson Papers: II. J. M. Heath's "Commonplace Book" ', in *Cornhill*, vol. 153, no. 916 (April 1936).

1833   One sonnet published in 'J. M. Heath's "Commonplace Book" '.

Six poems in Mary Ker's manuscript notebook in the Tennyson Collection in the Usher Gallery, Lincoln.

One poem published in *The Other Tennysons*, ed. Peter Hall.

7. ARTHUR (1814-99)

Collection of letters to Frederick Tennyson from various addresses c.1878-90. Originals at the University of Indiana, Bloomington, Indiana.

Letters to Sophie, wife of Julius, Frederick's son, from Malvern c.1881-90 at the University of Indiana.

One poem in *The Other Tennysons*, ed. Peter Hall.

Photocopies of letters at the Tennyson Research Centre.

Some letters in the Lincolnshire County Archives.

8. SEPTIMUS (1815-66)

1832/3 Four sonnets and a lyric in J. M. Heath's 'Commonplace Book'. Two of the sonnets were published by Charles Tennyson in his 'J. M. Heath's "Commonplace Book"', together with the lyric.

One sonnet in *The Other Tennysons*, ed. Peter Hall.

Eleven poems in Mary Ker's manuscript notebook in the Usher Gallery, Lincoln.

One letter to Frederick in *Letters to Frederick Tennyson*, ed. Hugh Schonfield, and other letters in the Lincolnshire County Archives.

9. MATILDA (1816-1913)

One fragment of poetry quoted by Charles Tennyson in *The Somersby Tennysons*.

One letter to Frederick in *Letters to Frederick Tennyson*, ed. Hugh Schonfield, and other letters at the Tennyson Research Centre.

10. CECILIA (1817-1909)

1880 *Fifty Years in Sandbourne* and *Two Pictures of Old Womanhood* (reprinted from *Good Words*) (London: Griffith & Farran).

1881 *Margaret the Moonbeam, A Story for the Young* (London: T. Fisher Unwin).

1882 *Over the Seas and Far Away* (London: Griffith & Farran).

One poem (from a novel) in *The Other Tennysons*, ed. Peter Hall.

Two letters to Frederick in *Letters to Frederick Tennyson*, ed. Hugh Schonfield, and other letters at the Tennyson Research Centre.

11. HORATIO (1819-99)

One letter to Frederick in *Letters to Frederick Tennyson*, ed. Hugh Schonfield, and others in the Lincolnshire County Archives.

12. BERTRAM (?-1890) (son of Horatio and Charlotte Maria Elwes)

1896 *The Land of Napoia and Other Essays in Prose and Verse* (Spectator Printing and Publishing Co., Moosomin, N.W. Territories).

13. WALTER KER (son of Mary Tennyson and Alan Ker)

c.1924   Three poems. Unpublished manuscript at the Tennyson Research Centre.

1928   'Poems Original and Translated'. Unpublished manuscript at the Tennyson Research Centre.

14. LUCIA MARIA LUSHINGTON (daughter of Cecilia Lushington, *née* Tennyson)

Verses (privately printed in Maidstone, n.d.)

B. *Some Books about the Tennyson Family*

(Catalogued in *Tennyson in Lincoln*, vol. II)

Benson, Arthur, *Genealogical History of the Family of Tennyson d'Eyncourt of Bayons Manor in the County of Lincolnshire* (privately printed, 1846). Bound with Charles Tennyson d'Eyncourt's *Bayons Manor*.

Fall, Christine, 'Frederick Tennyson: biographical and critical studies'. Typescript thesis, 1940.

George, T. J., and Richardson, William, *A History of Withernsea with Notices of Other Parishes in South Holderness* (Hull, 1911). Contains information on possible ancestors of the Tennyson family.

Hamilton, G. C., *Somersby Countryside and Tennyson: with extracts from early Lincolnshire poems* (privately printed, 1955).

Jesse, Eustace Tennyson d'Eyncourt, 'Annales Tennysoniani'. Collection of newscuttings, reviews and original material on the Tennyson and Jesse families 1873-1921.

Matthews, W., *The Poet Laureate's Early Homes* and *Tennyson's Village Portraits* (Manchester, 1884). Bound with Carpenter's *Message of Tennyson*.

Nicolson, Harold, *Tennyson's Two Brothers* (Frederick and Charles) (Cambridge University Press, 1947).

The Other Tennysons: a selection of poems written by the brothers and sisters of Alfred, Lord Tennyson, ed. Peter Hall (Invicta Press, 1967). Contains Mary Ker's 'The Spies' Report' and Edward Tennyson's 'Why do I weep' from Mary's notebook in the Usher Gallery, Lincoln.

Rawnsley, H. D., *Memories of the Tennysons* (Glasgow: James Mac-Lehose & Sons, 1900).

Scott-Gatty, Sir Alfred, 'Tennyson Family'. Typescript genealogical notes.

Smith, Henry Evan, *Notes on the Tennyson Families* (1892), ed. Peter Binnall (Goulding & Sons, Louth Almanack, 1941).

Tennyson, Sir Charles, *The Somersby Tennysons*, published by the Tennyson Society, no. 1, and in the Christmas supplement to *Victorian Studies*, 1963.

Tennyson Collection in the Usher Gallery, Lincoln (City of Lincoln Libraries, Museum and Art Gallery Committee, 1963). Pamphlet with foreword and annotations by Sir Charles Tennyson.

Of course, many of the books on the life of Alfred, Lord Tennyson contain references to his brothers, sisters, relatives and ancestors. Of these we would mention particularly Hallam, Lord Tennyson, *Tennyson: a memoir* (Macmillan, 1897); Charles Tennyson, *Alfred Tennyson* (Macmillan, 1949); Christopher Ricks, *Tennyson*, Masters of World Literature series (Macmillan, 1972). Mention may also be made of many books such as George Ambler, *Homes and Haunts of the Tennysons* (Jack, 1911), and John Cuming Walters, *In Tennyson Land* (Radway, 1890). There are articles on Frederick Tennyson and Charles Turner in *Tennyson and His Friends*, ed. Hallam, Lord Tennyson (Macmillan, 1911); on Frederick Tennyson in *Shorter Poems of Frederick Tennyson* (Macmillan, 1912); and on Charles Turner in Agnes Weld, *Glimpses of Tennyson* (Williams & Norgate, 1903), and in Charles Tennyson, 'The Vicar of Grasby', in *English*, vol. VIII (1950) pp. 117-20. Mention should also be made of *Letters to Frederick Tennyson*, ed. Hugh Schonfield (Hogarth Press, 1930).

INDEX

Ainslie, Sir Robert, 40
Alexander, Czar, 37
Alexandra, Queen, 206
Alington, Rev. Marmaduke, 24
Allen, Dr Matthew, 149-59
Allen, Mrs Matthew, 156-9
Allen, Oswald, 150
Allingham, William, 197
Amcotts, Sir Wharton, 27
Anderson, Evelyn, see Yarborough, Lord
Angerstein, John Julius, 24
Arabin, Sergeant, 93
Ashburton, Lord, 93

Baring, Rosa, 93, 114
Bayons Manor: bought by George Tennyson (1783-7), 27-8; rebuilding of, 84, 88-90, 92-3, 184-5; passes to Charles d'Eyncourt, 84-5
Beacons Manor, see Bayons Manor
Best family, 149
Bourne, John, 34, 39, 86
Bourne, Mary (b.1777), 32, 34, 55, 78, 88, 178, 180, 181, 182, 198
Bousfield, Dr, 61, 62, 66, 67, 68
Bowes, John, 18
Boyne, Emily, Lady, 33-4, 180
Brancepeth Castle, 33, 58, 61, 84, 90
Brookfield, W. H., 116
Brookfield, Mrs W. H., 168
Broughall, Marjorie (Pastel for Eliza), 140
Browning, Elizabeth Barrett, 101, 124
Browning, Robert, 101, 102, 103, 118, 124
Boucherett, Aynscough, 24
Bulwer, Henry, 124
Burke, John Bernard, 88, 189-90

Byerley, Sir John, 186

Carlyle, Jane, 152
Carlyle, Thomas, 117, 130, 150, 151, 152, 206
Cecil, Lord Thomas, 83
Chaplin, Rev. William, 66-7, 68
Charles, Mrs Rundle, 197
Clambers, Miss, 16
Clare, John, 149, 150
Clayton, Christopher (1687-1737), 15, 17
Clayton, Christopher (d.1794), 17, 19, 21, 22-3, 29
Clayton, David, 17-19
Clayton, Dorothy, 15, 28, 190
Clayton, Elizabeth (d.1755), see Tennyson, Elizabeth
Clayton, George (1694-1741?), 15, 16
Clayton, Susan, 16
Clayton family, 14-15, 21, 24, 27
Coleridge, Samuel Taylor, 109
Cook, Ann, 22-3
Cork, Lady, 205
Cornish, Blanche Warre, 165-6
Cotterell, Miss, 128

Dales, Betsy, 20, 27

Eccles, Miss, 74
Eden, Arthur, 93
Elwes, Charlotte Maria, see Tennyson, Charlotte Maria
Espin, 123
d'Eyncourt, Charles Tennyson (1784-1861), and family. See under Tennyson
d'Eyncourt, Walter, 189
d'Eyncourt, William, 189

d'Eyncourt family, 15, 83, 88, 185, 190
Eyre, Governor, 162

Fazackerley, Mr, 58
Field, Arthur, 128
FitzGerald, Edward, 95, 102, 103, 116, 117, 118, 121, 125, 197
Foster, Joseph, 17-19
Foster, Susannah, 17-19
ffytche, May, 144
Froude, J. A., 205
Fytche, Elizabeth (1781-1865), see Tennyson, Elizabeth
Fytche, John, 60, 66, 67
Fytche, Mrs John, 130
Fytche, Lewis, 109, 147
Fytche, Mary Anne, 75

Giuliotti, Maria, see Tennyson, Maria
Gladstone, W. E., 197
Gould family, 126-8
Gray, William, 20, 27
Greville, Mrs, 206
Grimsby: elections, 21-2, 58; docks scheme, 23-5, 183
Grove House, 26, 82

Haddelsey, Mr, 145, 153, 155
Haddelsey, Susan, 145, 148
Hallam, Arthur Henry (1811-33), 77, 85-6, 93, 114, 144-5, 146, 147, 166, 181
Hallam, Henry, 85-6, 120
Hamilton, Mrs, 75
Harrison, Dr, 66
Haslam, Mr, 154
Heath, John, 121, 145
Heneage family, 24, 40, 41, 64
High Beech: move from Somersby to, 93, 114, 145; family leave, 99, 149, 152
Hildyard, Christopher, 15
Hildyard, Dorothy, see Tennyson, Dorothy
Hildyard, William, 18
Hildyard family, 20, 27, 183
Horlins, 42
Houghton, Richard Monckton Milnes, Lord, 205, 206
Hunt, Leigh, 204
'Husks', 145-6, 147, 148, 168

Hutchinson, Mr, 35, 36
Hutton, Fanny, see Tennyson, Fanny

Irving, Henry, 144
Iveson, Mr, 20

James, Henry, 133
Jesse, Arthur Henry Hallam, 164
Jesse, Emilia (Emily) (1811-87): relations with father, 72, 73; love for A. H. Hallam, 85-6, 144-5, 181; marriage, 94, 99, 160; poetry, 144; 'Husks', 145-6; and Matthew Allen, 149-59; Church of the New Jerusalem, 161; spiritualism, 162; opinions, 164-5
Jesse, Eustace, 164
Jesse, Fryn Tennyson, 164
Jesse, Capt. Richard, 160, 164, 165, 168
Jowett, Benjamin, 197

Kemble, J. M., 116, 205
Ker, Alan, 160, 161, 163, 164
Ker, Mary (1810-84): marriage, 94, 160; in Cheltenham with mother, 95, 99; Church of the New Jerusalem, 101, 161, 164, 165; lameness, 143-4; poetry, 144, 162-3, 164; engagement to John Heath, 145; 'Husks', 145-6; visit to Channel Islands, 146, 148, 149; and Matthew Allen, 149-59; emigrates to Jamaica, 160; spiritualism, 162; death, 163
Ker, Walter, 161, 162, 163
Knight, Robert, 17

Langton, Bennet, 43
Lansdowne, Lord, 207
Lawrence, Sir Thomas, 26
Lecky, W. E. H., 197
Leinster, Duke of, 103
Lilly Library (Indiana University), 102, 103
Lloyd, Mrs, 116
Locker, Frederick, 197
Lovel and d'Eyncourt, Francis, Lord, 28

Lushington, Cecilia (1817-1909):
marriage, 94, 99, 160; poetry, 144,
173; 'Husks', 145-6, 147; sense of
humour, 147-8; and Matthew
Allen, 149-59; death of son, 162;
poor health, 168; books, 171-4;
eccentricity, 174-5
Lushington, Edmund (1843-56), 170,
174
Lushington, Edmund Law, 99, 138,
149, 156, 159, 160, 162, 168, 169,
170
Lushington, Emily (1849-68), 170
Lushington, Godfrey L., 174
Lushington, Henry, 168
Lushington, Lucia Maria (1852-73),
170-1
Lushington, Zilly, 170, 175
Lytton, Edward Bulwer, 92
Lytton, Emily, 184
Lytton, Robert, 1st Earl of, 124
Lytton, Rosina, 92

Maitland, F. W., 11
Maltby, Rev. Edward, 71-2, 74, 75
Marthion family, 68, 74, 75
Mayer, Mr, 154
Maynard, Emma Louisa, see Tennyson,
Emma Louisa
Melbourne, Lord, 207
Melville, Henry, 103
Mirabeau, Honoré, 205
Montagu, Mrs Basil, 152
Moore, Thomas, 198

Nell, Mr, 58
Neville, 'Mimosa', 148

Orme, Mr, 35

Palgrave, F. T., 197
Palmer, John, 194
Park House, 138, 149, 168, 169, 170,
172, 174, 175
Parkes, Joseph, 82
Parkinson, Dr, 23, 26, 27, 28
Paul, Emperor, 37
Pelham family, 20-1, 22, 23, 58. See
also Yarborough, Lord
Peterborough, Bishop of, 204
Pevsner, Sir Nikolaus, 184-5
Plunket, Judge, 207

Pope, Cecilia, 133
Potter, Rev. Brownlow, 28

Rader, R. W (Tennyson's Maud), 93,
115
Raines, Anne, 16
Ravensworth, Lord, 123
Rawnsley, Rev. H. D., 73, 79, 92,
149, 156, 181, 196; Memories of the
Tennysons, 116
Remigius, Bishop, 189, 190
Rennie, John, 25
Rhodes, Mr, 154
Rodenhurst, William, 22-3
Rogers, Samuel, 198
Rossetti, Dante Gabriel, 120
Ruskin, John, 204
Russell, Elizabeth (b.1776): marriage,
33; death of husband, 59; relations
with family, 60-1, 63, 69, 177-80;
in Paris, 75; head-dress on fire, 199
Russell, John, 28
Russell, Matthew, 33, 39, 58, 59, 84,
179-80

St Helens, Lord, 37
Sellwood, Anne, 146, 148, 149
Sellwood, Emily (1813-96), see
Tennyson, Emily, Lady
Sellwood, Henry, 153, 154, 155
Sellwood, Louisa, see Tennyson,
Louisa
Sheil, Richard Lalor, 101
Skipworth, Philip, 24
Smith, Henry, 123-4, 144
Somersby: family move to, 38, 42,
55; leave, 100, 114, 124, 125, 145
South Sea Bubble (1720), 17, 19
Spedding, James, 117
Spencer, Herbert, 204
Stephenson, Eliza, 140
Sussex, Augustus Frederick, Duke of,
186-7
Swinburne, Sir John, 205
Sydney, Sir William, 186
Symond, Dr, 197

Tenison, Edward, Bishop of Ossory
(1673-1735), 13
Tenison, Richard, Bishop of Meath
(1640-1705), 13

Tenison, Thomas, Archbishop of
Canterbury (1636-1715), 13
Tennyson, Alfred, 131
Tennyson, Alfred, Lord (1809-92):
conversation, 37, 197-208; poetry,
42, 45, 65, 74-5, 95, 96-7, 114, 140,
144-5, 169; Louth School, 55;
letters, 63, 77-8, 80-1, 120, 181; at
Cambridge, 68, 69, 72, 81, 116-17;
wins Chancellor's Gold Medal,
74-5; friendship with A. H. Hallam,
77, 85-6, 93, 114, 144-5, 147;
leaves Cambridge without a degree,
79; head of family, 79, 92; inherits
Grasby and Scartho properties, 88;
relations with Uncle Charles, 88;
marriage, 92, 99, 179; reluctance to
take up a profession, 92, 100; love
affair with Rosa Baring, 93, 114;
temperament, 94, 108-9, 114, 133;
relations with father, 94; and mother,
95, 96-7; move to High Beech, 114;
and Matthew Allen, 115, 149-59;
pension, 115, 159; becomes Poet
Laureate, 115; opinions of, 115-18;
drawings, 123; friendship with
Carlyle, 130, 152; and Governor
Eyre, 162; death, 170
Tennyson, Anne, 16
Tennyson, Arthur (1814-99); plan for
naval career, 69; grandfather's poor
opinion of, 77, 79-80, 123; in Italy,
99, 121, 124-5, 160; temperament,
122, 138; poetry, 123, 124;
drawings, 123; takes to drink, 124,
138; Crichton Institution, 124;
first marriage, 125, 137, 138, 139,
140, 143; religious conversion, 125,
128, 138, 140-1; second marriage,
139, 140; friendship with Eliza
Stephenson, 140; death, 143
Tennyson, Bertram (b. 1890), 133-7
Tennyson, Catherine, 125, 137, 143
Tennyson, Cecilia (1817-1909), see
Lushington, Cecilia
Tennyson, Cecilia, see Pope, Cecilia
Tennyson d'Eyncourt, Charles (1784-
1861): birth, 32, 34; father's
preference for, 34-5, 41, 183;
St Peter's Grammar School, 35;
Louth School, 35, 39; Cambridge,
35, 39; extravagance, 35; marriage,

55-6; relations with brother George,
57-8, 59; restoration of Brancepeth,
58, 84; parliamentary career, 58, 64,
75, 78, 82-3, 84, 91, 183, 184;
accompanies George to Paris, 68;
death of George, 78, 79; revival of
name of d'Eyncourt, 83, 89;
rebuilding of Bayons Manor, 84,
89-90, 92-3, 184-5, 190; takes
possession of Bayons, 84-5; death of
father, 87-8; Matthew Allen affair,
153-4; books, 178, 187-9; buys
house at Aincourt, 185; revival of
Knights Templar, 185-7; founds
'D'Eyncourt School and Institute',
190-4; death, 194
Tennyson Turner, Charles (1808-79):
Louth School, 55; poetry, 65, 95-6,
109, 110-14; love for Miss Watson,
68-9; Cambridge, 72, 75; ordained,
79, 80; opium addict, 80-1, 92, 109;
inherits Grasby and Caistor
properties, 87; takes name of
Turner, 87; marriage, 92, 109;
temperament, 93-4, 108
Tennyson, Charlotte Maria, 126, 133,
137, 143, 162
Tennyson d'Eyncourt, Clara, 81-2, 184
Tennyson, Dorothy, 16, 28, 190
Tennyson, Edward (1813-90): mental
illness, 73, 79, 80, 118; preparation
for Cambridge, 88; Lincoln
Asylum, 80, 118; death, 80;
inheritance from grandfather,
87-8; poetry, 118-20
Tennyson d'Eyncourt, Edwin, 82, 88,
184
Tennyson, Elizabeth (d.1755), 15, 16,
20, 190
Tennyson, Elizabeth (1781-1865):
marries George Tennyson, 38; his
illness, 62-3, 66-7, 68, 69, 72-3, 74;
unpractical nature, 70, 79; George's
death, 78; Edward's mental illness,
80; and father-in-law's funeral,
87; moves to High Beech, 93;
death, 94; family relationship, 94-9,
124; and Matthew Allen, 149-59;
moves to Cheltenham, 160, 179
Tennyson, Elizabeth (b.1776), see
Russell, Elizabeth
Tennyson d'Eyncourt, Ellen, 184

Tennyson, Emilia (Emily) (1811-87), see Jesse, Emilia

Tennyson, Emily, Lady (1813-96), 92, 99, 114, 115, 116, 117, 126, 152, 153, 170

Tennyson, Emma Louisa, 139, 140

Tennyson d'Eyncourt, Eustace, 82, 93, 146, 178, 184, 189

Tennyson d'Eyncourt, Fanny, 27, 55-6, 57, 58, 59, 60, 88, 89, 90, 177, 187, 189

Tennyson, Frederick (1807-98): Louth School, 55; Eton, 55; Cambridge, 63, 64, 68, 71, 74, 75, 81; poetry, 65, 71, 95, 97-9, 104-9, 166-7; temperament, 71-2, 93-4; relations with father, 71-3; agrees to study for Bar, 72; Continental trip, 77, 79; death of grandfather, 87-8; in Corfu, 87-8; inherits Grimsby property, 87, 92; love for mother, 97-9; goes to Italy, 99, 100, 121, 124; 160; marriage, 100; Church of the New Jerusalem, 101, 102-3, 161; friendship with Brownings, 101-2, 103; moves to Jersey, 102, 103, 125; Freemasonry and Melville, 103; drawings, 123; death of wife, 132; and Matthew Allen, 153, 154-5; spiritualism, 162; on the family genius, 196

Tennyson, George (1806), 55, 56

Tennyson d'Eyncourt, George, 57, 78, 87, 88, 91, 149, 184

Tennyson, George Clayton (1750-1835): inherits Clayton property, 16, 18; at Betsy Dales' school, 20; becomes solicitor, 20; settles in Market Rasen, 20; marriage, 20; partnership with Uncle William, 20; politics, 21-4; Grimsby dock scheme, 24-5; Tennyson & Main, 26; portrait, 26-7; character, 26-7, 30, 195; buys Bayons Manor, 27-8; leases Deloraine Court, 29; moves into Bayons, 29; death of wife, 30-1, 64; children, 32; preference for Charles, 34-5, 41, 183; relations with George, 39-40, 41, 55, 59, 60, 64-5, 73-4, 77; and revival of name of d'Eyncourt, 83; and rebuilding of Bayons, 84, 89; leaves Bayons,

84-5; death, 87, 120-1

Tennyson, Rev. Dr George Clayton (1778-1831): childhood, 32-3; relations with father, 34-5, 39-40, 41, 55, 59, 60, 64-5, 73-4, 77, 183; St Peter's Grammar School, 35; Cambridge, 35-6, 39; ordained, 37; Russian adventure, 37-8; marriage, 38; character, 42; writings, 42-3, 45-54; library, 43-5; educates Charles and Alfred himself, 55; doctorate, 57; illness, 59-69, 70-8, 94; death, 78, 100, 120; opinion of Alfred, 115; anecdotes, 207

Tennyson d'Eyncourt, George Hildyard, 184

Tennyson, Hallam, 2nd Lord (1852-1928) (Memoir), 13, 28, 37, 41, 45, 115, 117, 147, 197, 198, 199, 202, 206

Tennyson, Harriet, 125, 137, 138, 139, 140, 143

Tennyson, Horatio (1819-99): Louth School, 69, 79; plans for naval career, 79; Blackheath school, 92; character, 125-6, 128-31; farm in Tasmania, 125; first marriage, 126; religious feelings, 131-3, 138; children, 133; second marriage, 137-8

Tennyson d'Eyncourt, Julia, 84-5, 86, 92, 93, 184

Tennyson, Julius, 100, 104, 105

Tennyson, Lancelot, 13

Tennyson, Lionel (1854-86), 169, 170

Tennyson d'Eyncourt, Louis, 181, 184

Tennyson Turner, Louisa, 92, 109, 110

Tennyson, Maria, 100, 132

Tennyson, Mary (d.1825), 20, 27, 28, 29, 30-1, 32-9, 60, 61, 62, 64, 87, 118, 121, 195

Tennyson, Mary (b.1777), see Bourne, Mary

Tennyson, Mary (1810-84), see Ker, Mary

Tennyson, Matilda (1816-1913): in Cheltenham with mother, 95, 99, 160; childhood, 146-7; mysticism, 147; and Matthew Allen, 149-59; and Therese Tietjens, 169-70; at Farringford, 170; at Park House, 170, 175; death, 175

Tennyson, Maud, 129, 133
Tennyson, Michael, 14, 15-16, 17, 18,
    19, 20, 32, 33, 190
Tennyson, Ralph (d.1735), 13-14
Tennyson, Ralph II, 14, 15, 16, 17, 18
Tennyson, Septimus (1815-66): Louth
    School, 69; articled to solicitor, 79,
    80; temperament, 80, 94, 120;
    plans to study medicine, 81, 120;
    leaves solicitor, 92; goes to Italy, 99,
    121, 160; poetry, 121-2; planned
    trip to Demerara, 125; and
    Matthew Allen, 149-59
Tennyson, Susan, 16
Tennyson, Violet, 133
Tennyson, William, 14, 16, 18, 20, 21,
    25-6
Tennyson & Main, 26
Tennyson family: origins and name,
    11-13, 27
Tennyson Research Centre (Lincoln),
    11, 42, 43, 53, 118, 123, 143, 156,
    162, 173
Thackeray, Annie, 166, 197
Thompson, W. H., 116, 205
Turner, Charles Tennyson (1808-79),
    and family. See under Tennyson
Turner, Mary (d.1825), see Tennyson,
    Mary

Turner, Samuel, 28, 79, 87, 110

Usher Art Gallery (Lincoln), 13, 28
Usselby, 84-5, 88

Vallon, Annette, 204
Vere, Aubrey de, 118, 204

Watson, Miss, 68-9
Weld, Agnes Grace (Glimpses of
    Tennyson), 133
Wellesley-Pole, Hon. John, 22
West, Catherine, see Tennyson,
    Catherine
West, Harriet, see Tennyson, Harriet
Whewell, Mr, 69
Willis, Dr, 66
Winchester, Bishop of, 204
Withers, Thomas, 150
Wood, Robert, 22
Woolner, Thomas, 197
Wordsworth, William, 204
Wright, Susannah, see Foster,
    Susannah

Yarborough, Evelyn Anderson, Lord,
    21, 23, 24, 27